To Rich

Happy Xmas 1984

love Doo + Louise.

# SPARKS FLY!

# SPARKS FLY!
## A Trade Union Life

by

### FRANK CHAPPLE

**ERRATUM**

*On page 202, the sentence beginning on line 25 should read:*

'Down there, at the front of the hall, Barbara Switzer, number two to Communist Ken Gill in TASS, glared up at me throughout, or so it seemed to me.'

LONDON
MICHAEL JOSEPH

First published in Great Britain by Michael Joseph Ltd
44 Bedford Square, London WC1
1984

*British Library Cataloguing in Publication data*

Chapple, Frank
  Sparks Fly!
  1. Chapple, Frank
  2. Trade Unions — Great Britain — Officials and
  employees — Bibliography
  I. Title
  331.88′092′4    HD 6665.C5

ISBN 0 7181 2418 9 (H/B)
ISBN 0 7181 2512 6 (P/B)

Typeset by Alacrity Phototypesetters, Weston-super-Mare
Printed and bound in Great Britain by
Billings & Sons, Worcester

To Tommy Vetterlein
and all those who, like him,
stood up to be counted.

# CONTENTS

# ACKNOWLEDGEMENT

This book could not have been written without the immense amount of professional editorial help and guidance provided by my friend John Grant. He was necessarily a hard taskmaster whenever I sought to slacken; I am grateful to him for bringing this project to fruition.

## CHAPTER 1

# THE BIGGEST EVER FRAUD

There was a lack of belief in our case even among our own lawyers at the beginning. Gerald Gardiner, our QC and later to be a Labour Lord Chancellor, certainly started off with serious doubts about what we sought to achieve. He thought it was all little more than a power struggle between two rival groups for control of the union. I told him just how wrong he was. I wasn't the slightest bit interested in taking control, in power for power's sake. What I desperately wanted was for the Electrical Trades Union to be run in the members' interest, not in the interests of the Communist Party of Great Britain.

We set out to prove the public allegations that had mounted steadily since 1957 that there was conspiracy and fraud to rig the ETU's elections. We sought a declaration that the 1959 election for General Secretary, in which Frank Haxell supposedly defeated John Byrne, was null and void. We asked, too, for an order that future elections should be independently supervised.

I don't know that I convinced him then, but Gerald Gardiner certainly did us proud during the case. There is no doubt that, as the evidence amassed, he came round firmly to the view that we really had uncovered what he later pronounced to be 'the biggest fraud in the history of trade unionism'. Until this case exposed their aims and methods, the Communists were regarded as dedicated radical trade unionists, that's all. No one saw them as crooked, as habitual practitioners of the political double-cross. Yet they unscrupulously deceived working people, the organised labour, whom they purported to represent. We cut right through to their rotten core and showed them as they were – and still are.

My role in that High Court case was central and crucial. But for one man especially, the result was a total vindication of an unrelenting dedication to a cause – the public exposure, humiliation and overthrow of the Communist regime in the ETU. That man was the late Sir Leslie Cannon.

Les broke with the Communist Party over the Hungarian rising, though he reckoned he saw the light some while before that. The reprisals against him were swift and brutal. He was ousted from his job as the union's Education Officer. The Communist hierarchy closed the Education Department down and pretended that this justified his redundancy – the kind of warped decision that nowadays would see them arraigned before an Industrial Tribunal for unfair dismissal. They went on to swindle him out of an Executive Council seat, and his elected post on the union's TUC delegation. He was banned for five years from holding union office.

But this vindictive behaviour only enhanced his determination to fight back. He led the revolt against the Communists, and was the chief architect of their crushing defeat. It was a fitting reward that he later became the union's President, was knighted, and became a much respected figure in British industry. His tragic death in 1970 at the age of fifty-one robbed the British trade union movement of its most powerful and forceful intellect, and of the most far-sighted leader of the post-war era.

My own position after Hungary was different from that of Les Cannon. Disillusioned Communists quit in droves, but I was initially involved in meetings to try to persuade them to stay inside the Party, to democratise it, to alter its leadership, and to fight for policy changes. The Party's spies informed on me and I got the deep-freeze treatment. But they were too late to stop my election to the Executive Council in 1958, so they changed tack and turned on the heat. By then, though, I was shoulder to shoulder with Les, all the way to the High Court.

I do not pretend that I had a blinding flash of light that turned me overnight from a committed Communist to a fierce anti-Communist. Like most political decisions involving a fundamental shift of allegiance, this one evolved over a period. But once I fully realised the sick and squalid past in which I had shared and the gross injustice our members suffered as a consequence, I had no choice. There should have been no choice for anyone who held similar views.

I believed fervently in trade unionism. I still do. I believed in fraternity and brotherhood. I still do. The ETU as it was when our High Court case began, mocked those deep-seated beliefs. It had taken me all too long to wake up to that unpalatable fact, to reject, as a betrayal of

10

working people, the way Communists manipulated trade unions as a means of furthering the Party line.

Les was working as an electrician for Gaze's, the Kingston shopfitters, but got leave of absence so that he could work closely with Ben Hooberman, our solicitor, in preparing the case. We later appointed Ben as the union's lawyer and he is now widely recognised for his expertise in union affairs. His personal faith in our fight for justice went well beyond the bounds of legal duty and was another vital element in the success of our daunting undertaking. Les never missed a single courtroom session throughout the protracted hearings – he was absorbed, his application was total. He told me that he often got up at 5.00 a.m. to type out comments on the previous day's proceedings in order to help Counsel with union nuances. There was no doubt that he saw his future role in life changing spectacularly before him. I entertained no such thoughts. For me the battle I was currently engaged in was enough.

The hearing was in Divorce Court Four at the Royal Courts of Justice in the Strand. There can have been few cases where one side brought so many witnesses – ninety-seven of them for us. It was also the first time that the law on conspiracy had ever been applied to a trade union election, with working trade unionists acting against the officers of their own union. It was an incredible story, by any standards, that unfolded during the forty-two days of courtroom action. There was more than a ton of documentation, and there would have been far more if the defendants had come clean. The Communists had their hand-picked staff sifting through the mass of papers at the union's headquarters, Hayes Court, at Bromley, Kent. Their job was to suppress or dispose of anything incriminating before we got hold of it. Throughout the trial Mr Gardiner constantly had to call for more documents to be produced. Everything had to be dragged from our opponents.

We were entitled to documents as the plaintiffs, but who got what turned into something of a race. There were hundreds of thousands of letters and reports from union branches all over the country, some going back many years. We hired a huge hall in Lincoln's Inn Fields where the bumph was stacked from floor to ceiling. We burrowed away for endless hours and the sheer quantity of paper was our biggest enemy. Later, the documents would be conveyed to a basement below the Law Courts. Mark Young, another prominent member of our team and now General Secretary of the British Airline Pilots' Association, waded through

11

them, making copious notes to aid our attack. He too was an ex-Communist and like me was on unpaid leave of absence from his job as a London Transport electrician.

More sinister were the huts that were erected in the grounds of Hayes Court. They were manned by Communist Party union members working with those few members of the staff who could be trusted not only to 'regulate' the documents, but often to interview those branch secretaries and union members who might be called upon to give damning evidence about their branch voting. There is no doubt, too, that they were out to nobble any witnesses if they saw a chance of doing so. All this had the effect of making a monumental task more difficult.

It was not just paper that went missing: there were union members who could have backed us with telling details. Some of them quit the Communist Party in disgust, but, when it came to first-hand racket-busting, they simply lacked the guts to see it through. Yes, there was intimidation. These men had wives and families, and there was no certainty of ending up on the winning side. Some of them doubtless considered they would be throwing in their lot with surefire losers, or perhaps they just could not face the ugly prospect of standing in the witness box and confessing to their own past misdeeds. None of us relished that. Many of them had dirty hands. I know that I did.

Sitting in court I recalled a similar event that took place some years ago in our union. It was in 1939 at the time of a major contracting strike at Chorley. Joe Vigon, a disillusioned ETU Communist, made critical suggestions to the management which, after much argument, led to him making a report to the union's Executive Council. He alleged that the Communist Party held secret meetings with non-ETU Communists, designed to interfere with our policies and elections. Both Haxwell and Foulkes were among those charged by the union for their part in these underground activities. Haxell, then an Executive Councillor, was banned from union office for five years. Foulkes, an area official who was then running for General Secretary, escaped with a warning.

Joe Vigon, viciously abused by the Communists for telling the truth, was exonerated. But as a result of his disclosures to the Executive Council he was hounded for years after by every Communist electrician, and quite often by their sympathisers. They kept up their persecution until he finally left the trade.

What we were now fighting for was not only a verdict that would allow us to condemn and disown the past. At stake too was the future, for if we could not prove our case, if we were not believed, then we would all get the Joe Vigon treatment. We would become the pariahs of the Labour movement – driven out of our jobs, with the certain liability of a huge legal debt. I reflected that some of our witnesses might, like me, remember what had happened to Joe: they might have learnt their lesson. There were, however, forty or so brave local branch officials who willingly volunteered their help despite the grave risk. Afraid or not, we needed their evidence and got it. Here and there we subpoenaed a hostile witness; others, who were sympathetic, could have come forward voluntarily but deserted us. They were in a very different category in my book. I could sympathise, but I could not excuse them. They had taken from the union, and it was time to put something back.

There were sixteen defendants, though the case against two of them was dropped long before the trial was over. Of the other fourteen, the principal trio were Frank Foulkes, the union's President, Frank Haxell, the General Secretary, and Bob McLennan, the Assistant General Secretary. They were known as the 'Three Generals'. Eleven of those accused were Communist Party members and three were in the Labour Party, all of them fellow travellers. Names like Hendy, Frazer, Cosby, Davies, West, Feathers, Sell, Batchelor, Goldberg, Humphrey, Scott, mean little enough now, even to students of trade union form, but they were familiar enough in those days, both within the union and beyond it, through the extensive media coverage of both the trial and the events leading up to it.

The desperation of the Communists showed through well before the trial began. They did their utmost to push back the opening date, and to hinder the gathering of evidence they put out a circular to the union membership telling them that it would be wrong for them to give any information to the solicitors acting for me and for John Byrne. The fixers were at it, and it meant a preliminary legal skirmish to slap them down and establish our initial rights. The Lord Chief Justice in the Divisional Court dealt with the matter: he said that the circular was a clear contempt of court, warranting imprisonment. However, to avoid still more delay to the main trial, he only imposed a penalty of costs. Even so, the trial, originally due in February 1961, did not get under way until June.

It was, though, well worth waiting for. In the first five minutes of the very first day there was a major shock. Mr Neil (now Sir Neil) Lawson,

13

the defence QC, admitted that the Byrne–Haxell election result was invalid. They had conceded one of the main issues in our action at the outset – but it was only one of them, and there were plenty more. Gerald Gardiner was scintillating. He opened by explaining succinctly how elections were rigged by:

arranging that there was never more than one Communist candidate for a post, and fixing who it should be;

ensuring the maximum number of branch nominations for the favoured candidate;

sending National Officers to canvass for the Communist candidate in the branches;

making trivial charges against non-Communists so that they could be banned from office;

disqualifying non-Communist branches by using the union's complicated rules to claim irregularities while condoning the same irregularities in Communist-run branches;

and, when all else failed, altering the voting returns.

Mr Gardiner said the Communists 'actually excelled themselves' in the Byrne–Haxell contest. They used all seven methods and had already trumped up a charge against me to try to curb my constant challenges and embarrassing intrusions into their activities. The court was to hear a lot more about my deliberate provocation – it was a tactic I could not deny using, but it played its part in bringing my targets to justice. Yet despite all the fiddles, Mr Gardiner declared, Haxell still lost the election so 'there was only one way out left and that was to disqualify as many non-Communist branches as possible'.

Three days into the trial Mr Lawson tried again to get it adjourned for six months 'to amend the defence' and collect more evidence. Mr Justice Winn was clearly getting into the swing of it and was having none of that old bull.

Witness after witness testified to the existence of Communist Party advisory committees in the union and put the finger firmly on the ETU's own Communist advisory committee – a set-up with dictatorial powers. The court heard about the tight control of the ETU Communist advisory committee by the Three Generals. Foulkes, Haxell and McLennan were generals all right – conducting a no-holds-barred war in which they misrepresented both the laws of the country and the rules of the union as mere props for the capitalist classes. That way they could justify any kind of treachery and chalk it up to working class solidarity. Theirs was part of an endless war against compromise and tolerance.

One witness, Dick Reno, produced an interesting aside. During our campaign he courageously went on television to denounce the Communists. He told the court that he left the Communist Party and became a member of the Militant Industrial Group. He said that it produced a monthly journal, *The Militant*, and its total membership at the time was not more than twenty. That tiny, irrelevant band of backroom revolutionaries was among the progenitors of today's Militant Tendency, which has done so much damage to the Labour Party.

It was Thursday 27 April when I was called into the witness box, and well into the following day when I stepped down. I told my story at length – how I had joined the ETU twenty-six years earlier and the Communist Party in 1939. That I had been an electrician's mate to a Mr Stride in Liverpool and that it was Stride, later a full-time official of the union, who had introduced me to Communist advisory committee work. I presented a lot of detail about the advisory committees and how they held regular meetings to arrange the conduct of union elections and ballots. I explained how all the meetings began with a political statement which could last for anything from five minutes to an hour. This, I assured the court, was always the form at Communist Party meetings. Continual repetition and a coherent, centrally-dictated propaganda line throughout the Party was the established way to get the message across. It still is. That is why brainwashed Communists, wherever and whenever you meet them, all tend to spout the same things about the same people and events at the same time.

I explained too, how I had attended the union's 1949 Policy Conference as a delegate and put up a good case in defence of the Communist Party when I spoke. Frank Haxell had congratulated me and said 'you will be hearing from me'. Some months later I became a member of the Communist Party's ETU National Advisory Committee on Haxell's recommendation. I told the court how, before every ETU policy or rules revision conference, the most trustworthy Communist Party members met to decide what resolutions would be put through the branches and, later, to sort out which resolutions the Party wanted supported or opposed at the conference. Today, as then, rigging the conference agenda starts with pre-arranged Communist proposals in the branches. I dealt with my defection from the Communist Party and a subsequent phoney charge against me within the union, when I was censured by the Area Committee and inevitably had my appeal thrown out by the Executive Council.

I was questioned about a mass of correspondence between the union and the TUC. As public allegations of electoral malpractice and Communist influence mounted, the old TUC carthorse had finally stirred. One letter from the TUC General Secretary, Sir Vincent Tewson, to the union said of the various allegations: 'It is increasingly difficult for the General Council to ignore the possible effect of them on the prestige and public reputation of the trade union movement as a whole.' Haxell's response to Tewson, and to a series of other letters from the TUC, were also read into the court records. They showed that the TUC leadership, however belated its action, became more and more exasperated by the ETU's prevarication and evasion at a time when the press was running riot with criticisms and revelations.

Ploughing through the correspondence took some time. Then it was Mr Lawson's chance to grill me. He asked me whether I had not gone into the election for an Executive Council seat in 1957 as 'a very vigorous Communist'. I replied: 'The correct answer to that would be that I went to the members as a known member of the Communist Party but also as a man with an independent mind who did not always agree with either the Communist Party or the leadership of the union.' He pressed me on my brushes with Haxell and I told him that I disagreed with Haxell over his dictatorial use of advisory committee machinery within the union – which he used to his own advantage. Mr Lawson asked me pointedly whether I admitted that I had been a member of the Communist conspiracy. He got no cheer from my reply: 'I am saying not only that I was a member of that conspiracy, but that I am heartily ashamed of my part in it.'

I clashed sharply several times with Mr Lawson. I suggested that he should shorten the length of his questions if he really wanted 'Yes' and 'No' replies, as he claimed. My court-room manners may not have been Inner Temple standards, but I wasn't a lawyer raking in a big fat fee for inquisitorial eloquence. At one stage I was sufficiently riled to tell him: 'There are advisory committees of the Communist Party which deal with every facet of life in Britain, including all the trade unions and all the industries and all the things that are not industries, including the Law Courts.'

I knew about the sizeable Communist group among High Court lawyers. They operated through the Haldane Society, until a break-away led to the foundation of the Society of Labour Lawyers. I thought, and hoped, that I would be questioned about my assertion – I wanted the public to be fully aware of the implications of what I charged. But my comment went down like a lead balloon. I am sure that Mr Lawson winced; Mr Justice Winn and Mr Gardiner kept their heads down: it must have been the lawyers' self-protection society at work. It's a pretty good closed shop they run. But the pro-Communist Haldane Society still exists today, and there is plenty of evidence that the Communists still have no shortage of friends at court.

There was always something unexpected cropping up as the trial progressed. We even produced a private detective, William Cobbett, hired to demonstrate the theory that we had about postmarks on substituted ballot envelopes. We set out to prove that the Communists could have invalidated votes after receipt by putting them in fresh envelopes and re-posting them a week or so after the genuine envelopes were sent. We picked out pro-Byrne branch votes that were disqualified for late arrival and Cobbett drove around the country to the places postmarked to show that the election could have been fixed that way. 'Cobbett's Rides' were an important part of our evidence. We also hired the services of a firm specialising in market investigations, who interviewed the members of the union's London South West Branch and questioned them as to whether and how they had voted in the election.

John 'Jock' Byrne, the union's West of Scotland area official, was our last witness. He was my co-plaintiff in the action, a stocky, white-haired, taciturn Scot who had stood as the anti-Communist candidate for national office in a series of elections, without success, since 1947. He was not a popular choice among the ex-Communists as our candidate against Haxell. Many of them still saw themselves as left-wingers and were appalled at the prospect of backing a right-wing Catholic Labour Party man. I told them that was shortsighted, and declared: 'He is the man with both the right political background and the courage to beat them. We have to support him. He is our only chance to turn them over. We can only have a genuine political dialogue in the union when we have got rid of the Communists and that must be our sole policy at this stage.'

There were moments of real drama when the spotlight switched to the defendants. George Scott, an ETU National Officer, was a Labour Party stalwart, albeit of a very different kind from John Byrne. He began his career as a left-wing critic of the Communist leadership and at one time even backed Byrne. But he and Sam Goldberg, then a Trotskyite, went on a trip to the Polish 'People's Democracy', along with Haxell.

17

They promptly shifted their allegiance and became pro-Communists on the Haxell ticket. Looked at in the light of recent happenings in Poland, it is perhaps surprising that two trade unionists on the left of the Labour Party could have been so easily beguiled.

Mr Jonathan Sofer, Mr Gardiner's junior counsel, went for Scott over an article he wrote for the Communist *Daily Worker*, forerunner of the *Morning Star*, in which he claimed that the anti-Communist case was a press fantasy and said that even if all the votes of the disqualified branches were counted as valid, Haxell would still have won the election. Sofer failed to pin Scott to an admission that he was wrong over the figures. Mr Justice Winn joined in. He warned Scott not to argue, referred to the article and asked bluntly: 'You were being put forward there as an honest and upright Labour Party supporter telling the facts in connection with this smear campaign against the Communists?' Scott: 'I asked to do that, yes.' Mr Justice Winn: 'And the facts you gave were quite untrue?' Scott: 'It would appear that I was wrong by thirty-four votes.'

Scott then said he thought that he could have made an error, and the judge became increasingly irritated. He stabbed his pencil at Scott as if it was a dagger, and tartly adjourned the court for Scott to look at the relevant papers. When the court resumed ten minutes later Mr Lawson took over. He said Scott agreed that Mr Sofer's figures were correct – tantamount to acceptance that the *Daily Worker* article was false. But there was never any clear response over just what check Scott had made of the branch voting tallies before he wrote the offending article.

Scott featured in another curious incident when Mr Sofer accused him of helping a cover-up by deliberately failing to report ballot-rigging in the Southend Electronic Engineers' Branch. Scott had investigated the branch and reported to the union Executive. He was pressed several times by Mr Sofer and by Mr Justice Winn about his original report which appeared to be missing. He claimed he would very much like to produce it, but did not know where it was. Once John Byrne had been installed as General Secretary at Hayes Court, it took me a few minutes to discover that report. It was an unchallengeable example of vital evidence being suppressed by a Communist sympathiser who could genuinely claim that he had always been a loyal member of the Labour Party.

Frank Haxell, a Communist Party Executive Committee member, denied everything thrown at him. There were no ETU Communist advisory committees; he knew nothing about ballot-rigging. He trotted out a catalogue of his achievements on behalf of the union, but if he thought he was doing well, he was sadly in error. The judge cut in at one point to warn him that he was forming 'my own assessment of your intelligence and ability' – and it was no compliment. Later he called Haxell a sorry figure.

Frank Foulkes took the stand. He was the union's senior man: a renowned industrial negotiator whose wiles and ways secured both sympathy and respect, inside and outside the union. He had the furthest to fall, and he did just that – exposed on all counts. His evidence matched that of Scott for high drama, not least when he made the most startling, if ludicrous, suggestion of the trial – that Les Cannon and his associates rigged the whole election to achieve a null and void result because they didn't want John Byrne as General Secretary.

Mr Lawson contrived his own mini-marathon for the defendants in his summing up. He must have sensed it was a lost cause but they couldn't say he didn't try. He spent nearly two full days attempting to undermine our case. He sought to paint a picture of a group of ordinary working men plunged out of their depth into an administrative whirl-pool. It would have been more convincing if Foulkes, Haxell and their henchmen had not gone to such lengths to portray themselves as skilled negotiators of extraordinary sagacity and ability. They tried to have their cake and eat it.

Mr Gardiner was in splendid form in his last major fling for us. He ripped through all the bogus defence arguments with relish and gusto. He said: 'There are two lies which the defendants told on every possible occasion, including their appearance in the witness box. The first is that the criticisms which have been made are malicious, vile insinuations made by unscrupulous people who want to break up the union.' He said that Scott, Goldberg, Foulkes – 'any witness who had an opportunity made a little speech about these vicious attacks by the capitalist press, who wanted to break up the union. Far be it for me to say anything in defence of the capitalist press but this attack has not been on the union but on the defendants, a handful of Communists who have got this union in an iron grip. The second lie may be summarised in the phrase Mr Lawson made in his concluding speech when he described the whole thing as "a bitter feud between two groups". I utterly repudiate this.' It was then that Mr Gardiner called it all 'the biggest fraud in the history of British trade unionism'.

Mr Gardiner gave us a grandstand finish. Now it was up to Mr Justice

Winn. We could only sweat it out, fingers crossed and hoping like hell that the momentuous affair which we had lived with and even dreamed about for so long would be crowned with a verdict that warranted and justified our efforts.

## CHAPTER 2

# FROM PIGEONS TO POLITICS

We were lucky kids, my sister Emily and I – that's what father told us: separate bedrooms; a week's holiday at Southend-on-Sea each year. The only holiday most of my school chums had was two or three weeks with the family, hop-picking.

I suppose we really were lucky by the standards of those hard times. Father ran a one-man shoe repair shop in Pitfield Street, Hoxton. It was a typical poverty-stricken East End slum area of London, though it didn't seem that way to me at the time. I was born and bred to it. We lived in the flat over the shop and let off the two rooms at the top of the house to help the family budget.

We had a toilet in the outside yard, but no bath or running hot water, so we went to the public baths. Few working people were any better off then. What is depressing is to realise that there are still too many people living in Britain today in similarly unacceptable conditions. The main occupation for youngsters was to stand around on the street corners and to gamble for coppers with dice or cards. Fights broke out among the gangs of lads, many of them on the dole, and the police had to step in. Again, we don't seem to have made much progress.

Our shop premises was owned by my mother's family. In the depression years my father made precious little money from the business because shoes were cheap to buy new and people preferred to wear them out rather than pay a high price for a leather sole repair. Father couldn't run much of a slate for his hard-up customers because he had to have ready cash to buy materials. My mother, Emma, worked too – for her father. Mr Rook's greengrocery stall was a feature of Hoxton market. Mother used to get about thirty bob for a six-day week, and that was about as much as my father made from the shop. I think he rather resented that and thought that his wife's place was in the home – even though he didn't earn enough to sustain it.

Frank, my father, was invalided out of the Army in the First World

War after his knee cap was blown off at Ypres. Before the war he had been a painter and decorator, but his wound prevented him from climbing ladders so he learned shoe-making. But no one in Shoreditch or Hoxton bought hand-made shoes. They were for the toffs. So, he switched to repairs. One of his problems was that he couldn't read or write. He had difficulty in keeping proper accounts and it was easy for people to take advantage of him. My mother was an intelligent woman and I think my father's illiteracy was irritating to her. But it was hardly his fault – he was the youngest of twelve children and his opportunities were limited. His father was a chair-frame maker. My mother died when she was fifty-one and my father at sixty-five, but old Grannie Chapple lived to be ninety-two – I still remember her formidable appearance in her black bonnet and coat. I used to visit her every Saturday and she would give me tuppence. She was a tough old lady. So far as I know, my father's one claim to fame was that he was chosen to play the cat in one of Lupino Lane's shows at the old Britannia Theatre, Hoxton. That was the extent of his public performances. You could say I've more than made up for him.

Mother used to vote Tory, like her family, but I don't think father ever voted at all. He simply wasn't interested. Nonetheless, his shop was the centre of discussion for everything under the sun – from pigeons to politics. I've been involved with both ever since.

The local beat bobby often sat behind my father's machine partition while Mr Mordecai, the publican from the Ivy House next door, sent in a customary pint. It was a bribe to ensure that if they strayed a minute or two beyond closing time, there would be no summons. It certainly oiled the wheels of justice effectively, for there was never any nonsense with the beaks.

These were the days when illegal betting was rife. Every street had its bookie and 'dropsy' was a financial, not medical, term. Despite the dropsy, every bookie took his turn at being nicked. I can recall having a conversation with a Scottish copper as he sat behind the partition: he told me how spellbound he had been listening to a speech in Glasgow by Harry Pollitt, then the Communist Party's General Secretary. Pollitt had convinced my policeman friend that the Communists were not all wrong. I was still at school but his remarks were to have a great effect on my later life. Many years later, when the time came for me to make political decisions, that casual back-of-the-shop chat became decidedly relevant. It helped to push me along a political road which was at first exhilarating, but which I later came to abhor.

22

No doubt if any of my neighbours or friends from that time were asked what they remembered of me, they would describe a lad, sometimes cheeky, sometimes very serious, who could always give them advice about how they could treat their ailing pets. It was my father who passed on his love of animals to me. We had a backyard with a large shed that was always filled with a variety of animals – rabbits, white mice, ferrets – and I kept newts or fish in an old bath. We also had a fierce halfbreed bull terrier, called 'Buller'. I was always reading about animals. I had both practice and theory going for me and local people often found me useful when their own pets were ill.

My father liked to fish and in summer he would sometimes take me on a threepenny tram-ride to Chingford Mount. We would walk with rods and tackle to the River Lee. It was on one of these outings that I discovered a frog spawning ground: I collected the tadpoles and sold them back home at a halfpenny for a jam-jar of five.

There were other influences at work in those childhood years – two stand out. The first was my uncle, the greengrocer. He was a lifelong believer in socialism (though I suspect he always voted Conservative) and he filled me with anecdotal stories of the socialist orators of his youth. One he quoted as saying: 'Remember, lad, if you put all the gold in the world around the top of a coal-mine, it won't bring up a bucket of coal.' Another was: 'If you were dying of thirst in a desert, all the diamonds in the world would be no help to you.'

The second influence was of even more significance. My father and relatives were mostly shopkeepers and small businessmen, and I had a sallow complexion and dark hair. It was not surprising that some of my school chums thought I was Jewish. The word spread and I learned first-hand about the terror of racial prejudice. I was often referred to as a 'little Jew bastard'. I certainly need no lessons about the need for racial harmony.

I was an avid reader and particularly loved animals stories and travel books. But I ranged ever wider as I got older – from detective novels to socialist tracts. All this reading threw up question after question in my mind, not least about the incompatibility of surplus land and hungry workless people. Why, I mused, should life for so many be so miserable? I was never satisfied with the answers. The politician in me was stirring.

Another long-standing interest stems from these early days. I used to pay a fortnightly visit to the barber's shop, where Alf, the adopted son of Mr Watts, the barber, told me about the concerts he went to. So it was haircuts that introduced me to classical music. The only other thing I can remember about Alf now was that he had very smelly feet. I liked to hear about those concerts, but I was never sorry to escape from the barber's chair. I get great pleasure from classical music. Time has not been on my side and I have had to make do with the occasional concert, listening to records, and also tapes while driving. My Desert Island Discs would certainly include Sibelius's Fifth Symphony as well as Tchaikovsky, Rimsky-Korsakov and Rodrigues, the blind Spanish composer of guitar music.

Jim Reeves, a second-hand furniture dealer, lived opposite. His adult son was chair-bound and suffered badly from epileptic fits. He had the greatest collection of cigarette cards I have ever seen – books and books of them – which would be worth a fortune now. Jim was a founder member of the Socialist Party of Great Britain. His son-in-law was an official of the Transport and General Workers' Union and a pacifist who, according to my father, was pelted with horse manure by angry crowds when he spoke against the First World War from public platforms. That seemed to me to show a lot of pluck. I couldn't have imagined myself on a platform, addressing an audience, though I was to do so all too often in the years to come. If horse manure had remained as readily available, I would doubtless have received my share, though for different reasons.

I did gain one advantage in those days for my subsequent platform oratory. I have often been chided for speaking loudly, and in fact, all four of us – father, mother, sister and myself – were alike in this respect. The reason was simple enough. At a time when my father's business was prospering, he managed to buy a finishing machine which he used to polish the new soles and heels on his repairs with the colour of the upper. The shop parlour, where we ate all our meals, led directly from the shop, so to hear each other's conversation when the machine was running we had to pitch our voices as high as possible.

I mostly enjoyed my time at school. I still have my school leaving report: it described me as a bright boy, truthful and honest, who would do well. I did not finish my schooling in the highest possible class, but I did have, the report says, average ability. Towards the end of my school days I became very friendly with Mr Thoeday, the headmaster and one-time president of one of the teachers' unions. He was a fine, tall and impressive-looking man who had once been a Conservative Councillor at Ongar, Essex. He took a personal interest in boys who he thought could be doing better, and he thought that about me. His approach was 'onwards and upwards'. He was always particularly concerned for the welfare of the school-leavers and, where appropriate, did his best to steer them into jobs. I used to go back to visit him and it was a friendship which lasted until his death.

There was a teacher there called Jack Johnson, a formidable man with strange eyes, who terrified us. He was a strict disciplinarian who would whack boys at the slightest excuse. Mr Thoeday once told me that Johnson was the most brilliant teacher in the school. He said: 'The reason he has never been made headmaster is that he was a pacifist in the war.' I must say, you could have fooled me.

Before the Second World War, Shoreditch was a hotbed of Sir Oswald Mosley's fascists, just as today it is reckoned to be a source of considerable support for the National Front. The same sort of people who then attacked the Jews, now practise their race hatred at the expense of the blacks and other ethnic minorities. The pre-war fascists terrorised our neighbourhood with their regular marches in uniform to the beat of banging drums and clashing cymbals – I can think of no more frightening sound with which to disturb the traditional Sunday lunch and those turning out of the pubs. I saw too much of the black-shirted fascists because they had a headquarters in Mintern Street, opposite my father's shop. I am sorry to say that quite a few of my school chums joined them and the majority of the Shoreditch folk were, in a typically British way, largely indifferent to these dangerous extremists. They preferred to look the other way unless action was unavoidable.

Still, as a lad, I was much more interested in flora and fauna than fascism. I was especially involved with my pigeons. I still am. I kept about twenty and raced them when I was aged only twelve and was the youngest member of the local pigeon club. My father took no part in this because he reckoned that racing the birds was cruel; I have never agreed with that. In any event, I believe it was the pigeon club which indirectly encouraged me to argue and debate at subsequent political meetings. I had my say in club discussions, when we would sort out the season's racing programme and decide who would do what. We were all so hard up that we only had one pigeon clock between us. That was kept at the club headquarters in Hyde Road, Hoxton.

Imagine the scene on a race day. The pigeon would return to base, the rubber ring would be swiftly removed from it and a fleet-footed runner would dash with it to Hyde Road. Into the clock went the ring and a disc would then be pricked with the time your pigeon got home. The chore which always seemed to fall to me, as the youngest and most active member, was pushing the pigeons to be raced or trained by barrow to Kings Cross Station, all the way from Hoxton. It was several miles and hard work, but a barrow was the most our sparse resources would run to.

I never thought, as I pushed that barrow, that more than forty years on I would chat to the Queen about pigeons. It happened at a Buckingham Palace lunch where I was a guest, along with a famous playwright, a prison governess, a well-known steeplechase rider and a Fleet Street editor. I asked the Queen about the royal racing pigeons. I don't know whether she had been briefed about my interest but she certainly surprised me. She had a very considerable knowledge about pigeons and about the royal loft.

When my uncle, the greengrocer, opened a new shop, the firm that was doing the wiring for him took me on as an unindentured apprentice electrician. I was fifteen, and didn't really know what I wanted to do, but once in the job I got really keen. I had left school about a year earlier and done the various dead-end jobs that ill-educated working class youngsters of that time fell prey to. I worked as an errand boy, trundling furs or stationery in big cases around the City. I got to know that area very well and lived largely on chocolate bars. I did a couple of page boy jobs at hotels too, but I only stayed a few days in each. Most of the money I earned went on pigeon feed, but I kept a little to play cards with my friends.

It was all pretty frustrating, so starting work for the A to Zed electrical firm in the business hinterland at Vauxhall Bridge Road, off Victoria Street, was an exciting adventure. That job, too, meant plenty of walking: materials from the firm's store had to be pushed on a two-wheeled builders' barrow to the job on which we were working; material from the wholesalers was collected in the same way. Naturally, it was the apprentices who trundled the barrows, often all the way through the City. I remember with some nostalgia a wide teak counter in the basement of the GEC Aldwych office, where I often used to pick up orders. Years later, GEC's Lord Weinstock closed down that office. I managed to get a six foot length of the old counter from the demolition foreman before the building came down, and I still have it.

It was at this time that I had my first introduction to the world and language of trade unions. I plied the skilled men with questions about it. I wanted to know what a shop steward was. The reply: 'Just wait until you become one. You'll find out soon enough.' Those words were said with some bitterness and I learned later that the electrician who answered me was out of work for a long time after acting as shop steward on a previous job. The result was that he never became a shop steward again, although I have never met a more decent and diligent worker. I don't think there was a provable blacklist across the industry, but jobs were tight and employers checked whenever possible and played safe. Ex-shop stewards were regarded as a bit of a risk. I found too that one of the firm's managers was an ex-trade union activist and had been a union branch secretary. It was a pretty unusual move for those days and other workers felt he had sold out. Overall, it was not the most encouraging introduction to trade unionism.

It was not long before I reached my sixteenth birthday and became eligible for union membership. I was working then at Waterloo House, one of the few buildings I was employed at which is still standing today. It was from there that my attempts to join the union began. I was sponsored by Joe Saunders, the site shop steward and later a London Airport representative for the Association of Supervisory, Technical and Managerial Staffs. Unemployment was chronic and there were consequent restrictions on union membership. The local branch, Gray's Inn, met at Cloudesley Square in Islington and refused my application to join unless and until my employer guaranteed that he would employ me for five years, then the normal period for an indentured apprentice.

The firm was not prepared to give the necessary undertaking and I was left as the only non-unionist employed there. Joe Saunders took the view that I was unreasonably rejected as a member and hit on the idea that I should apply direct to ETU headquarters. The ploy worked and I was admitted. It was an inauspicious entry to the union and there was a spot more trouble. I immediately applied for a transfer to the branch which had turned me down and ETU headquarters took the necessary action.

I went along to my first branch meeting at the Cloudesley Tavern in Islington. It was a crowded session and many of the men there were unemployed. Charlie Perkins, the branch secretary, read out the letter from head office about my transfer and a fair old rumpus developed. It meant, after all, that the branch decision was overturned and feelings ran high. 'Who is he?' they demanded. It was at that point that I stood up and said: 'I'm here. I'm Chapple.' I was a decidedly nervous sixteen year old but my intervention succeeded. There was a bit more

27

muttering but it quickly subsided and they passed on to the next business.

I went fairly regularly to branch meetings after that. They were well attended – usually thirty or so people out of a total branch membership of about 120 turned up. The unemployed electricians were particularly keen to attend: they got twelve shillings a week unemployment benefit from the union which could be topped up from a branch contingency fund with, say, another three bob. We got the usual reports on negotiations and disputes and spent a fair bit of time kicking the Executive Council for its decisions.

The four or five Communists in the branch were extremely active, though not unduly successful with the policies they advocated, but they did manage to use the union to infiltrate the local Labour Party. One or two of them, Communist Party card-holders, nevertheless got themselves appointed as delegates to the East Islington Labour Party's General Management Committee. It was my first glimpse of the Communist Party's undercover operations, but it made no real impression on me at the time.

What had a marked effect was Franco's victory in the Spanish Civil War and the Communist Party's propaganda, embodied in slogans like 'Madrid today, London tomorrow'. All this was a catalyst for the political man that was growing inside me. I believed in the fight against fascism and for working class unity. If I had been older I would have gone to Spain.

I had joined the Labour League of Youth branch in Shoreditch – my first positive political step. Lord Ted Willis, the author and playwright, was then the League's vigorous young chairman. But the League of Youth was in trouble with Labour's Transport House headquarters – a situation often repeated since – and its National Advisory Committee was suspended. The details are pretty hazy now but I know that Ted Willis resigned and called on all League of Youth members to follow him into the ranks of the Young Communist League. Our Shoreditch branch did just that – en bloc. I made my own individual application to join the Communist Party and was promptly visited by a Communist member of my own union branch. I had put on my Party application form that I was an ETU member and the Party didn't miss a trick. My political concern could now be channelled through the union.

As with so many young people of that era, events and environment combined to place me on the political left. The threat of a new world war, fascism, poverty and unemployment, had to be fought. The Soviet denial of basic human rights and freedoms could be dismissed as capitalist lies aimed at undermining working class solidarity. Communism was the way ahead.

Thus, in 1939, I embarked upon political activity which has never ceased, though I later quit in disgust from the Party for which I had worked and to which I had belonged for nineteen years.

## CHAPTER 3

# BLOODY-MINDED – AND FIRED!

I was learning fast. Learning about politics and about life. I was still working for the A to Zed firm, but they ran out of work and transferred me temporarily to Troughton and Youngs, electrical contractors. I found myself working at a site in Horseferry Road, but when that contract was complete, I was unemployed. Another unindentured apprentice, Lennie Macausland, and I tramped around doing odd jobs. We had short spells of work and longer periods without, and it went on like that for some months.

It was at this time, while working for a firm called Hearsons, that I had my first taste of what it was like to be a shop steward. We couldn't meet in the firm's time without getting the sack, but during a lunch-break the men decided that I should be the steward. The reason was simple enough: none of the adults would take it on. They didn't want to be marked down, but I was only eighteen and didn't care. I didn't last long, either, and was one of the first to get my cards. The job was supposed to be coming to a close, but there's not much doubt that they got rid of me as soon as they could. They didn't appreciate my audacity in being the men's representative and arguing their case with the supervisors and foremen.

I had collected my shop steward's credentials from the ETU's London office at Rugby Chambers, off Theobalds Road. The office was often advised by employers about the availability of work and sent me on several short-term jobs. The shortest of the lot was at the Strand Palace Hotel, where I lasted two days. I couldn't stick the foreman there. He was a strange type, always breathing down my neck while I worked, and I got so sick of it I quit without even drawing my earnings. I reckon the Strand Palace still owes me two days' pay.

It didn't stop me getting a Royal Ordnance Factory job. I learned from the union office that H.J. Cash, another contracting outfit, wanted men for the ROF site at Kirkby, Liverpool. I saw Mr Jelly, the engineer in charge, at his offices off Victoria Street, London, and he hired me. He too was to have his regrets.

I became electrician's mate to Arthur Stride, deputy shop steward on the site and a keen Communist Party activist, who introduced me to the network of Communist cells. Then as now, Liverpool was a hotbed of far-left intrigue and action. Frank Foulkes was an ETU official there, although I didn't meet him at the time. He was keeping his political head down: the ETU Executive had just charged him with a breach of the union's rules which included collusion and holding meetings with members of the Communist Party during that electrical contracting dispute at Chorley, always referred to as the Vigon affair. Above all Liverpool was the home territory of the firebrand Communist Leo McGree, of the woodworkers' union. He ran the union cell meetings, mostly for builders and electricians, and had a hell-raiser's reputation. He earned it. He was a fine orator, made powerful speeches at TUC conferences and it was no coincidence that it was in Liverpool that the building workers got the highest rates in the trade.

McGree led the negotiations for all the building unions. Employers not only feared him but respected him, for he would turn up on the job and tell the men that they were wrong, if necessary - a tradition which union leaders have long since forgotten. But he would back the workers to the hilt if he thought them in the right. I was introduced to McGree at a Communist cell meeting.

It was on the Kirkby site that I experienced my first major strike. It was a big job with some 5,000 men on site and all the brickies came out - led by the Miles brothers, well-known in London for their disruptive tactics - and it caused chaos while it lasted. We had to remember that there was a war on, but since Russia had not yet come in, strikes were our contribution to the war effort. The authorities made it plain that they would play it tough and I got a tremendous jolt when they drafted in armed police from all over the north of England. Fortunately, there was a settlement before anything got out of hand.

Arthur Stride's role as shop steward didn't endear him to the gaffers. He seemed to collect all the worst jobs on the site and since I was his mate, that meant I got them too. If it was up a pole or in the mud, we got it. He had led a big dispute in London for electricians working in government departments and it looked as if the bosses were out to make things difficult for him.

I also shared digs with Arthur, living with a Liverpool docker and his family. One day Arthur told me Mr Jelly, now the resident site engineer, had informed the men's representatives that he had a problem over me. I had been paid so far at the adult mate's rate for over twenty-ones and overpayment was mounting up. I had realised this some while earlier and Arthur had advised me on what to do if I was challenged. He told me to pay it back or the firm would prosecute for recovery of the money. But he doubted if they would use the law since it only involved a few pounds and they wouldn't do so if I offered to pay it back weekly. If I made no offer, they would certainly sack me. Mr Jelly called me in and Arthur came with me. Mr Jelly called me a thief and said that I had stolen from the firm. Unless I repaid the money, they would prosecute. We worked long hours – about sixty weekly – and the gain to me, spread over the two months, couldn't have been much more than about £20. I said I would pay it off at a shilling a week. I said: 'After all, it's your accounting mistake. It costs a lot to live up here and I've spent the money. I can't pay it now because I don't have it. But I'll pay it back in time.' Mr Jelly got angry. 'If that's it, you're fired,' he shouted. He was a little bantam of a man, used to getting his own way. He wasn't going to be cheated by this cheeky juvenile.

Having pre-armed me and explained the alternatives, Arthur Stride said nothing throughout the interview. So I was out on my ear again. But the truth was that it was no penalty. I was thoroughly fed up with working on this cold and miserable job, squelching around in the mud, lining up with several thousand others for the early morning buses to take us to the site. It was mid-winter and I wanted out. I had had more than enough of Kirkby – including the turns I had to take at selling the *Daily Worker* to those crack-of-dawn bus queues. I was delighted to be sacked, especially since it meant that I got my fare home and my travelling time paid for. I shoved off home with glee.

I was taken on to go to another Royal Ordnance Factory site at Donnington, Shropshire, and it wasn't long before we were out on strike. This time I was one of the five-man strike committee – we were a real bunch of bloody-minded reds. A union official named Richardson was sent to try and sort it out but we refused to listen to him. He told us what he thought of troublemakers from London. We stayed out.

There were two other members of the committee that I remember well, Arthur Attwood and Dick Homewood. Arthur Attwood was a chargehand on the site. We recruited him to the Communist Party while he was there and he subsequently joined the RAF and led an airforce mutiny in India. After the war he became a fulltime ETU official and remained in his post until we banned Communists from office after the 1961 High Court Case. He refused to quit the Party and resigned from the union. His comrades fitted him up with a job in the press, with much better pay than he got from the union.

Dick Homewood didn't believe in supporting capitalism and spent most of his time sitting on a box, reading the *Daily Worker*. He never worked overtime on principle and he impressed me greatly until I discovered that his wife had a highly paid Civil Service job and he didn't need the money anyway. He was a very odd character, but likeable. Years after Donnington, when I was at Hayes Court head office, Dick moved to Littlehampton, Sussex. We knew he was there because the ETU Littlehampton branch started sending in resolutions attacking our anti-Communist Executive. We had never heard from them before, and I don't think we've had any more resolutions since he died.

The Donnington strike produced a military send-off for us, but not with any honours or flying colours. There was a war on, after all, so the Commanding Officer sent for the strike committee. We refused to budge. When the meeting was over, he told us that our tools had been collected from the job. We went outside and two lines of soldiers were ready. They marched us off the site pronto and another job was ignominiously over. Still, work was becoming much more plentiful now. Wartime demands meant jobs at the ordnance factories and on the extensions to munitions factories. Despite my youth I was accepted as a fairly experienced trade union Communist.

This was the time when the union negotiated with the government to allow trainees to come in as electricians and do skilled war work. They called them 'dilutees' and they were paid almost the same rate as skilled men as well as being exempt from war service. I reckoned it was unfair that the dilutees could get a 'skilled' card and I couldn't, even though I had worked for four years at the trade. I argued my case at the branch and they backed me, so I became what I thought at the time was the first nineteen-year-old electrician, though I later found that there were a few others of about the same age.

I was sent to a job converting flats at Regents Park which were to be used to house service personnel and also people being evacuated from Malta and Cyprus. The foreman, Charlie Haynes, nearly had an apoplectic fit when I presented my employment card – a skilled man and not yet twenty-one! – so we started off with a row, but he later came to regard me as rather more capable than some of the older men.

Once again I became a shop steward. Charlie, an ex-Labour councillor, who was also chairman of Camden Town ETU, posed a tricky problem: he wanted to get rid of some of the incompetents. As shop steward, I resisted, so he took me to see their handiwork and I had to agree with him. 'You're right. It's bloody awful,' I said. Eventually we settled for giving them a bit of instruction. Not that Charlie was happy with the compromise, for he was a proud, old-time craftsman and thought that any good trade unionist should be able to do his job well. I secretly admired his view at the time and I have acquired more and more respect for that approach as the years have passed.

It was 1940 and, like all good Communists, I was opposed to the war. The Communist-run People's Convention was campaigning on a 'stop the war' ticket. I had no wish to be called up to fight for a cause I didn't believe in so I got into the docks to work, which put me in an exempt industrial category. I worked for a firm of ship-repair electricians, Campbell Isherwood, on merchant ships, repairing damage, helping to fit guns and instal anti-magnetic mine wiring. Inevitably, I was a shop steward again; I also became secretary of the Poplar Young Communists. There were quite a few folk there who were to figure in my later life. One of my friends was John McLoughlin, who many years on achieved headlines as the 'bellringer' who brought the men out on strike at the Ford Motor Company in Dagenham. He too was a Young Communist and worked for another ship-repair firm where Frank Haxell headed a big cell and was regarded as the local 'guru'.

Most of London's leading Communists from the ETU were in the docks, carefully exempt from war service, but there was a remarkable lack of enthusiasm for war work. Whenever you walked into a ship's engineroom, you stepped over people sleeping or playing cards. Patriotism was a bit of a joke. But while I was there the Soviet line changed and so did ours. One moment the Communist Party was against the war, the next it was for it. I didn't find it easy to switch like that and we had to put up with a lot of ridicule from non-Communists. It was at this time that I first met Tommy Vetterlein who came to mean a lot to me. He was the ETU's East Ham branch secretary and a Communist ship-repair electrician, and I found that he shared many of my misgivings about Communist policy in industry. He was about ten years older than me and was able to put a lot of things in perspective – people and issues.

It was not my Communist faith that was shaken but my quizzical and rebellious nature led me to worry about Party policies and the behaviour of leading Communist figures. They didn't appear like true Communists to me. I have never been able to accept that people don't practise what they preach or to go along with the saying 'don't do what

I do, do what I tell you'. I was sceptical and critical. Why should leading Communists always get the good numbers to work at, corner weekend work at overtime rates, have something more important to do when it was time to get out and sell the *Daily Worker*?

Nevertheless, Poplar Young Communists were coming along nicely and my reputation as an organiser and speaker was beginning to spread. Ted Willis, by now the London District organiser for the Young Communist League, asked me to take a full-time job with the YCL and I became the East London and Essex organiser. I was uncertain about it, but Ted was a bit of a god in the YCL. He was brilliant on a platform – I have heard him speak for two hours without a note. I was once at a crowded open air meeting he addressed and a woman fainted. The copper next to me was so wrapped up in Ted's spouting he didn't even turn round to see what had happened.

The YCL launched a national recruiting campaign and I got a major role in running it. But no one wanted to join us and it was a pretty dismal flop. We were more successful socially. We organised socials and dances and made a lot of money for Party funds. We organised a Bank Holiday gala at Alexandra Palace – funfairs and the rest. There wasn't much of this kind going on in those early war years and we did a roaring trade. Next day Ted Willis and I counted the profits at our Bloomsbury headquarters: we had taken about £2,000 – but it was mostly in pennies. Our hands got filthier and filthier as we handled the bronze coins – and so did my language. I still swear a lot. I can't make excuses. I suppose it stems from a slum area upbringing where you foul-mouthed as kids to show you were as tough as anyone. It's a bad habit that I should have got rid of but haven't.

Of those who had joined the YCL during this period, several have surfaced in more important Party roles. Charlie Brewster, who was an apprentice at Briggs Bodies at the time and far more sceptical than any-one I have ever met, nevertheless clung on to the Communist Party and in more recent times became a *Morning Star* industrial reporter. But I guess his sceptism must have got him into bad odour because he did not last very long on the paper. Another was Tony Chater who is the present pro-Stalinist editor of the *Morning Star* and is currently in conflict with the Euro-Communists who have gained control of the party hierarchy.

While I did the YCL job my union activities were curtailed. I was minute secretary in the Gray's Inn branch but that was firmly controlled by the Party. So they transferred me to London station Engineers No. 10 branch to find out what went on there and to try to build a Communist cell. It was so right-wing that I couldn't even find a seconder for motions. One of the branch members was Ernie Bussey, the ETU's Assistant General Secretary who later became General Secretary. I was too busy in the YCL to do much more than attend union branch meetings, but that period of isolation taught me a great deal about the tactics of acquiring allies.

I stayed about eight months in the YCL post and got increasingly fed up with it. There was always some edict or other from the great planners at the Party's King Street national headquarters and it usually meant another useless campaign of some sort. They were deluding themselves: people just didn't want to become Communists, especially youngsters. YCL membership was falling and I was wasting my time. I was still living over my parents' shoe shop and had saved a bit of cash as an electrician but that all went while I was with the YCL. I needed it to supplement the peanuts I was paid.

I did manage to bring in quite a few Young Communists. We had a strong group among the apprentices at the old Briggs Motor Bodies plant and the Ford car plant at Dagenham. I organised meetings and dances at Dagenham but spending time there was no joy. It was a soul-destroying place, especially in the wartime blackouts – and still is. 'Cadre classes' ensured that I kept on the Communist straight and narrow. I regularly attended lectures on dialetical materialism, what the pronouncements of Lenin and Stalin meant in a British context and so on. I daresay I'm one of the few British union leaders to have read through *Das Kapital* and a lot of other Marx and Engels too.

But it all got too frustrating and I felt that the YCL would be better off if I went back to industry where I could do more for the Party. There was something else though: I started to enthuse for the war and wanted to get into action. Lovable 'Uncle Joe' Stalin had said it was all right for us to dislike fascists once again. If I returned to dock work I would still be exempt so I got a job instead as a site electrician for the Co-operative Wholesale Society at the new modern flour mill they were building at Silvertown Way, Canning Town. Meanwhile, I applied to join the Fleet Air Arm. They were particularly fussy and gave me special medical checks and tests, eventually failing me on eyesight. I carried on with my gruelling and boring job of plugging concrete for light fittings and pipework until my army call-up papers arrived.

## CHAPTER 4

# PRIVATE CHAPPLE'S SPECIAL WAR

It must have been the non-compliant shop steward in me; some would doubtless say the barrack-room lawyer. Whatever it was, it ensured that military service was eventful. And the Germans were the least of my troubles . . .

It was April 1943 when King and Country eventually sent for me. I did my square-bashing at Saighton Camp, Chester, then went for training as an electrician to learn Army methods. This consisted of a short spell of theory at Wandsworth Technical College, followed by training on vehicles and plant at Croydon. I was billeted out and managed to nip off in the evenings to meetings of my union branch. I also started going to a Toc H hall in Croydon where they had regular visits from a magnificent classical pianist. I loved it and was horrified to find when I got there one night that he had been replaced without notice with a 'brains trust'. The Bishop of Croydon was one of the panel and I really got stuck into them. I was full of smouldering resentment over missing my concert and gave the poor old Bishop a particular grilling over how much he got paid for doing his job.

Training complete, I was posted to Greenford, Middlesex, to a unit that maintained vehicles and equipment at a nearby ATS camp and at a hospital. I might have seen a relatively peaceful war out with that unit, but I fell out with the staff sergeant. Someone had to be allocated to do an assault course at Northolt and he picked on me. I let rip but I had no option. My displeasure at going was nothing to what I felt while I was there.

We did everything at the double. We climbed and jumped and strained. We crawled through stinking slime in tunnels and ditches and the NCOs stood up above and urinated on us. I stank so much that I went straight into the shower with all my gear on – tin hat, rifle, the lot. It all made a better soldier of me – or so I was officially informed. Back at the unit, that staff sergeant hadn't forgotten me. He put the boot in some

37

more and I was posted – to a Royal Electrical and Mechanical Engineers' active service unit. I had just lost one battle decisively. Now I was off to win the war.

There was a spot of personal business to attend to first. I went to a holding camp at Bicester, near Oxford, en route for France. And I applied for leave to get married.

I had courted Joan for quite a while. When she was a small child she lived near us in Hoxton and was a friend of my sister and my cousins. Her family moved to Camden Town and it was some years before I saw her again. I was visiting an aunt in Leyton and Joan called there by chance to see a cousin. The ugly duckling from Hoxton was transformed into a very attractive young woman – I insisted on taking her to the bus and then home. We dated regularly after that and she came with me to YCL outings and dances, though she didn't join the League. Her parents didn't like my politics. They were Labour and I was too far out for them. Her mother brought up five kids and was very strong-willed. Life could have been difficult if they had ever tried to stop the marriage.

I hitch-hiked home. Joan was in the ATS by then and she scrounged a few days leave, too. We had a church wedding at Camden Town. I was an agnostic so the religious aspect didn't mean anything to me, but it pleased everyone else, so I went along with it. It was a typical wartime wedding: a tearful parting and back to camp for me, ready for invasion.

It was Gosport this time, with a REME base workshop, already loaded on lorries and waiting to be shipped across the Channel to reinforce the D-Day landings. We were held up by bad weather and it was D-Day plus twenty when we arrived on the beach at Arromanches. We made our way slowly through France and into Belgium, Holland, and eventually Germany. The daftest thing I did was in Holland where the Germans opened the dykes to flood the land ahead of our advance. I slept one night under a tank. Next day I realised that the ground was getting softer all the time and that the tank could easily have sunk down with me beneath it. We were under enemy fire for much of the time but I would have been much safer sleeping in the open. It was also in Holland that I got my only mention in despatches – nothing heroic. We were out of the front line for a rest and the brigadier's car broke down. I fixed it fast and earned my commendation.

It was life without the *Daily Worker*, which was impossible to come by, so I made do with *The Times*. But there was some consolation: Joan knew I was fond of the works of the poet Percy Bysshe Shelley, so when she came across a copy of his collected works on a Charing Cross Road bookstall she sent it to me. It cost her a couple of quid, a high price in those days, but when I got it, it was a real bonus. I started reading the poems to the other lads as we camped on our way through France and Holland. My favourites were *The Banquet of Plato* and *Peter Bell the Third*. The poetry readings became a regular thing and I involved my mates in Shakespeare, too, getting them to read parts from the plays. It was fascinating to see their interest in Shelley: they had never heard his works before or read any of the classics. The Party line would have said it was my proletarian duty to try to raise the cultural level of the masses, but it wasn't that at all. It was all about comfort and comradeship.

Animosity and indignation were building up in the ranks over the lousy conditions. Ever since our landing in France the food had been abominable. There were problems over the massive tent in which we worked under lights to repair trucks and tanks. The most bile was raised, though, over the careful segregation of and privileges for the officers. The lieutenant-colonel who commanded us was even reputed to be acquiring the spoils of war and shipping them back to England in crates. It all came to a head when he disappeared for a few days, presumably on leave, and was said to have gone to Paris where he had a wife or maybe a mistress. The rumblings of discontent got so bad that his deputy, a major, assembled the entire unit on parade, officers in front and a couple of hundred troops in a long line behind. The major paced up and down, lecturing us angrily about ill-based rumours and criticisms. He told us we were a disgrace to the British Army. Then he made his biggest mistake: he demanded to know just what we were complaining about.

I don't quite know why I did it. Someone had to and I knew the appropriate behaviour. Private Chapple snapped into action. I shouted 'Sir!', came smartly to attention and took three paces forward. I listed all those grumbles in a very loud voice so that everyone on parade could hear. As soon as I finished, the squaddies broke into a cheer. Everyone realised that the major should never have called the parade. The sergeant major sensed danger and stepped in quickly to dismiss us and put an end to it. There is no doubt what the squaddies thought of me: they were agog at my audacity.

The major posed the question and got his answer, but it didn't end there for me. A few days later, when the lieutenant-colonel was back, I was posted to a light aid detachment attached to a fighting unit of the 15th Scottish. I never did find out whether any of those complaints bore fruit for the lads I left behind.

The light aid detachment proved to be a rum lot. It was a fourteen-man unit, with a captain in charge, split up into four or five groups, and they were at each other's throats the whole time. I first met them in their bivouacs in a field near the front; they had grouped themselves around the various trucks and wagons that made up the unit's workshop complement and were certainly not talking to each other. It was some time before I managed to ease the situation. The fact that we were going to go through some rough times together was of some help.

The first big event for me was to be sent forward under a gun barrage in the Reichwold Forest as an advance unit, in case our tanks or vehicles broke down. It meant going out into no-man's-land to try to recover the vehicles and it was no picnic. Still, we were not very far into Germany when the armistice was signed. We moved on and at Celle we saw our first concentration camps and the starving prisoners. The German civilians were terrified of us and did their best to tell us that they didn't know what went on behind the wire in those camps. I don't think that they convinced anyone.

Finally, the 15th Scottish came to rest at Lubeck, an old trading town on the Baltic coast and almost on the border with the Russians. Before we encountered any Russian troops, we heard all the horror stories about their rape and pillage from refugees who had fled before them. Our first Russians were mostly Mongolians. They seemed to have wristwatches up to their elbows and they certainly were fearsome-looking fellows. There were Russian and Yugoslav prisoners-of-war in camps near us and it was difficult for me to understand their reluctance to be repatriated to their Communist homelands. They must have feared that they would be shot as traitors or deserters, as we later learned happened to many who did go back.

Many of the Yugoslavs in the refugee camp near us were so determined not to be sent home that they went on a violent rampage. It was the most frightening incident of my whole life. An officer took three of us out with sten guns to quell the riot. We were surrounded by a huge, fierce crowd and I was sure we would be lynched. We lifted our guns and fired into the air. It was a terrifying moment, but the crowd melted away.

I talked to as many Russians as I could, but language was a problem. I met one Russian ex-soldier who worked as a virtual slave for a German farmer. He lived and slept rough in a stable. In a mixture of English and broken German, I tried to enthuse him with the idea of returning to Communist Russia and a new and better society. It was very clear, though, that he was sure he would be better off staying put. It was a reaction that was to take on a special importance for me in later years.

We were in Lubeck for some months and I became politically active again. I made no secret of my Communism and was known as a 'bloody Red': through this, and contacts at the Army Education Centre, I got involved with a cell of about forty army Communists, including several staff sergeants and a couple of officers. We collected hundred of pounds from the troops for the *Daily Worker* and one of the officers got it changed into postal orders so that we could send it off. Barbara Niven, the person responsible for sending us the paper from England, was continuously singing our praises.

We used to meet in a private house in Lubeck, but it was all a risky business. The officers kept away and we stayed in touch with them through the staff sergeants. Army field security got wind of the cell and the meetings and raided the house, but we evaded them by climbing over a back wall. I also established contact with the German Communist Party in Lubeck. My link man was August Michel and I was able to help them, in particular, with an occasional jerry can of British Army petrol – a precious commodity for them. When I left Germany I received a letter of commendation from the German Communist Party, thanking the British Communist Party for my services.

Our light aid detachment was dispersed and I applied for a staff sergeant's training course. I did the course and was offered the rank if I signed on for either three or five years further army service. I didn't want that – home appealed too much. I had only seen Joan for a single weekend leave in Brussels in about three years. I was sent to Osnabruck to work on tanks for a Desert Rats unit there and, once more, I got in touch with the local Communists. Then, in early 1947, I was demobbed. The German Communists' loss was the British Communists' gain – or so they and I thought at the time.

# CHAPTER 5

# THE STRANDS OF DISCORD

The soldier was home. Like so many, I had a wife, a demob suit, and precious little else – certainly no home and no job.

It meant starting married life together in a room over my parents' Pitfield Street shop. Getting work was a bigger problem. I was entitled to go back to my last civvy employer, the Co-operative Wholesale Society, so I applied to them, but they were far from pleased to see me back in one piece. The only work that lousy lot offered me was in Northern Ireland. It was a rotten deal and I thought I had some rights, so I did it the trade union way and took them to a tribunal. It met at Hackney Labour Exchange and, to my chagrin, it found that the firm's offer was reasonable. Four years away soldiering and I was supposed to shove off again. I had a go at the tribunal's trade union member but got no sympathy. I turned down the job.

I was unemployed and angry which gave me a double incentive to get back to my union and political activities. I hadn't been home long before I learned through the union branch about a one-year sponsored scholarship for an ETU member to attend the London School of Economics. There were several eligible candidates but it ended up between Sid Maitland and myself. Sid was later a prominent, if unsuccessful, opponent of my leadership, but he got to the LSE.

However, the ETU Executive Council decided that the runner-up should go to Prague as one of the union's two representatives at a huge jamboree to be held under the auspices of the Communist-run World Federation of Democratic Youth. The other ETU delegate turned out to be Les Cannon, then the union's Liverpool area Executive Councillor. I met him for the first time when he called at Pitfield Street to introduce himself and to discuss the trip. That started a political alliance and a close personal friendship that lasted until his untimely death. It was a meeting that was to lead to spectacular changes in the course of the ETU's history.

Les impressed upon me straightaway that those of us who were Communists must play the main roles in the delegation, certainly among the trade unionists, not all of whom would be Party members. It was supposed to be a non-political occasion but the Labour Party knew better and refused to take part officially. All sorts of youth organisations were involved, including a strong contingent of Young Tories who thought they could expose this Communist set-up. We were there for a purpose: the Communist Party wanted feedback and as much control as possible from within the UK delegation.

There was a London meeting of pro-Communist delegates before we left for Prague, at which Les was elected delegation leader and I was made his deputy. The journey to Prague was a nightmare: we lumbered across Europe in trains that made wartime troop transport seem streamlined; the Prague leg took thirty-six hours on a train with no water aboard. When we arrived it was chaos. Les and I had to find and allocate hostel rooms, ration cards for food and sort out the extraordinary muddle.

We were there for five weeks. It was a mad scramble for food in the student restaurants and, when you got it, it was hardly edible. Fortunately, Les, then unmarried, had an eye for the girls. He struck up a friendship with a Czech girl interpreter and, through her help, eating became less of an ordeal. She even took us to her home where we got some decent meals at last. It was a poor advertisement for burgeoning Communism but those of us who were Party members got some privileges once we had established our identities. We were invited to better meals and parties – the Czech Prime Minister, Gottwald, signed my Party card for me at one of the junkets.

Those of us who were delegation leaders were involved in the political meetings rather than the folk dancing, sports and parades that occupied most of the youngsters. Shelepin led the Russian Young Communists – he was to become head of the infamous Soviet secret police, the KGB, before switching to lead the Soviet puppet trade unions. Les clashed sharply with him at one gathering where we made speeches about our own countries' policies and problems.

There was an abortive attempt to persuade me to go back to full-time work for the Party. Bill Brooks, the YCL's National Secretary, was in Prague; he was leaving his job and wanted me to take it on. I was non-committal, but when he got home he recommended me to the Party Executive. I was approached, but my earlier YCL job was no inspiration. Besides, I had a wife who expected our first child and the pay was poor – I decided to stick to the industrial path.

The practice of Communism so often undermines the theory. Even sympathisers are alienated. I can't believe that the Prague event made any converts to the cause, for it was an abject lesson in indoctrination gone wrong. I was reminded of that Prague visit when I heard about the 1983 World Peace Assembly run by the World Peace Council, a major Soviet front organisation. The Assembly was in Prague and the Czech hosts prevented any criticism of Soviet missile deployment which might have balanced the virulent anti-Americanism, so much so that they upset some of the non-Communist West European peace groups. The West German Greens walked out in protest at Czech police suppression of a peace demonstration and the refusal of their hosts to allow them to meet with the Charter 77 dissidents.

Home again, work was hard to come by, and the situation was made worse by a postwar shortage of electricians' materials. A car breakdown firm took me on for a few months and I then got a job with London Transport on the electrification of the tube out to Ongar. I pestered the local council for a flat and, after the birth of my elder son, Roger, they allocated us a place over a sweet shop very near to my parents' shop. It had a leaking roof and was in a squalid state, but it was our first home of our own.

Inside the union branch I at last had a couple more Party members and we got a few debates going. It was an uphill struggle but I knew much more about the union than most of the others, and I was winning the arguments. Despite being in a small political minority, I was elected as chairman. Ernie Bussey, that right-wing pillar who had been the big man in the LSE No. 10 Branch, had become ETU General Secretary. Clem Attlee gave him a job after the war in the nationalised electricity industry, but the branch stayed firmly on the political right. Ernie's son, Foster, was now the assistant secretary and I became a thorn in his side. Even though I never missed a weekly meeting and my union record was excellent, my bedrock support was minimal and when I upset an influential right-wing shop steward, it wasn't long before I was ousted from the chair. But shifting me out was a mistake. I was uninhibited and could be consistently awkward from the floor – Foster Bussey had a torrid time and no real stomach for it. He lost interest in the branch and the union, and pulled right out.

The Communist group was four-strong now and we got some team-work going. We kept our politics low key and made our pitch on industrial matters, so that we came to be seen as concerned and active trade unionists, as indeed we were. We attracted increasing non-Communist support and Foster Bussey's departure left the way clear for me to take over. No one wanted the post, which was a bit of a chore, but it was useful to the Party and there was an additional attraction: a £12 quarterly expenses payment to help me with repayments on the small terraced house in Stamford Hill for which I had scraped up the cash deposit.

Ours wasn't the only solidly right-wing branch in the area. I went to a nearby branch where Frank Haxell, then an Executive Councillor, was under attack. As a visitor, I could speak but not vote. I did my best, but the verdict against Haxell and the left-led Executive was massive – two votes for him and about 160 against. We Communists had a long way to travel.

We did, however, get a fillip during this period when Ernie Bussey was replaced as ETU General Secretary by Walter Stevens. Stevens was not a Party card-holder but the Communists backed his candidacy on the secret understanding that he would announce, once elected, that he had joined them. He got the job and delivered his part of the bargain. There was nothing philosophical about his Communism – he was in the Party because of the union situation, that was all – but his declaration was useful to those like me who were doing our utmost to build up the Party at branch level.

Like every good Communist, I never neglected my Party political work, and before I left Hoxton for my new home I worked vigorously to strengthen the Shoreditch Communist Party. I was Communist candidate for the local council and polled fewer votes than the fascist. When the result was declared at the Town Hall, the fascist tried to make a speech and I loudly interrupted him. The fascists went wild and a screaming mob of them chased me out of the hall. Only one of my Communist comrades stuck with me and the two of us fled across the road and into the local police station. There was a police car parked outside and one quite elderly fascist woman gave the driver a right-hander through the window. She was soon in clink. But the police didn't want to know; they cleared us out of the station and we had to run for it again, chased by a sizeable posse of neo-Nazi thugs carrying lumps of wood and other vicious-looking weapons. I hadn't moved so fast since that Army assault course at Northolt; fortunately for us, we outstripped them and got away.

I left London Transport and through the late 1940s and early 1950s did a variety of electrical contracting jobs, mostly around London. I worked at Broadcasting House, at the Alexandra Palace television studios, and on rewiring the public library at Essex Road, Islington. I went to Venice as a lighting electrician on the set of a film starring Trevor Howard and didn't do a day's work in the six weeks I stayed there because of some dispute with the Italians. I opted out for a couple of days half-way through to get to an ETU conference, paying my own each-way fare to do so. I was a dead keen member.

We had a second son, Barry, now and there were still spells of unemployment which hit the family budget hard. There was one fifteen-week period from which I spent five weeks on strike from a job at the Earls Court exhibition centre. I marched in torchlight procession during guerrilla strikes throughout the electrical contracting industry and I clashed with union officials at our Camden Town strike centre for their failure to get strike pay out properly to the lads who needed it. On another occasion I led a march of 2,000 electricians from Hyde Park to the Bloomsbury headquarters of the National Federated Electrical Association and handed over a petition to back our demands. There was a staggering number of police on duty but we avoided any trouble. It was all very necessary militant activity for it was important to be involved in industrial action of all kinds and to be seen to be involved. The Communist Party believes that if anything industrially significant is happening, then Party members should get out onto the streets to back it, particularly strikes and demonstrations. Marx teaches that revolution, not criticism, is the motive force of history.

All the while I consistently supported the ETU Communist top brass. I attended the union's Communist Advisory Committee for London regularly over the years and was eventually invited onto the National Advisory body as well, following that conference speech which Haxell thought earned me a promising rating. Communist advisory committees were busy manipulating all the ETU elections, without too much success in Scotland and the north-east but very effectively elsewhere and especially in London and Liverpool – Communists and their sympathisers were grabbing nearly all the official positions in the union. Yet doubts about the ETU leadership crept in. They tended to ignore or brush aside matters raised from the branch which not only irritated us, it provoked us into demanding further probes and sowed the seeds of much deeper dissension than any of us foresaw.

One of my branch Communists was Jim Watson, a Yorkshireman

and a stickler for financial propriety. He took a keen interest in union accounts and expenses, and scrutinised Hayes Court as best he could from long range, promoting a series of tricky questions. He even got outside help from an accountant and found what appeared to be various examples of double bookings by officials for expenses and other potential cash fiddles. The branch took up his requests for more information with Head Office. Foulkes, Haxell and company clearly thought that these queries were mine and were inspired by Les Cannon, whose relationship with them was becoming very strained. The truth is that I rarely saw Les and it was the persistent Jim Watson who was mainly responsible. Mostly, we got very dusty answers or no answers at all. We felt we were spitting in the wind.

These days I was a regular branch delegate at all the ETU national policy and rules revision conferences. My first was in 1948, a rules revision conference at Ayr, but it was the next year's Worthing policy conference which produced a couple of annoying incidents that heightened my gathering doubts and anxieties.

I made some criticism of union officials in a private chat with another delegate and my remarks were overheard by a full-time officer who got together with some of the others to challenge me. 'What do you mean by it? What are you trying to stir up? You're supposed to be a Communist,' I was told. If they expected a crawling apology, they got a very rude awakening: I tore into them, both for over-reacting to some pretty minor grousing and even more for their blatant eavesdropping. They backed off in some disorder, but they coloured a view that was taking a hold – that what we had was not a union serving the members, but one in which the members were in a sort of bondage to the leadership, one in which any voice of dissent was speedily crushed by the Party machine.

This heretical thinking was only underlined by the second incident. There was an habitual whip-round at such conferences for the *Daily Worker*. Ordinarily, I would have stumped up readily enough but I had lost my registered envelope which contained my money for the fares to and from the conference, and I had to tell them that I just didn't have the money to give. They wouldn't believe that I had lost it and we had quite a barney. I was guilty of dereliction of duty, they said; but I had paid over plenty in the past and this distrust and pressure left me feeling both hurt and indignant.

Overall, I was more and more discomforted by the treatment meted out. Some of us who had been in the forefront of swinging the union leftwards now found ourselves disregarded as a source of opinion. We seemed to be dealing with a bunch of Communists who were corrupted by capitalism and behaved just like those they condemned, now that they had seized control. There was a struggle under way for the union's soul which was not easily recognisable at the time. It was between Haxell and his favoured henchmen, on the one hand, and on the other, those who opposed his personalised and elitist way of conducting the union's affairs. Haxell, as Assistant General Secretary, was relentless in his quest for full power. His arrogance really showed through when Walter Stevens was killed in a car crash shortly before our 1954 Bournemouth rules revision conference, and Haxell assumed the key job of putting rule changes to the fifty delegates. His detailed proposals were instigated by Jack Gaster, a solicitor and member of the Communist Party's London District Committee: here came the pay-off for all that dedicated organisation and deception. The Communists had their coveted Executive majority, and the rules could now be tailored to tighten centralisation, to give Haxell and his Executive tools untrammelled control – and to ensure that things stayed that way.

My faith and belief that the members would benefit from Communist rule was steadily disappearing. It was not just politics. Pay rates slipped by comparison with other groups of workers. The electricians, regarded among the aristocrats of labour, dropped from eighth to thirtieth on the industrial pay ladder during this period, even though electronics was increasing in importance. There was less and less consultation with the members, even those who, like me, helped the leadership by rigging meetings and ballots. For much of my time as LSE No 10 assistant branch secretary, our secretary was unwell and left balloting arrangements to me to deal with, and there were several occasions when I fiddled branch votes by one or other of the methods later disclosed in the High Court. It was simple enough to do with the slapdash voting arrangements we had – arrangements which most unions irresponsibly still permit.

Yet I was uneasy. As my doubts about the leadership intensified, I reflected more and more on the morality of it all: what was a political system worth that could only succeed if it was backed by these unsavoury means? The Party grip seemed to be suffocating the union. They didn't have the numbers, but at any ETU conference they had the platform in their grip and enough backers of my kind on the floor to see that what they wanted was secured. Careful co-ordination, predetermined agendas, votes rigged where necessary: very little ever happened by accident. The right-wing was not averse to a spot of fiddling if they could get away with it, but it was only a hobby for them. The Communists made it into a science. I overhead two right-wingers talking in the toilet at one conference. One said to the other: 'There's only about twenty of them, but, by Christ, it seems like two hundred.' We didn't need two hundred – the right couldn't match us for effort or sheer professionalism. The cracks began to show, though. The various strands of discord were beginning to draw together.

Les Cannon, still an Executive Councillor, began to emerge as a focus for dissent. He was highly ambitious and had no doubt that he should lead the union rather than those he saw as unable to make good use of the power they had illicitly acquired. He could already see that corruption and incompetence together could bring the whole dangerous structure down, and he had no intention of being brought down with it. Rather, he would help it on its way.

There was much more to his shift to the right than that, as I discovered by chance. Arthur Payne, one of my veteran non-Communist branch stalwarts, asked me if I could help to get an elderly Czechoslovakian couple out of their homeland, where they were suffering as a consequence of their contacts with people like Arthur in England. I had great respect for Arthur, a decent and sensible man, and wanted to assist. Knowing of his Czech connections, I thought it best to ask Les to intercede and was shocked when he said: 'Forget it. If we try to do anything from here, it will only make their lives more miserable.' Then he unburdened himself: his Czech wife, Olga, had been a prominent Communist in her own country but her parents, small shopkeepers, were treated there as petty bourgeois – the Communists drove them from their business and their home. It was that brutal treatment which caused Les to question the whole philosophy of Communism. Too ashamed of the Communist Party to tell him that we could do nothing, I went back and told Arthur Payne that we would set things in motion and do what we could. The whole episode made a deep and disturbing impression on me.

Our own commissars at the head of the ETU 'people's democracy' aggravated that resentment. Despite their bland protectiveness we were sure that the union's funds were misused, that drunkenness and other misbehaviour were commonplace. Jim Watson, a left-wing Mary Whitehouse of his day, stuck tenaciously to his inquiries. Les Cannon tried to counsel caution before he switched sides, declaring: 'You aren't just attacking union officials. You are attacking the Communist Party.'

That was the orthodox Communist line to deflect, contain or suppress criticism.

There were other peculiar events. Union members who niggled at the Hayes Court regime were mysteriously sacked from their jobs. Employers, wanting an easy life, could be very compliant under pressure. Patronage was an even more serious cause for disquiet: only Haxell's recommended people became sponsored Communist candidates, and if you weren't among his favourites your prospect of election through the advisory committees was remote – they could always dream up a reason for finding someone was unsuitable. Still, Haxell could be beaten. One Communist Executive Councillor was Tommy Vetterlein, my old and respected friend from war-time dockland. ETU Executive work was part-time, with not much more than a monthly meeting to attend unless Haxell placed you on sub-committees. Tommy was not one of his kind or one of his clique.

A full-time London officer's post was vacant and Tommy opted to run for it. There was a tacit understanding between us that if he got it he would back my nomination to succeed him on the Executive Council. He was easily the most popular member the union ever had in East London and was the obvious Party choice, but Haxell wanted to put in his own lickspittle, Jim Humphrey, to perfect his control of ETU organisation in London. For once, we turned Haxell over. We mustered the branch nominations for Tommy and got him accepted by the Communist advisory committee. Haxell had to swallow it – along with the certain knowledge that I would be a front runner for that vacant Executive seat. It was a personal setback for Haxell, but it didn't alter the fact that through him, Foulkes and their cronies, the Communists ran the union. All their activities were designed to see that their authority was permanent, every criticism was a bleat in the wilderness. But beneath the surface discontent and disenchantment festered away.

My major misgivings about the ETU situation were becoming dwarfed by the mounting turmoil over Soviet Communism. The Moscow Jewish doctors' plot, in which the Jews were accused of poisoning Stalin, led to unheard of discussion in my local Stamford Hill Communist Party branch. Only a couple of us in the branch were not Jewish and charges of Soviet anti-semitism struck home forcibly. There was more controversy over Poland and the Poznan riots, where workers demonstrated under the slogan 'We want bread'. Most of all, there was the remarkable denunciation by Kruschev of Stalin and the cult of personality. Kruschev's speech shattered a multitude of fond illusions and revealed for the first time to the world what so many British Communists until then didn't know, or didn't want to know – that Soviet Communism had been based on murder, torture, mendacity, duplicity and every possible violation of human rights.

It compelled a fundamental reappraisal of Communist theory and practice, and initiated an outbreak of intellectual dissent. E P Thompson, who today gives comfort to the old men in the Kremlin through his unilateral nuclear disarmament campaigning, was a Yorkshire Communist, and co-editor of a short-lived duplicated 'rebel' discussion journal called *The Reasoner*. Its masthead quoted Marx: 'To leave error unabated is to encourage intellectual immorality'. The Communist Party executive tried to ban it. Thompson and his co-editor were careful to condemn the 'repeated betrayals of both working class interests and of Socialist principles by reformist Labour leaders' and to sneer at 'the mock battles of Gaitskellism'. But their real target was Britain's Stalinist Communist leadership who they accused of 'a cult of authority'. They rejected as a myth the 'utopian propaganda about the Soviet Union as the land of Socialism-realised'.

Many other prominent intellectual voices were raised. The author Doris Lessing was one, though she excused the impossible silence of those with previous knowledge of the Stalin business by claiming that if they had denounced it, they would have been cast out as traitors and isolated from a world movement in which they believed. It was less convincing than the non-intellectual contribution of Lawrence Daly, only recently retired as the National Union of Mineworkers' General Secretary. He quit the Communist Party after sixteen years and then wrote in *The Reasoner*: 'However inadequate and hypocritical British capitalist democracy may be, the average worker does feel that he has the right, more or less, to express his own opinion freely on political and other affairs, worship freely in his own way, get a fair trial if he is arrested, listen to different points of view and make up his own mind, travel almost where he likes (if he can afford it) and so on.' He concluded that workers feared that many of these rights would disappear if the Communists got power – 'it would now appear that their fears were justified'. It was an argument I could not honestly deny.

This mid-fifties period saw a brawling, squabbling and bitter debate inside the Communist Party which we activists had never believed possible, which indeed we had always been warned against as gross treachery. Now I was part and parcel of it. I thought back to the hypocrisy of the 1939 Nazi-Soviet pact, to the sudden switch by the Russians to our side. I recalled Lubeck and those Russian soldiers, determined not to return to life under Communism.

It all began to telescope in 1956, with internal problems in the union and our own undemocratic personality cult combining with the political upheaval in the Party to make one point abundantly clear: our British Communist policy was patented in Moscow, where Kruschev vilified Stalin but failed to abolish the secret police, the one-party state and the vital control of the Party over the public mind. Would a revolution in Britain, which we were taught was our aim, resolve moral and material corruption any more than it had in Soviet Russia? Communism was under question, lock, stock and barrel.

I was working at Vauxhall Motors, Luton, where they were building a new press shop and installing new machinery in a £36,000,000 plant expansion programme. I was on site for several months, among twenty-one men employed by the contracting firm, May and Robertson, seventeen of whom were Communists. I was chairman of the electricians' shop and of the joint unions' shop stewards' committee for the whole site. Mark Young was another of our stewards and so was Lew Britz, now on the EETPU Executive Council and another robust supporter throughout the battle for the union. He was a Trotskyite but I recruited him on the spot to Communism. We were quite a ginger group, stirring it up, still broadly subscribing to the Communist theory that you created revolution to demonstrate the emptiness of the capitalist system. Our demands on pay and conditions were tough.

Vauxhalls were very fed up with us. We were troublemakers and they took the contract away from May and Robertson to get rid of us. It wasn't that simple: the men on the site reckoned their chairman should stay and I was found a job with another contractor, much to Vauxhall's annoyance. Moreover, I scored a considerable industrial triumph. The contractors with whom we negotiated argued that Vauxhalls were preventing them from meeting our pay claim, so I insisted on taking a shop stewards' team to meet the motor firm's American management. It was the first time that anyone could recollect where a site grievance resulted in the unions confronting the client company direct. It was quite a feather in my industrial cap and enhanced my reputation with the members.

And then came Hungary. Almost overnight, there were Russian tanks on the street of Budapest, Hungarian workers and students resisting behind their makeshift barricades, and us stuck there in Luton like a small irrelevant group of theologians. The electricians were far and away the most politically advanced of the workers on the site, yet our solidarity with the Hungarian workers was least. Other union men were clearly with them and a fundamental divide opened up in our own ranks. The old guard Stalinists clung to the British Communist Party line for comfort and refused to associate with calls for the withdrawal of Soviet troops. All that emerged from the Party's King Street head-quarters was the usual pro-Soviet smokescreen, blaming imperialist agents and frantically trying to divert attention to Eden's undoubtedly reckless Suez gamble.

The Lord Mayor of London opened a fund for Hungarian refugees and we had collecting buckets in our works canteen. British workers threw a lot of money into those buckets, knowing that an oppressive regime had imprisoned many good Socialists and trade unionists and had killed free speech. They recognised the appalling effects of the combination of Communist Hungarian secret police and Soviet generals, and they coughed up. I said to my ETU mates: 'Look at them. The whole British working class, except us, can't be wrong about it. They understand it. Why don't we?'

There was a particularly nasty moment for me as we Communists sat around the canteen discussing Hungary. It got a bit heated. Then one Party hard-liner, Harry Woolf, said: 'The trouble with the Russians is that they didn't shoot enough of these Hungarian bastards.' I have never been a physically violent man but I lost control. No doubt the politically traumatic time I was having was part of it. Woolf sat opposite me, across the table. I upped and punched him on the jaw. I don't think I did much damage. He was too dazed – and perhaps too scared – to retaliate. That little fracas ended the debate. My flash of temper may have been no cause for pride, but I must say that I have no regrets.

The whole business sickened me. Like a good many other British Communists, I still argued that we could democratise the Party and change the leadership, yet I had trouble convincing myself, never mind others who wavered. I began to feel that I had lived a lie for so long that along with thousands of other Party members I had suppressed my individual conscience through gravely misplaced loyalty to a phoney war.

Back in London I went to a Communist meeting at Holborn Hall to hear Party doyen Harry Pollitt report back on a visit that he, John Gollan, the General Secretary, and others, had made to Moscow.

Several questioners expressed anxiety over Hungary. Pollitt said dismissively: 'If you're worried about it, comrade, take an aspirin.' Was this what I had worked to hear? Did this pave the way to the brave new Communist society? Once again I felt anger and revulsion.

## CHAPTER 6

# OUT OF PRISON, INTO BATTLE

The battle under way inside the union was almost a microcosm of what was happening in the Soviet Union. London's ETU dissidents began to group around me, and also Tommy Vetterlein, the other mainstay for those disenchanted with the way the union was being run. His record was formidable: a Communist since 1924, he spent eight years on the union's Executive Council and was now elected as a London official, with nearly twice as many votes as his two opponents put together.

Tommy had to leave his seat on the Executive Council and a row broke out over who was to succeed him. Haxell and his supporters wanted to keep me out: they knew my views on Hungary and there were embarrassing enquiries still arising from my branch about their expenses. Haxell clashed with me when I came within a hair's breadth of overturning a pay deal he had negotiated by trading in a claim for shorter hours in exchange for more money – a trend I opposed then and still do. When the stewards met they almost rejected the agreement, and my part in the rebellion rankled with him.

Under Haxell's guidance, a big effort was made to persuade the comrades that in the aftermath of Hungary it would be best to back a pliant non-Communist for the Executive – someone who could be fooled and manipulated. Haxell was highly skilled in the art of using front men and he considered that Alf McBrowse fitted the bill. Haxell was aware that he had made too many enemies on the Party's ETU London Advisory Committee to beat me there so he called a larger meeting of the union Reds from East London and the surrounding area. But it just wasn't on for him: this was my neck of the woods and once more he had to admit defeat. I was one of life's awkward squad, and everyone knew it, but I was also known as a worker for the union with a long history of activity around those parts, including that full-time YCL post; there was very little support for McBrowse.

I became the candidate of the left, but Haxell made sure that it did nothing to help. Nevertheless, the contest boiled down to a straight fight between me and the moderate Bill Sullivan and I won comfortably enough by 2,239 votes to 1,527. Bill had taken a lot of stick from me in the past and I couldn't have blamed him for outright hostility. Instead, he recognised my misgivings, accepted that my days in the Party were numbered, and established a rapport with me that was to prove extremely valuable when we later joined forces.

Unless I got a seat on the Executive Council there was scant chance of reform, or of genuine consultation by the leadership with the rank and file which would allow them adequate participation in the union's affairs. That was how it seemed, but I was soon to discover that I was unable to do much as an Executive member either, with the Three Generals and most of the other ten Executive men ganging up to thwart me. My election late in 1957 meant that I took my seat towards the end of 1958, and I quickly got a foretaste of what was in store. A rules revision conference was due and it was past practice to invite incoming Executive members to attend, so when no invitation arrived I phoned Haxell to ask if it had been overlooked. His response was terse – and negative. The gauntlet was down already, and I hadn't even reached Hayes Court.

My apparent deviations brought me trouble inside the Communist Party. My predominantly Jewish Stamford Hill branch were mostly with me, and the majority of them ultimately quit the Party, but it was different in the Earls Court industrial branch, a multi-union set-up covering London Transport. The comrades there used to get up to the usual conspiratorial tricks. One prominent Communist shop steward once got me to fill in spare ballot papers for union elections – and he was in the National Union of Railwaymen. Now my Party membership was in question and I was summoned to a meeting to discuss my errant ways. A fair sprinkling of electricians who worked with me turned up and the frustrated hard-liners couldn't muster a majority for disciplinary action. I might have guessed that a little matter like democracy wouldn't stop them: two weeks after the meeting I got a letter to say that a further meeting had recommended my expulsion from the branch. They must have been a very exclusive bunch of brethren for no one had troubled to tell me or my supporters that the second meeting was on.

It was typical sharp practice but it didn't really matter. I was shaping up to resign and this was merely one more instance of Communist double-dealing to help me on my way. Les Cannon had already left the Party and was now heading the ETU college at Esher, Surrey, where his credit was high with the stream of union members who passed through on courses. He was seething at the outcome of his bid to regain his Executive seat: he lost to Jack Frazer, the Communist choice, by 2,023 votes to 1,451 and he was in no doubt that he had been robbed by a rigged result. Proving it was another matter, but he was really on his mettle now.

Making the break with the Communist Party was no overnight decision for me, for it betrayed all those youthful hopes and dreams which caused me to join. I have never been indecisive but I approached that breakpoint many times, hanging on, in part, to bring out others with me who shared my concerns. It was surprising just how many Communists quietly let me know that they felt the same way, and this was an important factor in my decision to leave – I knew that I would be in very good company as a member of the largest party in the world – that of the ex-Communists.

I considered the role of all those other traitors to the Party and the working class, people I had condemned countless times – some of them friends or family. Some I had cut dead; some had ceased to exist, except to be used to prove how insidious was the corruption of capitalism. Then, slowly and painfully, came the realisation that they couldn't all be wrong. Yet although I vowed that, in spite of everything, I would keep to the socialist path, I had still failed to come to a clear-cut decision. I continued to seek reassurance, hoping to resolve my doubts and make the final act of departure unnecessary.

Yet the machinery I had helped to build was relentless, and it became plain to me that I was no longer a Communist. I no longer subscribed to the elitist concept of the leading role of the party; it had become the antithesis of my beliefs. I began to see those who were supposed to be my political allies as a backward, barbarous and murderous brotherhood, a political mafia, a mutation of democratic man, seeking not liberation or the end of the exploitation of man by man, but determined on the intellectual and physical enslavement of man. The theories of Communism were the source of practices I had grown to abhor: the collective state only liberates its leadership; for the rest it is the conformity of the anthill or the beehive.

There was still a last flickering chance for the Party to reclaim me, or so they must have thought. An entertainment unions' delegation was due to visit the Soviet Union and the Executive Council decided to send Bert Batchelor, the National Officer for our entertainment industry members, together with a Communist shop steward from one of the film studios. I let slip the tentative suggestion that a trip to the socialist fatherland might yet provide me with some answers, and that unfortunate shop steward was promptly dropped in my favour.

It was true enough that I was keen to hear first-hand explanations of Stalinism, the Polish and Hungarian suppressions and so on, and that I needed to test my drastically changed views against a practical example. The only unvarnished account of the Soviet dictatorship that I had ever had was from those Russian soldiers in Lubeck. Perhaps I was really only seeking confirmation that my giant stride away from Communism was truly justified, that I hadn't made a grave mistake. I certainly found that confirmation.

Our delegation was led by Sir Tom O'Brien, rascally Labour MP, theatre workers' leader and a TUC General Council member, and included Hardie Ratcliffe, the General Secretary of the Musicians' Union; Equity, the actors' union, sent Jimmy Edwards, the comedian, and Rosamund John, actress wife of Labour MP John Silkin. We endured numerous boring lectures, referred to as discussions, and all the while, my antagonism to Communism was strengthening. For a start, I found it very odd that at all the meetings we appeared to be placed around the table in some sort of hierarchical order. Indeed, everything seemed to be done that way. The deference was very disconcerting and decidedly unsocialist.

The delegation was taken to see Lenin's Tomb in Red Square and was ushered straight to the head of a long straggling queue of Russian citizens, waiting to file past in homage to their hero. There wasn't a murmur of protest from them about this bunch of queue-jumping foreigners. They knew their place. I simply couldn't imagine that kind of unhealthy passivity at home. Another time, I had some official photographs of us at dinner with our Soviet hosts and was looking at a print in the hotel lift. I showed it to a friendly member of the hotel staff and simply couldn't convince her that it was snapped in Moscow. The sight of a Russian table so loaded with food and drink was unbelievable to her.

We were given the old line by one Russian union official that there were no strikes there, a sweeping statement amended after questioning to acknowledge that a few broke out, fomented by 'enemies of the people'. The same official claimed that every worker in a particular category got exactly the same pay, and handed over a percentage of it in union dues. More questioning produced the somewhat shamefaced admission that our Russian trade union host picked up four salaries from different jobs and lived in a special privileged compound. It was 'I'm all right Ivan' with a vengeance. We managed to chat to some ordinary workers and discovered that some of them actually had appalling hours and conditions, but their accounts tended to be very different if the trade union official was in earshot. We learned from hotel staff and our car drivers that some of them often worked round-the-clock. British workers would never have put up with it.

I did finish up with a better grasp of Russia's problems and with great sympathy for the plight of the Russian people, but the trip hardened my enmity to the one-party totalitarian state. The Soviet Union had taken the road to a new kind of serfdom. So many ordinary Russians had the peasant mentality which made them easy victims of those in power, allowing the Communists to gain and maintain the ascendancy. My opposition to all this was cemented and was never again in any doubt. The visit was a disaster for the Communist Party so far as my convictions were concerned. Party officials began to see me, not merely as a lost cause, but as the enemy. Party members, many of them my erstwhile friends, determined to give me no peace, and everything I did was questioned in a constant attempt to undermine me and to punish me.

A campaign of character assassination was initiated, and it was made crystal clear that everything possible would be done to oust me from my London Transport job. I told one of them: 'The best thing you can do is to leave me alone or you will force me to fight you.' But they wouldn't back off. I worked nights but had to take some time off to get to ETU Executive Council meetings. The London Transport Communists, most of them NUR men, carped about my absences and kept up a running campaign of threats and harrassment, using any old pretext, to make me pack up and go.

So the Communist Party had my card carefully marked. A two-year spell on the union's Executive Council and then I would have to face re-election. They were busily laying the groundwork for my forthcoming defeat. The pressure got to me, depression set in, and I toyed with the idea of emigrating to New Zealand to build a new life. Instead, I became more and more entwined in the small band fighting to democratise the union.

I was now a member of the Stoke Newington and Hackney North Labour Party. It was riddled with the same old faction fighting that has dogged the Party over the years, especially in the big cities, and has brought Labour to its present sorry condition. I didn't get involved because of my union activities, but Hugh Gaitskell was fighting against unilateral nuclear disarmament and I warned one meeting that the end product of a 'ban the bomb' policy was a world under Soviet domination. It didn't make me popular, but it was true then and it is true now, when the very same argument rages.

Those who broke with the Communist Party had to organise resolutely if we were to break their stranglehold on the union. Les Cannon spurred us on and we set up the ETU Reform Group, with Mark Young as Secretary and link man with the rest of the country. We still saw ourselves as staunch left-wingers and we could have had some strange bedfellows. Gerry Healey, the Irish-born Trotskyite leader of the Socialist Labour League (now the Workers' Revolutionary Party), came to my home to persuade me that what I disagreed with in the Communist Party didn't exist in his organisation. He was a nasty, unsmiling, cloak-and-dagger type whose followers called themselves professional revolutionaries. I went to one of his meetings which convinced me that these people were not for me – they were too much like the fascist left I had just walked out on.

Ted Grant, now best known as the founding father of today's Militant Tendency, was another suitor, a far more affable character than Gerry Healey. It was hard not to like Ted. He adhered to a French branch of Trotskyism and was a comic political figure, incompetent and inefficient. It is incredible that he should now lead young people – in those days he couldn't get up in the mornings and worked after lunch as a brush salesman. I'm told he hasn't changed much. He turned up on my doorstep a few times and was always hungry; he got a cuppa and a bite from me but there was no political affinity, although I did once write an article for him.

The ETU Reform Group was small and scattered. We had no more than one hundred contacts in the union throughout the country and few of them were prepared to act. It was like a soldier doing 'jankers' and being ordered to clean the parade ground with a toothbrush. Almost all the full-time officials opposed us or shied away – Tommy Vetterlein, Jock Byrne and the other two Scottish area officials were the exceptions, but we had no close contact with Jock at that stage, since his right-wing Catholic position was anathema to us. Les Cannon, sacked from his ETU college post at Esher, was back working as an electrician, and he and Mark Young did most of the leg work in building a case against the union leadership. Those of us who could manage it, chipped in with a bit of cash to help defray expenses. As an Executive Councillor, I was unable to stray too far from my own division without being challenged by the Communists for trespassing outside my area of responsibility. They looked for any excuse to discipline me and hopefully to ban me from office; we couldn't afford to slip up.

I expected a fierce contest to retain my Executive seat in 1959, but it turned out to be a strange affair in which I was greatly helped by my former opponent, Bill Sullivan. He was nominated to run against me again but withdrew at a late stage in my favour; he must have swallowed some pride to do it, but he was ready to throw in his lot with the Reform Group. The Communists, originally hopeful that my Russian trip might yet bring me back to the fold, apparently found Alf McBrowse reluctant to run and left it too late to field a candidate. It was a bad error on their part and a stroke of good luck for me – I got back to the Executive Council unopposed.

There was a more important election in the offing: Frank Foulkes was seeking to retain the Presidency. The Reform Group fielded Bill Blairford, a Scottish ex-Communist who had left the Party over Hungary but, despite the hard work we put in, Foulkes got back with a majority of nearly 3,000. We were sure it was another fraud, but we couldn't prove how it had been done and the Group split on what to do next. Some of us wanted to 'keep it in the union': we said the outcome of the election should be contested through the union's own appeals system. Les Cannon, on the other hand, was adamant: 'It's no good,' he declared. 'The machinery is rigged. It has to be the courts.' He carried the doubters with him, including me. 'I know what will happen now,' I said. 'I'll be the first bloody one with a case in court.' It was an accurate enough prophesy: we were still two years off the main case but I was to chalk up our first significant legal victory well ahead of that.

The intimidation against me continued unabated. I was put up to speak for the Executive Council at one policy conference on the fairly uncontroversial subject of a national rate for electricians. The Communists were out to roast me. Foulkes announced: 'Brother Chapple, for the Executive Council,' knowing full well what was coming. It seemed that the whole conference was booing and jeering. I hadn't said a word and couldn't, until Foulkes intervened with some relish to quell the uproar that he and his comrades had arranged. He revelled in my discomfort, but that hooligan behaviour was not without advantage to me: quite a few delegates told me privately afterwards that I had shown courage in sticking it out. There wasn't much else I could have done, but I won a few waverers to our cause.

It was a discouraging occasion and not just because of the rumpus. Our policies could only pick up about half-a-dozen votes from the delegates. Yet Les Cannon told us: 'Don't worry, they're beaten. They've thrown everything at us. If that's the best they can do, we're winning. We've lost the votes, but won the arguments.' I don't know whether he really believed what he was saying or was just whistling to keep our spirits up, but either way it showed considerable leadership and, what's more, he was proved right.

I was regularly slagged off at Executive Council meetings in those days – accused of leaking to the press, of spilling the beans to the TUC, of generally letting down the union – and inevitably, I faced disciplinary action. The truth was that I had had no direct press contacts for a long while, and had only met Vic Feather, the TUC's Assistant General Secretary, a couple of times in the four years leading up to the High Court hearing. On one of those occasions I most certainly told Vic that Haxell and Co. appeared to be untouched by our efforts: 'It's as though no one has laid a glove on them,' I said. I urged the TUC to stop moving like a blinkered carthorse. Vic retorted: 'Don't worry, lad. They've got to keep going now, else they'll fall down.' It sounded reassuring, but we Reform Group members felt the strain on our finances, our family life and even on our health. We needed more than soothing, folksy, Yorkshire soft-soap, however well-meaning.

TUC General Secretary, Sir Vincent Tewson, did ask the ETU about Communist influence and Haxell agreed with his union cronies to set up a three-man internal inquiry committee. Unsurprisingly, it discovered 'no evidence whatsoever of Communist interference'. As for the press, well I talked to Les and Mark after our Executive meetings and they did the rest. They had to. The spotlight was essential, but my own direct involvement would have been fatal: the Communists would have used it to kick me off the Executive Council and that would have been a hammer blow to our prospects.

Some of the journalists covering the affair tried to help; others disliked renegade ex-Communists; others still were drinking pals of Foulkes who denied all the charges they put to him and quashed a good many stories that way. ETU conferences, in particular, were always swimming in booze at the ordinary members' expense, and the journalists were well looked after, capitalist lackeys or not. Frank Foulkes was adept at his public relations: *Daily Worker* people got their full

conference expenses paid from union funds – one more concealed dona-
tion to the Communist Party. A touch of media scepticism was not out of
place, since no rank and file grouping had ever before combined to
successfully combat Communist activities inside the Labour movement.
There had been sporadic attempts in the past to do so in the ETU, but
the Communists had emerged stronger than ever.

Media cynicism, justified or not, was well matched by the behaviour
of a number of major employers who were anxious to keep in with the
Hayes Court regime, and certainly did not expect a change of leadership. The electrical contracting employers connived with Haxell who
was allowed to negotiate the biggest-ever rise in that industry for our
members; concessions by other weak-kneed managements also aided
the Communists in enhancing their reputations as tough and astute
negotiators. I could hardly complain, but there were some suspiciously
cosy relationships across the negotiating table which were primarily of
short-term value to the ETU leaders rather than of long-term value to
our members.

At least there is no doubting our best media friend – Woodrow Wyatt.
He wrote an article in 1956 in the magazine *Illustrated*, exposing the
ETU's election procedures; the next year he stimulated and took part in
two BBC 'Panorama' programmes which forced the whole affair into
national prominence; he followed up with a fierce article in the *New
Statesman*, which became our main platform. Woodrow, the maverick
Labour MP for Bosworth and a former junior minister, was in contact
with Les Cannon during this period but his reputation for vehemently
right-wing politics put me off.

However, I got into a position in which I lost so much time from work
that I badly needed some financial help. My wife, Joan, made her
contribution as a homeworker, stitching neckties at a meagre sixpence
each so that they could then be sold for three pounds a time at Harrods,
but the cash problem was serious. The biggest cost was the expense of
travelling round to build up support and gather evidence of ballot-
rigging. Twice I went to meetings of one Suffolk Branch in my division:
each time the chairman closed the meeting as I walked in. It was a
deliberate snub that had more to do with some funny branch book-
keeping than with left politics, but it was wasted time and money for me.
There was the uncomfortable ride to visit another East Anglian branch
secretary, this time on the back of a motorcycle driven by Seymour
Moss, another Reform Group activist who is now a full-time EETPU
official. It poured with rain and I got soaked, so much so that when I got

to that secretary's home I had to borrow some socks from him. Those socks were all I did get for he was too windy to help with evidence. It was another fruitless errand.

The financial pressure led Les to take me to see Woodrow Wyatt. Woodrow didn't quibble. He gave me the first instalment of some thirty to forty pounds, which he generously donated over several months to tide me over. It was a decent sum in those days and he gave it willingly, making no attempt to extract any political promises in turn. Ever since then I have had enormous respect for him and we have become firm personal friends. Woodrow has lifted me out of the doldrums many times and his ultimate defeat in the general election of 1970 was a sad mistake by the people of Bosworth. He is a radical eccentric who might have stepped out of an earlier period of British political and parliamentary history – always ready to challenge conventional wisdom and champion unpopular causes.

He is also a man of vision and perspicacity. He was proved correct in his well-known and long-standing opposition to the re-nationalisation of the steel industry, an honestly held view that pitchforked him into trouble inside the Labour Party. Extreme left-wingers always got by in the Labour ranks; today they prosper. Yet a right-wing or simply a common-sense approach was perilous for a Labour MP and, in the current climate, is a threat to political survival. Yet on steel, events since Woodrow's stand show that the industry needed modernising and pruning, not re-nationalising. Millions of pounds have been poured into the state-owned industry and have produced fewer jobs, ever-mounting losses and a continuing crisis. Private industry may have done no better, but at least the taxpayers would not have had to foot the enormous bill for mismanagement and incompetence. Steel has performed as though it is hooked on drugs – not dying but carrying on in indefinite agony.

Woodrow's comments and writings often seem to fly in the face of reason but he usually turns out to be much more far-sighted than his many critics. His unsparing support for our case did more than any other single outside source to put us on the map and promote our eventual success. The newspapers, television and radio could not ignore us or write us off as a bunch of troublesome and irrelevant ne'er-do-wells. We kept the tap full on: Mark Young had a revealing letter published in the *New Statesman*, members like Dick Reno made allegations of rigging on television and radio. Dick was banned from office by the Communists – though he was later elected as a full-time official when we won control and scrapped the ban.

It was all boiling up. In February 1960, Foulkes made a disastrous 'Panorama' appearance in which he was pilloried by John Freeman, another ex-Labour MP and former junior Minister who became Ambassador to Washington. Freeman challenged the evasive Foulkes to sue the BBC and himself for libel if the assertions made against him were false; even the slothful TUC General Council demanded that the union should take legal action to protect the movement's good name. As the pressure mounted against the Reds, so they got more vicious. My two anti-Communist Executive Council companions were Colin Walker, from Scotland, and Ernie Hadley, from Yorkshire. Colin, who had been a member before I took my place, told me when I arrived that he was terrified by every Hayes Court meeting he attended. Initially, I put it down to funk and was unimpressed, but I found out what he meant: the Communists dripped with venom and the atmosphere at the meetings was oppressive and intimidatory.

Colin departed for a personnel management job shortly before the 1961 High Court case and couldn't wait to leave. Ernie was a little fellow whose heart was in the right place: he didn't scare easily but he was no match for the wiles of Haxell and the sheer weight of numbers thrown against us at meetings. All the important decisions were taken by the Three Generals and their mates before the full Executive Council met and we were supposed to rubber stamp their deals. We lost any and every contentious vote by eight to three.

Not that I was averse to a bit of rough stuff myself to keep them on their toes. I angrily denounced Sam Goldberg as a 'renegade Jew' and was accused of anti-Semitism. I told them they stood the argument on its head – that it was Goldberg who was anti-Semitic for supporting the Soviet regime that persecuted the Jews. All the time, I niggled away at procedures, insisted that things should be properly recorded in the minutes, and was especially careful to jump in on issues about candidates' election addresses. I reckoned that this latter concern might be vital to our campaign and it certainly was.

The Reform Group met to decide who to run against Bob McLennan, up for re-election in mid-1960 as Assistant General Secretary. He was one of the best-liked Communist personalities and would be hard to shift. We opted for Bill Blair, long-standing secretary of our Ruislip branch, Justice of the Peace, Labour Party activist, a man with an impeccably honest union record. He was at the meeting and, knowing he could command considerable backing from the branches, agreed to be our man. Next day I got a shock: a telegram from Bill to say he had changed his mind and didn't want to stand. There was no time to call the Group together again, so I phoned Les and Mark and we concluded that I must be the candidate. We were up against the clock and it was far from certain that I could rustle up enough branch nominations in time to allow me to run. It was a hectic business and we began with a decided handicap.

We were on tenterhooks because we could see that unless the Reform Group could register a worthwhile victory soon, it might well collapse. It was now my firm opinion that we had to get to court and I could see just how to bait the trap. Oddly enough, Les wasn't in favour at the outset: he thought my plan wouldn't work and, although he didn't say so, I think that he doubted my capacity to carry out such a tricky operation. I was acutely conscious of how the ETU leaders bridled at any forthright criticism of their control which candidates put into their election addresses – I had seen their scissors at work. They had censored Jock Byrne's address on one occasion for daring to advocate independently-scrutinised, one-member, one-vote postal ballots. Candidates found their addresses chopped about and left as though written by illiterate idiots and that was how the membership received them.

It is ironic that these days the EETPU left-wing grouse that our system for vetting election addresses is harsh: their memories are selectively short on this, as with so many other matters. Nowadays every candidate gets up to 500 words and only libel is automatically cut out after legal advice. If we failed to take that basic precaution, both the individual and the union, as publisher of the offending remarks, would risk litigation. Factual errors can be challenged and removed (but only by the full Executive Council), opinions are not doctored, and candidates can re-write their addresses where necessary. It was very different in 1960. Past form suggested that Haxell could be counted on to clamp down if I included certain provocative comments in my address. I went to a solicitor for preliminary advice on my chances in court if my address was mutilated and what I heard raised my hopes.

I posted the address to Haxell and sure enough, at the next Executive Council meeting, he announced that a sub-committee should be formed to deal with candidates' addresses; what he was really after was technical backing for his censorship. Ernie Hadley got onto the sub-committee, but although he made his protest he was unable to prevent the cuts in my address. We knew that they would take no notice of him, but Ernie was able to let me know what they were up to before the sub-committee reported to the full Executive. They deleted my attack on those who 'never tire of boasting about our union's democracy yet lay an ever ready tongue to slander those who dare to take advantage of this democracy in offering themselves as candidates for office', and removed several other spicily-suggestive bits. Inevitably, they couldn't resist knocking out my banker, a reference to practices 'only a short step from totalitarianism'.

We slapped in an immediate writ, demanding postponement of the election. Haxell got quite different legal advice and the Executive Council decided, by the usual eight-to-three vote, that the ballot should go ahead. It was a tense and angry session. I spoke of 'trickery' and warned them against doctoring the tape of our Executive proceedings. Haxell protested and Ron Sell called me 'a bloody rat' who was undermining the union.

They were badly rattled. We went for an interim injunction to freeze the situation and our application came before Mr Justice Danckwerts in the High Court. Labour MP Williams Wells, Q.C., appeared for me, while the ETU was represented by the formidable pro-Soviet QC, D.N. Pritt, who was expelled from the Labour Party. Mr Wells stuttered along and more than once Mr Pritt helped him out by interpreting his remarks to the Judge; Pritt was on excellent form. It looked pretty bad to me, but I was using the wrong yardstick. Mr Justice Danckwerts didn't bother to hear Mr Wells respond to Mr Pritt's slick offering, but granted the interim injunction without hesitation. Les Cannon and I left that court feeling fifteen feet high. It was the first major triumph, our first big blow for freedom, and a desperately needed tonic for the Reform Group.

The Judge instructed the union to reinstate my address in its original form and to postpone the election until the main action could be tried. The Executive Council had no option and complied during yet another bitter and snarling session. In the event, the case was overtaken by the subsequent Byrne–Haxell contest and the all-important High Court case that unravelled and revealed the entire sordid Communist conspiracy, but this earlier courtroom success revived our people's flagging spirits and pointed the way forward. I had outguessed the Reds, set them up and used their own prejudices to defeat them.

We headed for the real test with renewed vigour and optimism, determined to unseat the machine-man himself: it was Frank Haxell's turn to be the target. Not all the Reform Group wanted Jock Byrne as our candidate for General Secretary, for he was not a fit man. Yet if we had ditched him we might never have made the final breakthrough. His prolonged and well-known struggle against the Communists was of immense value and we needed him and relied on him at that time rather more than he has ever received credit for. The Communists made private overtures to try to persuade him to back off and even attempted to trump up a charge against him. They got nowhere.

I can't pretend that I liked Jock Byrne. He was a stubborn and difficult man who thought provincially rather than in terms of the union as a whole. He distrusted us ex-Communists and once, in our Hayes Court days together, he called me 'an insolent cur'. His distaste for Les Cannon was marked but it was Les who did most to bring him along with us. Les once motored overnight to Scotland to see him and arrived on Sunday morning as Jock was leaving home with his wife to go to church. He told Les he must wait until after the service if he wanted to talk, but Les, tired and angry, threatened to drive straight back to London and Jock relented. His wife went to church alone. It sometimes seemed that Jock thought that what was happening in the union was all the will of God. We put it down to human sweat and strife. But Jock Byrne, for all his faults, had guts and was an instrumental part of our ultimate conquest.

It was all coming together – nothing succeeds like success. The lawyers wanted an extraordinary amount of detailed work done before they would move. They still doubted us and had to have 190 per cent proof of everything, but we began to pick up more and more evidence of branch fiddles as the Byrne–Haxell election progressed. The Communists went over the top and as the panic set in, so their mistakes mounted. It was a fractious and fateful Executive Council that met to hear the election result declared. It was all carefully schemed in advance – the premature adoption of the scrutineers' report returning Haxell to office, the stifled questions and Foulkes' refusal to respond to my request for a slow reading of the branch disqualifications, the speech by Sell to divert attention and obstruct my probing. They reckoned they had out-smarted me, but when I met the Reform Group later it was like a celebration. I was laughing and said: 'It had to end up in court. They hammered the nails in their own coffin today.'

The writs were issued, the Communists were on the run, and they knew it. I went by car with 'Honest' John Hendy to inspect conditions at a site in Essex where our members worked. As we travelled, he said to me in a gruff manner:

'What will it take to end this battle in the union?'

'What you have to do,' I replied, 'is to declare Byrne elected.'

Hendy said bitterly: 'We aren't going to have a reactionary Catholic running this union.'

There was only one response. I said: 'If the members want him, that's what we will have. And that's where I stand.'

Hendy has reminded me of that conversation several times over the years since 1961. But it is another of the cardinal weaknesses of those who believe their activities are justified by destiny that they don't know how to retreat.

## CHAPTER 7

# JUDGEMENT DAY

There have been many colourful and controversial highlights in my life since Wednesday 28 June 1961. It's been brickbats and battles all the way. I have fought my corner inside the union, the Trades Union Congress, the Labour Party, with employers and with both Tory and Labour governments, but that summer day, twenty-three years ago, was the incomparable turning point for me.

I sat in the High Court in London as the late Mr Justice Winn fired legal torpedoes as relatively devastating as any that one-time submarine commander ever launched in his wartime naval career. He delivered an historic and damning 40,000-word judgment that irretrievably and irrefutably scuppered and sank the Communist ballot-riggers in the ETU. The robed and bewigged judge rattled on at a truly remarkable and sustained high speed through page after page of his findings. His sheer pace confounded some of those in court and they needed the exact outcome spelled out to them afterwards; even the official court short-hand writer had trouble keeping up. But, as one of the two plaintiffs, it was clear to me, long before he finished his marathon verdict, that we had won. Our prolonged and bitter struggle had smashed the spider's web of fraud and conspiracy through which the Communists had dominated the union and maintained their stranglehold upon it.

It was an amazing triumph against all the odds that were so over-whelmingly stacked up against us when we set out on our task to replace union corruption with union democracy. For that was our aim, and that was our ultimate achievement.

At the very outset of his judgment, Mr Justice Winn drew particular attention to a rank anomaly: Communist Party membership in the ETU could hardly have been more than about one in a hundred of our 250,000 membership at the time. Yet, he pointed out, the President, General Secretary, Assistant General Secretary, five Executive Coun-cillors, the office manager and four of the five National Officers were

Communists. It was, he said, a representation markedly out of line with the votes of those 'on whom no cogent persuasion had been brought to bear'.

He explained a problem he faced in considering the case: proof of conspiracy could seldom be achieved by direct evidence since conspirators didn't run tape recorders or cameras. Then he went on to give us his own definition of Communists and their like: 'Only a recluse in an ivory tower would fail to appreciate the tendency of all forms of single-minded devotion to ideology, whether religious, political or economic, to degenerate into fanaticism and a state of obsessive delusion that the only criterion of good and ill in conduct is utility for the achievement of chosen ends.' The witnesses, he said, no doubt seemed to themselves to be honest and accordingly presented the general appearance of being frank and straightforward. Assessing them was a very much more difficult task than detecting the lies of wholly dishonest rogues.

But Mr Justice Winn showed that, difficult or not, his perception of the trial and the defendants had led him to unequivocal decisions. He declared: 'I find that not only was the ETU managed and controlled by Communists and pliant sympathisers but it was so managed in the service of the Communist Party of the United Kingdom and the ideas of the Party. In my judgement, it is nothing but what has sometimes been called double-talk to speak of servicing the ETU by aiming to achieve for its members the aims and objects regarded as *optima* by Communists; simplified that means rallying the union in the Communist struggle for those objects.'

He made searing comments about the defendants. His comments on Executive Council member 'Honest' John Hendy bared to the bone that unquestioning and compulsive devotion to Communism, among other ideological extremes, which can twist an otherwise decent individual until he is blind to any other standards and considerations. The judge called Hendy 'a man who is inspired, if not possessed, by a fervent faith that the Communist creed is the ultimate truth, an appeal to which will afford an answer logically solving any problem of behaviour or choice of action ... personally honourable to the extent that he would not adopt any course of conduct which seemed to him to be unjust to an individual unless the demands of loyalty to Communist tenets or consideration of advantage to the Communist Party left him no choice.' Just to rub in how Hendy's undiluted faith took precedence, Mr Justice Winn added that throughout his evidence Hendy gave 'a wonderful performance of adroit sidestepping and circumlocution'.

71

If Hendy was a well-intentioned if dangerous political nut, there were no qualifications to the judicial condemnation of Messrs Foulkes and Haxell. Haxell, said the judge, was a 'most markedly dominant type of man, shrewd, ruthless and persuasive'. Both Haxell and Executive Councillor Frazer put forward 'puerile mendacities and gave untrue evidence', and McLennan's evidence was similarly dismissed. Foulkes evaded the substance of questions and had the idea that he could save himself 'technically from committing perjury'. He had lied on television and both he and Haxell 'preferred expediency to truth'.

The judge highlighted another pernicious Communist tactic by quoting a passage from one union document which read: 'Politics. Up against Rules of the Labour Party. No such rules for TUC industrial affiliations. Our members must not sign documents. May be necessary to modify our attitude as witch-hunt develops, for example, Stooge TC.' Said the judge: 'This clearly means that controlled sympathisers who could sign a statement that they were not Communists should be sent to Trades Councils.'

He dealt swiftly with the Executive Council's disciplinary charges against me: one he brushed aside as trumpery – 'a desire to clip the wings of a stormy petrel'; the other charge, on which I was convicted, 'was not the same charge as that which it was resolved should be laid against him'. That wangle didn't stop them finding me guilty, but the judge added: 'I have the firm impression that he so infuriated the members of the Executive Council by his adoption of a position independent of their own ... that the judges were not judicial towards him.' I did come in for some criticism, though: the judge referred to my evidence that the Communist advisory committee meetings were set up by written notice to those who could be trusted to destroy them and by word of mouth to the others, and said that my statement had 'the appearance of picturesque embroidery'. All the notes I got for those meetings had 'please destroy this note' written on the bottom – and I had, so there was no evidence to support my claim.

Piece by piece Mr Justice Winn took the tattered defence apart. He picked out 'a wicked fraud upon the members of the ETU' by Haxell when he distracted delegates' attention at a rules conference and slipped through changes to enhance his own powers. He tackled the various rigged branch ballots and Haxell's suppression of branch demands for special investigations.

Coming to the all-important 1959 Byrne–Haxell election and the

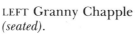

LEFT Granny Chapple *(seated)*.

RIGHT Private Chapple of the REME.

.ow Sir Leslie Cannon,
vital figure in the fight
.inst Communism in the
U.

LEFT In Worthing
with my wife Joan and
sons Roger and Barry.

ЭHT Moscow 1958:
*o r)* Sir Tom O'Brien *(in dark
t)*, Rosamund John, Jimmy
wards, the author, George
vin and Bert Batchelor
*ith camera)*.

ABOVE A Communist-dominated ETU conference delegation with: *front row*, Gen. Sec. Frank Haxell *(second from left)*, Pres. Frank Foulkes *(third from left)*, Asst Gen. Sec. Bob McLennan *(third from right)*, and Jock Byrne *(far right)*; *back row*, Sam Goldberg *(far left)*, Bill Blair *(second from left)*, Jack Frazer *(third from left)*, Bill Sullivan *(fourth from left)*, Bill Blairford *(fifth from right)* and Jack Hendy *(fourth from right)*.

LEFT At the 1961 TUC conference, Foulkes pleads for the ETU to be allowed to stay within the Trade Union movement.

'sinister' over-ordering of ballot papers from the printers, he said that extra voting papers, already marked with Haxell votes, had been sent to Communist branch secretaries for them to include in their returns as votes received by post from their members. But despite all the fiddling, disaster threatened Haxell, his two 'myrmidons', and the prestige of the Communist Party in trade union circles. They knew that Byrne was ahead and panic set in. Envelopes in which fifty-five branches had sent in their returns were destroyed, or switched to other returns, and new substitute postings were arranged from the same place where the original envelope had been posted. When these further envelopes arrived, the returns they contained were disqualified for arriving too late, but from forty of the fifty-five branches witnesses gave evidence of posting a substantial time before the dates on the envelopes produced by the defendents at the trial.

The judge found that twenty-seven out of the forty cases of alleged substitution were established to his complete satisfaction and four more on the balance of probability. In every case the majority vote was for Byrne, who would have led by 2,107 votes, yet the published result was Byrne 18,577, Haxell 19,611. Out of 109 branches whose votes were disqualified, 106 produced a majority for Byrne. Fraud, including forged votes, was used to make the union's scrutineers give their return in Haxell's favour.

So, whodunnit? Mr Justice Winn said the result had been contrived by a combination of dishonest trickery through selective indulgences over late arrivals and disqualifications of branch returns, and through Foulkes and McLennan distorting the presentation of material to the union's scrutineers. If he did not devise the scheme, Haxell directed it, and Foulkes and McLennan were guiltily complicit. He said the scheme for substitute envelopes bore the hallmarks of Haxell and Frazer, both of whom were 'blunt, unsubtle and ruthless. Agents must have been used whom it is impossible to identify . . . it would not be inconsistent with the general probabilities that the aid of the Communist Party network was invoked.'

The judge recalled too that, at the union's Executive Council meeting, Foulkes had prematurely put through a motion to record Haxell's victory – he was out to stifle any discussion of the disqualifications. Referring to my interrupted attempt to argue at the pre-election meeting that 'we are entitled to have a scrutineers' report which includes . .', Mr Justice Winn said: 'No doubt he was going to say "the disqualifications". Just so.' And, the judge surmised, Foulkes played it that way not just because he was tired of the troubles I caused inside the Executive Council, but because he knew that the disqualifications were wholly abnormal in number and were symptomatic of rigging.

He said there were further attempts to hush up the facts inside that meeting. Two Executive Councillors, Frazer and Sell, agreed in advance to propose adoption of the statement about the result and Sell made a speech to try to divert attention and obstruct me. Mr Justice Winn reckoned though, that Sell was a 'raw hand', not fully in the confidence of the others. Cosby, Davies, Feathers, Goldberg, Hendy and West were also there and supported the proposal to endorse Haxell's election. Mr Gardiner submitted that they should be found guilty as parties to the conspiracy, but, despite considerable doubt, the judge thought the evidence and inferences to be drawn in these cases (and for Scott and Batchelor), by contrast with those of the other defendants, 'do not come up to the standard required to establish so grave a charge'. Even so, he thought that Goldberg and Hendy had such intelligence and experience of union affairs that 'it is contrary to the balance of probability that they were ignorant of the rigging'. Each gave materially untrue evidence and Goldberg was 'a not very scrupulous henchman of Haxell'.

Oddly enough, the unquestionable culprits were decimated in only a sentence or so. It was enough. Mr Justice Winn found that Foulkes, Haxell, McLennan, Frazer and Humphrey had acted in breach of the union's rules and 'conspired together to prevent by fraudulent and unlawful devices the election of the plaintiff Byrne in the place of the defendant Haxell as General Secretary of the defendant union'. There were still some loose ends to tie up, but the Communist reign was effectively over.

We were back with Mr Justice Winn on 3 July. The Communists were fighting their rearguard action and we had to establish quite unequivocally what that court verdict meant. Mr Lawson's arguments were swept aside and the judge formally declared that John Byrne was elected as General Secretary in December 1959 and that 'as from this moment of time' is the General Secretary of the union. We also asked that the fresh Executive Council elections to be held the following September should be conducted by the independent Electoral Reform Society. It was a modest enough request in view of everything that had happened, but Mr Lawson contested it. He said that the judge should not sweep away the union's rules about elections and claimed that the existing Executive Council would ensure impartiality. He must have been kidding; he was paid to do a job for his clients, but this was ridiculous.

Mr Justice Winn clobbered him hard. He admitted that he no longer had an unprejudiced and open mind about the individuals on trial and regarded the whole lot of them with the greatest suspicion. He could not leave the fortunes of the union members in their hands, nor could he trust anyone at Head Office to conduct a straightforward election, so the court 'must take drastic measures here'. Mr Gardiner stepped in. He referred to another pending court action alleging similar frauds in a current election for Assistant General Secretary, in which I was standing against McLennan, and said the defendants would be in control of that election and there was already fraud at branch and headquarters level. He wanted to ensure that members got their ballot papers from an independent person and returned them to that person so that they were not dealt with by Communist branch secretaries.

Eventually, the problem was resolved when Mr Lawson gave an assurance, sought by the judge, that chartered accountants not associated with the Communist Party would be used to supervise the elections. It was not quite the watertight arrangement I would have liked, but it seemed likely to be good enough to produce the first fair elections in the union for very many years.

There was a little matter of cash to sort out, and Mr Justice Winn ruled that our costs could be recovered from the union and the defendants. Goldberg and Hendy, who were acquitted, got no costs – a clear indication of the judge's view of their involvement. The other five successful defendants were told to get their costs from their guilty pals. In a way, it seemed unfair that the union should have to foot the bill. The ordinary dues-paying members were innocent of everything, except perhaps the apathy which is always the best friend of extremists and rogues.

Mr Lawson – or his alert clerk – must have been uncomfortably aware from the start that the judge might order those found guilty to pay the huge costs of the case from their own pockets, rather than from union funds, so he received his counsel's retainer each day as the hearing progressed – in cash in brown paper envelopes. It was understandable. After all, the defendants admitted at the outset that the election was invalid, and any disgruntled individual union member might have claimed that it was a misuse of union funds to pay for the action from them rather than make the conspirators fully liable for their own misdeeds. They could never have met their £250,000 costs from their own resources.

Mr Lawson gave notice that an appeal was likely, though I should think he was merely going through the legal motions. Mr Justice Winn's trenchant, lucid and censorious determination should have left no room for gestures of that kind, but that was reckoning without the curious mixture of cunning, conceit and stubbornness that was found in Frank Foulkes. Doubtless feeling there was nothing to lose, he insisted on a new challenge, claiming that he was not a party to any fraud. It was the following January before the case reached the Court of Appeal, where it was heard by Lord Justice Sellers, Lord Justice Donovan and Lord Justice Pearson. By then we had decided to toss in a cross-appeal against Scott's acquittal on the basis of fresh evidence – his own report on the investigation into Southend Electronics Branch which had suppressed evidence of ballot-rigging.

Foulkes cut a sorrier and sorrier figure; the judges were withering. Lord Justice Sellers gave Mr Justice Winn a pat on the back for his 'mastery of the complicated details of the case', then dealt with Foulkes. He said: 'It is with regret that, as this appeal has been unfolded and the evidence revealed, I conclude and would hold, as did Mr Justice Winn, that the appellant played his part – not an unimportant part – in the rigging of this election.' He added that but for the 'vigilance and persistence' of John Byrne and I, the fraud might have remained concealed.

I came directly into the reckoning again when he referred to that Executive Council meeting at which the election result had been declared and at which Foulkes had stifled the opposition. Said the judge: 'It has been submitted that anger or annoyance with the provocative Mr Frank Chapple explains, or might explain, Mr Foulkes' conduct. I do not regard this as a reasonable view.' All three judges concurred and Foulkes' ill-conceived appeal was thrown out.

The cross-appeal against George Scott was more of a teaser, so much so that it split the judges. Lord Justice Sellers said that Scott's report that 'went missing' during the trial was found by us as soon as we took over, but it was 'too remote' to have a direct bearing on the case, and he refused to accept it as further evidence. He said Scott was only on the fringe of the matter – he may have been a tool but that would not justify a decision that Mr Justice Winn was wrong to acquit him. Lord Justice Donovan disagreed. He believed that Scott's report was clearly relevant to the general conspiracy alleged, and thought that if Mr Justice Winn had had the report, 'it must have been decisive against Mr Scott'. He suggested that the new evidence should be admitted and that Scott should have another opportunity to explain it so that the court could then decide on whether the judgement should stand.

That said, Donovan – later to head the important Royal Commission on trade unions and employers' organisations set up by the Wilson Government – recognised that his two fellow judges considered the report should not be admitted, so he pursued the matter 'no further', and agreed that without the report they could not reverse the judge's findings. The score was two to one against us, but Scott was not awarded his costs – another sign of what their Lordships thought about it all.

The ETU case was a body blow from which the Communist Party has never recovered. I doubt if it ever will. Ever since the case, the Communists and their broad sweep of allies throughout the trade union movement have tried to turn back the clock, and they still seek to foster the illusion that, in the good old days, the Communists led a fighting, democratic organisation which used its industrial strength skilfully on behalf of the membership. Their propaganda sounds attractive, well-meaning and even forward-looking, but there are too many who have learned nothing. They have ensured that a stream of mindless and often vicious abuse has been directed against the union's leadership in general, and against me in particular.

They have their media friends – much of the mythology about the old Red leadership is well doctored and carefully released to coincide with important union events – and the 'progressives' in Fleet Street and television play an unscrupulous game. They choose to ignore the facts. Those facts underline the success story which has followed the eviction of the ballot-riggers who, often with the backing of those who now criticise us, stole our members' democratic rights: our membership has doubled; there has been enormous growth in the members' participation in union affairs and we offer our membership a service second to none; the Communist and Trotskyite based opposition have consistently lost in genuinely held elections, although at every rules revision conference they have tried to recapture power through manipulation and intimidation.

There is a wider-than-ever variety of political gangsters of the far left around today, but all things are relative. For all the insidious efforts of the ragbag of extremist Trotskyite groups in modern Britain, the emaciated Communist Party remains the best-organised, best-

77

disciplined and hence most potent long-term threat to our democratic way of life. Yet its political clout is less than ever: its Parliamentary candidates at the last General Election were humbled; it is strained by internal jealousy and dissension; its daily newspaper, the *Morning Star*, survives by courtesy of the bulk purchases made by the Soviet Union and its East European satellites, who between them buy about 18,000 copies of the paper each day – more than are sold to the entire UK readership. It is the best example of 'laundered' funds from Moscow finding their way to Britain's Communists.

Industrially, the Communist Party cannot be dismissed so lightly. It was Lenin who said the unions are the transmission belts for the Party, and inside the unions Communism retains an influence far in excess of its numerical strength. A number of top union officials – General Secretaries and Presidents among them – are Communists, and they control several major unions, often through fellow travellers and their stooges – though only the Amalgamated Engineering Workers' Technical, Administrative and Supervisory Section (TASS) labours under the kind of iron grip which once bedevilled the ETU. Communists are well entrenched throughout the unions, all the way to the TUC General Council where last year's swing to the right in the contest for seats still left two Communist card-carriers at our movement's top table. A Communist Party industrial organiser once claimed that the Communist Party could formulate a policy in the spring and it would become the policy of the TUC and the Labour Party by the autumn.

Today's favoured tactic is to work through the Labour Party, with which the Communists now have few policy differences. It is all a very far cry from the days when the official Communist line was for a programme of struggle against Labour, and for a Party which assumed 'the independent leadership of the proletariat', but there is no need for that with the current policies of the Labour Party.

My fight to rid my union of the fraudsters has made a difficult job, representing my members, an onerous one at times. The Communists in the union, and outside it, have never forgiven me for exposing them in the courts and never will. They have plenty of backing – the Scargills, the Benns and their ilk – and I'm the man they all love to hate. It is just as well that I have broad shoulders: sometimes I have shoulder-charged, but mostly I have been able to shrug off my misleading detractors – literally and metaphorically. They have never been able to silence me and that has maddened them. Nor can they challenge my working class origins. I was born in a seedy street in London's cheerfully tough East

End in August 1921 and it was thirty-five years later when I first lived in a house with a bath. My two sons, Roger, now aged thirty-five, and Barrie, thirty-two, were both apprenticed electricians, are both EETPU members and Labour Party activists and Barry is a union branch secretary. I can swop colourful expletives with anyone and I am always ready to buck the establishment if it needs it.

But the biggest irritant to the Communists and their allies comes from the consistent support I get from the overwhelming bulk of my members. I have trusted the members and they have trusted me. I have stayed one of them, have done my best to represent their hopes, needs and aspirations, and they have regularly and overwhelmingly returned me to office with ever-increasing majorities, a claim that very few union leaders can make. And I reckon that the majority of the ordinary members of other trade unions are with me, too.

## CHAPTER 8

# INTO THE SADDLE,
# OUT WITH THE REDS

There were sweeping repercussions from the High Court verdict. We had won a momentous battle but the war was far from over. Jock Byrne was established as General Secretary, but the pro-Communist Executive Council majority were out to make him pay for victory and to give him the roughest possible ride. There were still only three of us to support him – myself, Ernie Hadley and Bill Blairford, elected to replace Colin Walker. The fresh Executive elections were several months off and even if we ousted the Communists then, it would be the end of the year before our people could take their seats.

Meanwhile, the union must be managed. The bulk of the full-time officials were hostile to us, as were most of the staff at Head Office, known as the 'little Kremlin', since they were all the old regime's appointees. Unless we moved quickly Jock would be ensnared. It was vital for him to assert the authority his office commanded. He did so by suspending Jim Humphrey, the Hayes Court office manager who was among those found guilty by Mr Justice Winn, and by appointing Les Cannon and myself as his personal assistants. Foulkes swiftly counter-attacked by calling a meeting of all the ETU officials. It was held at London's Russell Hotel and was a put up job to keep us stretched, strained and, hopefully, on the defensive. The officials lambasted Les as the mastermind behind the court case and passed a vitriolic resolution demanding that Jock should sack him; at the same time they tried to force Humphrey's reinstatement. They couldn't object to my role as Byrne's aide since I was an elected Executive Councillor. Jock pluckily refused to budge from the decision he had made.

The Communists shifted their ground to try to hamstring him: on the pretext that the High Court was critical of its past failure to accept full responsibility for conduct of the union's affairs, the Executive Council set up a series of sub-committees to cover every function that mattered. There were sub-committees for ballots, for litigation and one for establishment concerns, which had the right to hire and fire and would clearly be used for a renewed bid to pick off Les Cannon. The powers of the General Secretary were subject to the say-so of the Executive Council and this action virtually stripped Jock of his authority.

He ignored these shackles and complained to the TUC where George Woodcock was now the General Secretary, not that we entertained any great hopes of help from that quarter. We despaired of TUC prevarication, one good example of which followed our suggestion during the court hearings that the TUC might appoint an acting General Secretary to look after the members' interests until the judgement. After all, there had been an early admission that Haxell's election was invalid. Woodcock turned us down flat. But now that the case was over the TUC felt able to toughen up: it announced its own investigation and began to shape up to kick the union from its ranks. The Labour Party followed suit.

The five-hour meeting that was held between the TUC General Council and the full ETU Executive was a stormy and utterly futile occasion. Foulkes and his followers continued to protest their innocence and to insist that they would all appeal against the High Court verdict. Woodcock said later that he had 'never in my life had a more miserable experience', and any decent, caring trade unionist would have felt that way about the arrogance, bluster and whingeing of Foulkes and his allies. The TUC made a last attempt to soft-pedal, compromise and avoid the drastic step of expulsion by calling on Foulkes to resign and seek re-election, and demanding action to bar five of the other conspiratorial ringleaders from union office for at least five years. They wanted the sub-committees to be scrapped and they insisted that Jock's staff appointments and suspensions should be ratified. True to form, our Executive met and voted by the customary eight votes to three to defy the TUC's 'unwarranted interference'.

At the TUC's 1961 Portsmouth conference George Woodcock had the job of moving, on behalf of the General Council, that the ETU should be expelled. There was no alternative. I listened intently from the body of the hall as he claimed that the General Council had been patient, tolerant and that there had 'never been at any stage any rushing in here'. That was the understatement of the year: the TUC's lack of any sense of urgency had always been a lamentable bonus for the Communists. Woodcock told of the ETU's pitiable non-answers and evasions. The issue for the TUC was fraud, not Communism, and he declared: 'Trade unions are the protectors of working people and nobody has the right to pervert the trade unions to other purposes and functions.'

There was high drama as Foulkes took the rostrum and lashed at those 'determined to wreck my union'. He accused Les – without naming him – of a personal vendetta and there could have been few delegates in the hall who failed to identify his target. No contrition, no remorse; once again Foulkes denied everything that the court had proved so decisively. Sam Goldberg's conference contribution reeked of even greater hypocrisy, contending that the Executive Council regarded ballot-rigging with 'loathing and disgust . . . a crime against democracy'. Jack Frazer, the third of our old guard to get a hearing, did the Communist cause no good by tactlessly rounding on the General Council for bias and intimidation. If there were any floating votes, the trio who spoke for the fraudsters must have lost them.

Of course, the Communists had their apologists. The belligerent Danny McGarvey, of the boilermakers, described Foulkes as 'one of the most highly respected men in the Movement'. Spokesmen for the pro-Communist draughtsmen's union (now TASS) and the Association of Cinematograph, Television and Allied Technicians, joined him in opposing the ETU's exit. Leaders of these unions, along with Clive Jenkins of the supervisory staffs, had sponsored a Haxell defence fund during the court case. They were prepared for a forlorn last-ditch stand. Clive has backed as many wrong horses as anyone during his long trade union career. Haxell was an early 'wrong-un' for him, but age and experience seem to have taught Clive very little and his judgements remain as inappropriate as his lifestyle is affluent.

There was more drama at the TUC conference when Jock Byrne was called to speak. He was brief, but he shot down the phoney Communist claim that they now sought unity in the union, telling Congress sternly that the Communists and Trotskyites had already formed a campaign committee to try to destroy him. He won considerable applause for his stand. George Woodcock had the last word: 'It is wrong by every standard of trade unionism as I know it that people should seek to change rules and procedures and one thing and another to deprive unionists of the right to manage their own affairs. I say that to governments as well as to other people.'

The conference was compelled to square up to the massive damage that the ETU tricksters had done to the entire British trade union movement, and it voted by an overwhelming 7,320,000 to 735,000 to throw the union out. Our delegation was asked to withdraw and to surrender our credentials. We had again made trade union history – in the sorriest fashion.

The rigmarole was repeated a month later when it was the Labour Party's turn. We had met Labour's National Executive Committee for another vicious and acrimonious session during which I put the boot in hard and undoubtedly shocked some of the Labour leaders with my candid revelations. I recalled my own Communist past and how we used to fix candidates for union office; I rubbed in the role of the Communist ETU Advisory Committee in choosing union delegates to Labour's annual conference; I said of those delegates: 'One of them did, in fact, make an application to join the Communist Party and was instructed to remain within the Labour Party because he could do a better job.' There was no challenge to my disclosures from the ETU Communists and the Labour Party representatives got the clearest possible message.

Twenty-four hours before our Executive Council assembled in Blackpool for Labour's 1961 conference, the Labour Party National Executive Committee agreed that we should be disaffiliated. Even Labour's pro-Communist Executive members felt unable to vote to keep us in and offered no worthwhile opposition to the punitive proposal. Jock Byrne explained to our Executive that the disaffiliation took immediate effect – it would be reported to the opening conference session next day but our delegation would not be allowed to attend. Our delegation sat in the visitors' gallery that morning. The Communists had friends in the hall and had ensured that an appeal would be made for the Conference to suspend its standing orders so that an ETU representative could put the case against expulsion. Justice had to be seen to be done and the Conference agreed to the request.

A Labour Party member had to do the job and Sam Goldberg was briefed, ready and waiting. At the conference rostrum he asserted that the Labour leadership's recommendation, like the TUC decision, was a device to influence the forthcoming union elections for a new Executive Council. He claimed that the actions of George Woodcock, the Liberal Party, the *Daily Mirror* and the Trade Union Group of Labour MPs in tendering their advice to ETU voters constituted widespread interference. He might as well have chucked in the kitchen sink – and the *Daily Worker*.

Ray Gunter, who became Minister of Labour in the subsequent Wilson Government, put the Labour Executive's proposition. He portrayed the meeting with the ETU Executive as 'the most dismal and disturbing' he had ever attended, and talked about the naked bitterness and anger between members of our Executive. He made particular mention of my remarks about the Red influence inside the Labour Party, insisting that Labour must 'keep the Party clean'; the Party stood for tolerance, not witch-hunting, but tolerance must not 'undermine our principles and our faith'.

Once more the pro-Communists did their best to preserve their comrades. Left delegates called expulsion 'a stab in the back for the working class' and Gunter, admittedly a wily and somewhat unctous man, was accused of glibness and 'Welsh tears'. It was left to Charlie Pannell, the down-to-earth veteran MP for Leeds West and secretary of the Trade Union Group of MPs, to demolish the Communists and the Labour hacks. He was pretty familiar with our troubles, having attended some of the courtroom sessions. He denounced Goldberg's 'brass cheek' and said that the union should have sent Jock Byrne to the rostrum to speak for it: that, he said, would have earned a standing ovation. The Labour Party was not asked to disaffiliate the union for fraud, but because of Communist domination. He referred to our sham elections and drove home a wounding shaft that has rightly been often repeated: 'Show me a Communist,' he rapped 'and I will show you a crook.' That was music to my ears – I couldn't have put it better or more accurately.

We were tossed out of the Labour Party by a majority of 5,337,000 to 642,000. It was perhaps rough justice for many of our decent ETU members in Labour's ranks around the country, and some of them certainly felt sore about it. Our union was in the original Labour Representation Committee of 1900 set up to take working people's views to Parliament and to promote them there; we had been affiliated to the Labour Party since 1902. Any other decision by that conference, however, would have been twisted and misrepresented by the Communists as a gesture of approval for them in this rearguard action to keep in their grasp the most important industrial gain they had ever made. It would have been a disastrous error.

We were still on a knife-edge, for the union was deeply divided. Letters from our branches received at Head Office showed 350 for Byrne and 330 against; not the most precise reflection of the members' views but nevertheless indicating that the Reds retained substantial backing.

They ran a smear campaign based on two myths. The first was that we were the beneficiaries of secret right-wing funds which enabled us to crawl to the biased capitalist courts. The facts were very different: we welcomed donations to our cause but they were scarce and the struggle cost us all 'dear – in cash and countless other ways. Les Cannon's expenses for his essential extensive travel to gather evidence from branch officers was properly paid for by our lawyers who could never have managed to do the job themselves and freely admitted it, but the real key to our funding was the legal aid certificates granted long before we reached the High Court. Without that assistance it is unlikely that we would ever have got there. The second myth, peddled hard by the Communists, was that Jock Byrne was appointed to his post by a prejudiced establishment judge. Some foolish and misguided people believed it, rather than accept the reality: that Jock was deprived by fraud of the members' votes which elected him to the office he would have assumed from February 1960.

Fortunately, the Executive election results gave us the overall control we needed. There was no postal voting, but the enormous publicity following the court case ensured that the members knew what was going on, and mass participation was possible for ETU members for the first time in many years. Independent accountants were appointed to supervise the balloting in accordance with the undertaking given in court. The Communists dare not risk rigging this one. From the union's 1961 strength of 250,000 members, 49,000 took part, a high figure for any union ballot – especially as we later discovered that only about 180,000 members were paying their dues.

The Reds were swept from office – only two of their supporters, Harry West and Jim McKernan, retained their seats. We had a nine-to-two majority on the Executive Council though we had a waverer or two to give us eight to three or seven to four on occasion. Nevertheless, we were firmly in the saddle, poised to cleanse the union, introduce genuine democracy in the interests of the entire membership, and dispense for good with rule by a dirty and dishonest political clique. But that cleansing was to be opposed by what remained of the Communist/Trotskyite alliance at every turn.

Foulkes hung grimly to his position, but Haxell was washed up. The Communist Party typically decided that it could best save face by disowning this one-time star member of its own leadership, and it borrowed union-owned High Court transcripts – which it has yet to return – and used them to conduct an internal inquiry. It expelled first Haxell and then Frazer, who tried to defend him. Naturally, the King

Street comrades found themselves not guilty, and did not feel compelled to apologise for their conspiratorial role. Haxell and Frazer were convenient scapegoats to allow the Party chiefs to escape any responsibility for what they had helped to create through their willing ETU tools.

Before the newly-elected Executive could take over we suffered another setback: Les found Jock Byrne collapsed on the floor of his lodgings. There can be no doubt that his stroke was the direct toll exacted by the punishing strain of his prolonged fight against the Reds and by eventually securing the union's top job so late in his working life. His illness posed us a tricky problem and we were ultra-cautious in breaking the news. We knew that the Communists would seize the opportunity to declare Jock unfit to carry on if they got half a chance, so we played down his condition and assured everyone that he would soon be back in harness. As it turned out, he was not out of action for very long, but the stroke left him weakened and unable to play more than a part-time role.

Our anti-Communist Executive Council held its first session at Hayes Court on 2 January 1962. President Foulkes offered a tongue in cheek welcome to the new members; McLennan, still acting Assistant General Secretary, also attended – we smartly discontinued his appointment. One immediate issue was the presence at the meeting of all five Communist and pro-Communist National Officers. Jock Byrne said that they should be out working for the members and could be called in for such meetings when required. Foulkes refused to ask them to leave and was over-ruled. It was the familiar eight-to-three vote, only this time we had the built-in majority. The National Officers trooped from the meeting. We put out a press statement after that first meeting, pledging ourselves to 'stamp out any remnants of fraud and conspiracy', and also set in motion our successful applications for reaffiliation to the TUC and Labour Party.

Soon, we began to uncover a catalogue of financial irregularities that showed callous disregard of the members' interests and an extensive officials' gravy train at the members' expense. There was Haxell's house at Bickley, Kent, restored from dilapidation by the union at heavy cost and later sold by him at a nice profit. Haxell categorically denied the charge when it was initially raised by Dick Reno at a union conference in 1959, calling the accusation 'low and despicable' and winning an ovation for his hypocrisy. He was later forced to admit the sordid affair in a further High Court case and had to apologise publicly to Reno, who had been pilloried by the Communists for his determined attempts to bring out the truth.

There was the unsavoury behaviour of Maurice Tarlo, the union's solicitor, who got a regular retainer from the union for his work and charged normal solicitor's fees and costs as well. He was effectively being paid twice. We fired him but had to get a court order to get him to return 625 of our members' accident cases. Many of the cases were stale and had been neglected by Tarlo, who had nonetheless pocketed his union salary. Members who needed and were entitled to help from the union had been denied it.

There were the delegation fees collected by Foulkes for crossing the office corridor to meet Haxell in his office. There were the out-of-town allowances paid to one Communist National Officer for supposedly living in Liverpool when he was really based full-time at Hayes Court. There was the rent charged by officials for garaging their union cars even though they kept them at home. It was a record of fiddling, big and small, all thoroughly in line with that gross fraud and conspiracy which had been revealed in the High Court. There was plenty more murky and disreputable business, some of it provable, some of it just highly suspicious.

The ordinary members paid for all this, and those who fooled and deceived them were the self-styled champions of working people, ever-ready to attack robber-employers while quietly putting their hands in the union till. It would be foolish for me to pretend that it is only Communist officials in British trade unions that ever behave that way, but it is the Communists, above all, who place themselves on a pedestal of ideological purity and who all too often practise in the political and material gutter. Some of our officials think me stingy and unduly scrupulous in guarding the union's resources and I admit that I am conditioned by what I saw happen under the Red regime. We do get our trade unionism on the cheap in Britain, but cheap or not I have made very sure that those membership dues have not been frittered away.

The Communists may have been chastened but they maintained their abuse against us. Supporters from one of the area committees turned up uninvited at Hayes Court and demanded to see Jock Byrne. He simply wasn't up to it and I met them in his place. They swore and shouted at me and I was hustled as I left the room in disgust. Their grievances were phoney, dreamed up so that they could demonstrate against us anti-Communists. It was the kind of behaviour that made us more determined than ever to purge our union of its corrupt and hooligan elements.

We had already charged the ringleaders in the ballot-rigging episode – Haxell, Frazer, McLennan and Humphrey were dealt with under the ETU Rules and expelled from membership. Some of the other prime movers got similar treatment, but Foulkes remained a stumbling block. I was deputed to go and talk to him and to tell him that the Executive Council wanted him to retire early. We did not want vengeance against an elderly man who was running out of time and could never regain his past power, nor did we seek to jeopardise his union pension, but I had to let him know that we would be obliged to charge him under the union's rules if he clung to office. How could we possibly act otherwise on behalf of the members he had defrauded?

He was intransigent and claimed publicly that we sought to blackmail him into going. Some journalists were stupid enough, or sufficiently hostile to us to accept his warped interpretation. It was as though we were the guilty parties, not Foulkes. He stayed away from Hayes Court Executive meetings for about four months, giving illness as his reason, and only resumed the chair at the June 1962 Executive meeting, a whole year after the verdict condemning him in the High Court. All that time he had remained titular President on full pay.

We had been generous long enough. We waited until the normal business of the meeting was over, then Foulkes was asked why, after the failure of his appeal, he had not resigned. We got nowhere with him. He stubbornly insisted that he had no intention of quitting, so my Executive colleague, Tom Breakell, and I moved that he should be formally asked to resign and should have twenty-four hours to think it over. That was agreed by seven votes to four. Foulkes remained adamant that resignation was out of the question, and Jock Byrne gave Counsel's opinion which indicated that our rules gave us no alternative to charging him if he refused to go voluntarily. It was a weird display of cussedness and vanity.

A month later the Executive dealt with the formal charge that was laid against Foulkes. He was at last ready to shop his guilty comrades and for the very first time conceded that the Byrne-Haxell election was rigged, though he still proclaimed that he knew nothing about the fixing until the election was over. It was a belated and pathetic bid to save his own skin and it just wasn't on. He failed to convince the judge and he could hardly hope to convince us. He lost the vote, again by seven to four, and his long reign was ended – dishonourably by expulsion. We were attacked for hounding him, yet he had presided over harsh disciplinary action against decent anti-Red ETU members based on false charges. He was guilty as hell himself, yet his boozing pals whipped-up public sympathy denied to any of those earlier victims of Communist persecution. We had given him every chance to go quietly and, after the expulsion, even found a way to give him a temporary pension on humanitarian grounds.

Still Foulkes was no more than a distraction from the main task ahead. True democracy in the ETU had to be sanctioned by the entire membership since, although the Executive Council was in our hands, we still needed to bust the Communist hold on the rules and policy conferences if we were not to be continually hamstrung. The customary fifty conference delegates made it easy for the Reds to get their people into place to run the show, but there was a legitimate way to bypass those conferences: we were entitled to ballot the membership. The Executive agreed to ask their approval to hold a special rules revision conference to which each of the union's 700 branches could send a delegate. The Communists could sow up fifty delegates, but 700 was a very different proposition. The vote went our way by a thumping 26,458 to 6,206. The lesson is simple enough: the more participative democracy is extended, the more the extremists are cut down to size. We held the rules revision conference at Margate and, since there was no General President in office, I was appointed by the Executive Council to chair the immensely important gathering.

The Communists did their utmost to thwart me from the outset. A succession of their supporters came to the rostrum to protest vehemently about the arrangements before we had even got under way. A big conference is difficult for any chairman to manage, but the bulk of those delegates were decent sensible trade unionists who were not going to be manipulated. They could smell deliberate sabotage and they backed me in getting the business moving. I made a short opening statement, warning of a widening gap between workers on the shopfloor and the trade union leadership, a theme I have pursued many times since and dealt with in my TUC President's address more than twenty years on. I told that 1962 conference that the ETU had evolved a rule book of 'such complexity as to be incomprehensible to any logical mind and for that reason a rule book that has been particularly open to abuse'. I said that the Executive Council's proposed rule changes were 'all designed to ensure that the membership gets the leadership that it wants and that it has the facilities to control the policy of the union in its own interests'.

Our major proposals included elections by post to and from the members' homes; transferable votes and independent supervision; a new type of conference with delegates from every branch; and an independent appeals committee of rank and file members. We got the whole package through, although there were some tight votes: democracy was on the march in the ETU and the pace was quickening.

We were back in the TUC and Labour Party folds now, and Les Cannon had been reappointed to his old job as Education Officer. But while we were getting our new act together, every Communist, inside and outside the union, continued to do everything possible to obstruct our efforts. Strikes in industries where we were involved were directed as much at the Executive Council as against the employers. The winter of 1962-3 brought widespread electricity cuts because of unofficial action in the power stations. The wildcats were led by Charlie Doyle, formerly a prominent American Communist Party member, who was kicked out of the United States and had hardly set foot in England before he started to make trouble. He got a job at Battersea Power Station and set up a shop stewards' organisation to link all the power stations and to ignore the official trade unions; it was no coincidence that it should be formed just after the Communists lost control of the ETU, the industry's main union. We warned our members that they breached our rules if they got mixed up with this rebel gang, but the so-called National Committee of Shop Stewards defiantly carried on its destructive efforts for some years.

It was not just Doyle, later thrown out of the union, who gave us trouble. I headed the multi-union negotiating team at the Electricity Council for official pay talks. We rejected two pay offers as inadequate and also turned down arbitration, but we could see that the Tory Government had nobbled the Electricity Boards. The ETU Executive backed an industry-wide overtime ban but the other unions backed down, and voted by four to one for a deal. They subsequently refused to support my bid to re-open negotiations for a better offer; we could hardly go-it-alone for long, but the settlement to which I objected gave the unofficial movement a useful stick to beat me with. I would be depicted as the union leader responsible for a sell-out. It has been a boringly incessant cry against me in negotiations ever since, though fortunately its irrelevance has become increasingly apparent to my union members.

We were into another ETU election and the left, as usual, hotted up its campaign. The contest for Assistant General Secretary had been

90

shelved following the court rumpus over my censored election address, but McLennan, appointed to carry on in an acting capacity by the old Red Executive, was no longer a union member. I was the obvious anti-Communist candidate to take his place and cantered home with 27,445 votes to the 13,846 of my nearest rival, Albert Wallis from Bradford, who had the Communists' support. I opted for my first break in years from the day-to-day pressure of our battle. Some two years earlier I had won a Ford Foundation scholarship for a six-week sponsored visit to the USA, but felt unable to abandon the ETU at such a critical time. No one is indispensable, but it would have been no relaxation for me to be away whilst uncertainty ruled. Now that things were more settled and my own election was complete, I could safely make the visit. By the time I returned we were shaping up for a far more vital tussle – it was time to pick the successor to Foulkes as General President.

The first and biggest hurdle to jump was the anti-Communists' choice of candidate. Communists have their political dogma which teaches them that unity is essential at such times for survival, but non-Communists have no such creed and may fail to stick together. The Reform Group was rapidly in disarray. It was scarcely credible to me that Les Cannon should not be our automatic selection; yet, however formidable his abilities, he made enemies easily and not just among our political opponents. He did not suffer fools: his lip curled and his eyes, beneath the domed balding head, betrayed his scorn.

Jock Byrne was in poor health, but he was reluctant to share his power with Les. The ETU General Secretaryship was always the principal office, although the President, as chief industrial negotiator, tended to get most of the publicity. Jock feared he would be completely over-shadowed with Les as President and he was dead right. Les was a stern assessor and saw our problem as one of mediocrity: he didn't only mean Jock and his mornings-only work capacity; the Executive members were mostly raw material without national negotiating experience. Les had long made it clear that he would run for President. He was intensely ambitious, but there was much more to it than that: our foundations were far from secure and we still had mountains to climb; there could be no respite; he was convinced that his personal leadership was a necessity, not mere conceit, but simple realism. Bill Blairford, Foulkes' original opponent, never pushed to be the candidate on this occasion, but several Executive members and other Reform Group members said that they preferred him to Les.

We met in a cliff-top hotel in Scarborough, where one of our conferences was being held, and Les Tuck, an Executive man, said pugnaciously that Les would be 'like a racehorse that no-one can control'. I retorted: 'That's better than having a lumbering old cart-horse who would take us nowhere but oblivion.' It was not Bill Blairford I was getting at, but Jock Byrne and his allies. It was a regrettable and bitter occasion. Mark Young, who had succeeded Les Cannon as Jock Byrne's personal assistant, argued for Bill Blairford, although Bill really supported Les. It then emerged that Mark was ready to run himself and had apparently secured Jock's backing. Harry Gittins, another Executive Councillor, made one of his familiar speeches about 'Communist leopards who don't really change their spots'. I lost my rag and tore into him; he took my remarks badly and left the meeting. The whole event would have been farcical if it hadn't been so outrageous and so dangerous to our cause.

Les clinched it for himself in the end, saying he would stand whatever happened: 'And I'll beat the lot of you, if I have to.' His opposition began to back down – they could see he wasn't bluffing and knew that he could do it. Influential Executive members like Bill Blair, Tom Breakell and Bill Blairford all got behind Les and discretion being the better part of valour, the rest came into line. It was a sorry business and the Reform Group was never quite the same again. It was mainly about personalities and it weakened us needlessly. Whatever Les Cannon's failings – he was overbearing at times and eventually he became too fond of the high life for me – he was undoubtedly the man we needed.

Our preference was soon vindicated by the members. In September 1963 the result of the postal ballot was announced: Les had 34,978 votes, an overall majority of 14,502 over his two rivals, Les Gregory, a National Officer who had resigned from the Communist Party, and Eric Elsom, Communist Area Secretary from Sheffield. It was the highest vote for office in the ETU's history and no one deserved it more.

We also had fresh elections for the Executive Council and managed to hold our position. There was one significant result which the *Daily Worker* reported enthusiastically as 'Shock for ETU Rightwing' – Les Tuck lost his seat to a challenge from newcomer Eric Hammond, then a branch secretary and a shop steward at West Thurrock power station. Eric was regarded as the left candidate and got Communist support, but it was a result that the Reds bitterly regret today. Eric, my successor as General Secretary, is as unswervingly dedicated as I have been to keeping the union free of all Communist and other extremist influence and infiltration.

Les Cannon's victory and the re-election of a moderate Executive Council kept us rolling along. These successes were followed by another body blow for our opponents which Les and I felt must be delivered, since the Communists still considered themselves free as ever to organise their factions, to predetermine ETU affairs according to their Party edicts and to run a union within our union. No self-respecting independent and free organisation can permit that – it was tantamount to giving them extra rights because they were Communists. The last straw was a circular they sent round to our branches, proposing rule amendments to strip the Executive Council of its authority. We retaliated with interest. We could have dealt with individuals within the existing rules, but that would have been messy, protracted and would only have offered a partial solution. We were out to smash them once and for all and we balloted the membership to outlaw Communists from holding ETU office.

It was not a step taken lightly. Only the Transport and General Workers' Union operated a similar ban at the time and has since mistakenly lifted it. The TGWU, the biggest union, has long been the Communist Party's coveted industrial prize. Communists and their backers have become a force within the union's leadership and their activities are clearly reflected in the union's policies and decisions. The repercussions in the broad Labour and trade union movement have caused both anguish and shame.

Bans and proscriptions on trade unionists, whatever their political views, are nothing to celebrate – they are at best a necessary evil – but my personal experience of the Communist Party has led me to one conclusion: that Communists should not hold office in any trade union. They will use the power and influence they gain to further the interests of the Party as a priority and to undermine, if not overthrow, genuine democracy. They are not innocents, seeking to forge a better understanding among trade unionists. Their first loyalty and allegiance is not to the union but to their outside political masters.

The members endorsed our view and voted by 43,197 to 13,932 to ban Communists from office. It was the clearest possible rebuff for Communist and left-wing elitism and their theory that they always know what's good for the rest of us. It was an unmistakable pronouncement, delivered in the teeth of a fierce and sustained Communist campaign against such a move. The free voice of the mass of ordinary members is always a stake in the heart of extremism. It was an example that others should have followed – and still could.

There was a plaintive twitch from the Party's King Street head-quarters: they instructed our full-time officials who were Communists to quit their jobs with the union. Instead, twenty of them resigned from the Party to stay with the union. Only one solitary official stuck it out to the point where the rules were breached and he effectively sacked himself.

Communism takes the path of fratricide, not brotherhood; Communists report on each other; they accept the supremacy of the political tier above them; most of all, they are a conspiracy against the majority. If that is not so, why must they meet in clandestine groups to fix things in advance? Why do they consistently treat ordinary trade unionists as mugs whose spontaneity can never be trusted and who must therefore be manoeuvered into doing what is good for them? Why are they not prepared to win or lose on the merits of the argument?

They work in this sinister way in every organisation in which they have membership. Other extremist left-wing groups have copied them, though they lack that firm discipline and worldwide Communist regimentation which ensures that from Sydney to Salford, from Bombay to Berlin, they can trot out the same Party line at the same moment. There are no British Communists, Russian Communists or even Euro-Communists, despite the present superficial fallout in the United Kingdom Communist Party; there are just Communists, bred on a diet of hatred for America and love for Russia. Trade unionists must understand and appreciate what drives these people on.

Working people frequently have first-hand experience that trade union leaders choose to shut their eyes to and do not wish to be reminded about. They may tolerate Communists as shop stewards where they often do useful industrial work, but derisory Red votes at election times show that the members balk at giving them real policy-making power. Sadly, in too many unions, Communists slip into office unrecognised and by the use of dubious procedures. The members should all have a chance to decide by postal ballot, exercised in the secrecy of their own homes and free from any undue pressure or intimidation. That way, Communists would be out in the cold, as any union bold enough to test the proposition would find.

Does it matter? True, the Communist Party has shrunk from more than 30,000 members in the 1960s to a paltry 15,000 now, but the figures are misleading. It retains an incredibly high proportion of union office holders among its members – around one in ten Executive members and officers in the big unions are either Party members or work hand-in-glove with them. The Party has maintained that position over many years, whatever its other setbacks. The Transport Workers and UCATT (construction workers) each have strong Communist minorities on their Executives, while ASLEF, the train drivers' union, is reckoned to have three Communists and three sympathisers on its seven-man Executive. The miners in Scotland, Wales, Kent and South Yorkshire are Communist-dominated, and the left-wing hold on Ken Gill's TASS (the draughtsmen) will not be weakened by the merger with the sheet metal workers' union, led by George Guy, another Party member. The link-up makes little industrial sense, but the politics are real enough.

The Communist Party's advisory committees are all in place in unions like our own EETPU, in TASS, UCATT, the National Union of Public Employees, the Civil and Public Services Association, and the Society of Civil and Public Servants. There are active advisories based on key industries like engineering and railways, as well as a network of work-place branches; in major plants – such as the British Leyland car factories – there are several branches.

All Communists are under an obligation to belong to their trade unions, which are seen as the Party's vital weapon. One of their most hackneyed slogans derives from Lenin's view that trade unions 'decide everything'. Communists are told to get into their unions and to do a good job industrially – but as a means to aiding the Party. Their policy does not generally favour manufacturing disputes unless there is a genuine grievance to be exploited, but that still leaves plenty of scope. Wrong-headed managements are the Reds' biggest allies in creating shop-floor dissension. If it is necessary to abuse the loyalty of British workers towards their unions, no matter. The Communists have the same attitude towards union rules as they have towards the laws of the country. These are the trappings of protection for the capitalist classes, so breaking them is neither treachery nor treason for a Communist.

Union Communists work incessantly to determine their slates of candidates for elections, to prepare for conferences and to frame resolutions. Every autumn the Party produces a document, usually called *Needs of the Hour*, cooked up for the forthcoming trade union and Labour Party conference season. It sets out Communist priorities: for example, pressure for unilateral nuclear disarmament, withdrawal from the EEC and hostility to any wages policy. It is not brandished openly, but is for use at district, advisory or work-place committees. The aim: to achieve a socialist government and through it to gain control. The tactic: to work within the system and through the unions to subvert the Labour Party. As Mick Costello, former Communist Party industrial organiser, told the *Guardian* in 1978, the Communists had been 'a very serious factor' in the move to the left inside the Labour Party and the TUC.

The Communist Party now has a split in its ranks: the pro-Soviet hardliners, trade union based, want to keep the emphasis on mobilising the working class through the unions; the so-called Euro-Communists see the way forward through the peace movement, women's groups and so on. The Euro-Communists have the whip hand on the Party Executive though the Moscow men still control the *Morning Star*, the Party's ailing newspaper. Their internal troubles and the nation's contempt for their political creed were reflected in the 1983 General Election – they could only muster 11,598 votes in thirty-five constituencies fought throughout the country. That compares with 16,858 votes in the thirty-nine constituencies fought in 1979.

One outcome of all this is that the Communist Party has been forced to co-operate with broad left groupings and, in particular, to act on occasions with the Trotskyite Militant Tendency, undoubtedly its most serious rival for the allegiance of the far left. Militant, with its policy of Labour Party entryism, has its own newspaper, about 4,000 members and an industrial department with several full-time staff. It has had a few trade union successes, notably in capturing the Post Office Engineering Union's Executive in 1983, and in getting a supporter elected for a brief spell as President of the CPSA, the biggest civil service union.

By and large, though, the Communist Party is engaged in trench warfare with Militant over who is to lead the union left. The Communists have warded off the Trotskyites in the Engineering and Miners' unions and have squabbled fiercely with Militant in NUPE. Broad left trade unionists have come together under the umbrella of B.L.O.C. (the Broad Left Organisation Committee), but the Communists have joined from necessity, not choice. They cannot afford to ignore it and to spurn a share in its control.

The rest of the ragbag of left-wing Trotskyite revolutionary outfits, dedicated to overthrow the system, are of scant industrial consequence, but the Communist Party, for all its divisions and pathetic political performance, is the one stable entity on the far left of the British industrial scene. Stalinist, Euroist, call its members what you will, their

ABOVE After the fall of 'The Three Generals', a new Executive Council for the ETU: *(l to r)* Jimmy O'Neill, Harry Gittins, Bill Blair, the author, Jock Byrne, Ernie Hadley, Jim McKernan, Bill Blairford, Tom Breakell and *(backs to camera)* Harry West and Les Tuck.

BELOW In 1967, masked demonstrators protest against disciplinary action imposed to curb a rebellion against an electrical contracting agreement.

Examining a
champion race
pigeon in New York;
fellwalking in
Derbyshire.

ABOVE A meeting
with Lane Kirkland,
President of the AFL/
CIO (the American
TUC) in their
Washington
boardroom, with
British TUC leaders
Len Murray, Tom
Jackson and Alan
Sapper.

LEFT The strong arm
of the law contains
left-wing
demonstrators at the
union's Hayes Court
Headquarters.

tactics may differ but they are all Communists with common long-term objectives: not only the end of capitalism but the permanent destruction of our democratic way of life.

That message cannot be shouted too loudly. Those who brand active anti-Communists as McCarthyites, who speak of witch-hunts, or hysteria, stand the arguments conveniently on their head, sometimes from vested interest, sometimes from ignorance, sometimes through woolly-headed and simplistic liberalism.

CHAPTER 9

# LABOUR PAINS

The autumn 1964 TUC Conference was a pre-election rally for Labour. Congress offered the Party Leader, Harold Wilson, no blank cheque if he took over at 10 Downing Street the following month, but he knew that he could count on broad support for his economic policies, including an incomes policy. By November, when we assembled at Southport for one of our ETU industrial conferences, Wilson was Prime Minister. Les Cannon used the opportunity of Southport to be the first union leader to give a public post-election pledge of his organisation's support for the Labour government. It was a conference at which I made my own somewhat unexpected impact with a trenchant attack on the 'chaos and indiscipline' on Britain's building sites. I called for agreements to be honoured so that the union had greater bargaining power to press for rises for its members and I blasted slipshod and uncaring employers for allowing appalling and often dangerous site conditions. I was warmly applauded by the stewards for my home truths, which made quite a change from catcalls.

I was well versed in what was wrong on those sites from first-hand experience over the years. Now I believed that we faced unparalleled economic difficulties unless we resolved the industrial relations problems that were fed by supine management and inept trade union leadership – and the building industry was perhaps the most culpable of all. Power stations, oil and chemical plants and other major site projects were vital to economic growth and development, but their extravagant construction costs was draining the economy and costing the nation billions of pounds. Construction times were absurd – eight to ten years for a power station – and industrial disruption threw schedules into disarray. Some of this disruption could be attributed to the reaction to indescribably bad working conditions, some of it to sheer bloody-mindedness by the men. There were too many small firms, often 'cowboy' employers. Leapfrog earnings situations would develop, with workers chasing each other up the wages ladder and undermining fair and rational negotiations. There were phoney productivity deals; there was technical disruption by the management, such as design changes in the middle of a job; sometimes, workers spun out the project to keep their jobs going. The Barbican project in the City of London is perhaps the best-known and amongst the most costly of all the building industry scandals.

Many of the major defects remain. The reluctance by management and men at local level to adapt and to modernise has been marked. There has been an unhealthy conservatism which is too typically British, whereby people take impossibly long to wake up to the need for change and to appreciate the benefits that can accrue from it. Management and foremen in the building industry carry on in the same old slapdash way at site level, exactly as they did in my youth, and wonder why they get the same old reactions from disgruntled workers. Too often, weak employers take the easy way out and buy an uneasy short-term peace, thus storing up far greater trouble for the future. Every time a management succumbs to blatant industrial blackmail, whatever the immediate and measurable gain to company or workers, the nation is sold short. There are some shocking examples.

On one housing site in the north-west a few years ago, the company operated a bonus scheme that was so bad that when the men worked to rule they still earned their bonus. They had an unofficial dispute and half-a-dozen of the electricians ran a successful picket line which stopped the job for about a year. They got several thousands of pounds, raised through union branches, and were also drawing social security benefit while picketing. The company were in deep financial difficulty because of the strike and liquidation loomed. They were desperate to end the stoppage and offered the electricians £12,000 each to clear off. However, when the men arrived for the buy-out, after prolonged haggling, the company could only afford to sign individual cheques for £6,000 a man. The scaled-down offer was grudgingly accepted and the company reinstated the men for a quarter-of-an-hour and handed over the money as redundancy pay so that a state refund could be obtained. Some of the same workers moved on to Manchester and repeated their tactic; once again, it worked for them. The employer was windy at the time and later ashamed of his capitulation.

Around the same time I was phoned in the middle of the night from Chicago by a director of an American firm which was building a factory on Merseyside. He wanted me to know that they too had decided to pay off a bunch of troublemakers. 'For us,' he said, 'it's the lesser evil. We must get the job finished.' My language was ripe and not just because he had woken me up.

There was an on–off unofficial strike by electricians at the £7,000,000 Inland Revenue complex at Bootle, near Liverpool, which spread over five years, earning it a place in the *Guinness Book of Records* as the country's longest-running dispute. It cost the taxpayers an estimated £5,000,000. The final six-months stoppage involved nine electricians, who drew unemployment and social security benefits while the branches collected £30,000 for them. No wonder they sat it out.

We were a modern and well-disciplined union, compared with most, but we could not prevent weak-kneed employers making settlements of which we strongly disapproved, nor could we compel men to go back to work in these situations. The pressure on a firm to do a shabby deal can be immense but every time they are blackmailed into submission, they only ensure that their industrial tormentors will be back for more, admittedly usually at the expense of a new victim. The building industry is now in the doldrums – workers are more cautious and management is a bit more efficient than hitherto. The generally depressed economic climate has had a sobering effect, yet the same impediments remain. The underlying problems have not really been dealt with and an economic upturn would quickly expose the industrial anarchy that simmers away, just below the surface.

These difficulties cannot be effectively legislated away; what they do need is strong leadership on both sides of industry and a new climate based on mutual understanding and trust. There is precious little evidence of that about and few of today's politicians, industrialists or trade union leaders measure up to the task. There is very limited progress to report since my outburst at Southport some twenty years ago.

If that speech was a success, there was another at that time which proved a source of embarrassment. The Amalgamated Union of Engineering Workers called for a one-day token strike throughout the Engineering Industry and I reckoned that we should back them. I went to an Engineering Industry shop stewards' conference for ETU members and promised support for our AUEW brothers. Our Executive Council, initially sceptical, swung behind me but what I had failed to realise was that the stoppage wouldn't cost the Engineers a bean – they provided no strike pay to their members for actions of less than three days. Our strike bill for that one-day demonstration was £10,000. It was an expensive display of solidarity that achieved very little, except to teach me a costly lesson about when to keep my mouth closed.

Before the end of 1964, we made ourselves distinctly unpopular with the Labour Government and with other unions by opposing a three-year pay and holidays deal in engineering which was seen as helping the Wilson incomes policy. Les Cannon said it only enshrined the anomalies that gave a skilled man in one industry up to three times as much as his counterpart elsewhere, who offered no extra skill or additional hard work, and he refused to reconcile that with an incomes policy. It was the kind of argument that was to recur many times over the years, but there was something else behind our apparent obduracy. If people wanted our help over incomes policy, they had better talk to us about it. Our nominees were pointedly kept off both the TUC General Council and the Labour Party's National Executive Committee, and we resented the ETU's effective exclusion from direct discussions between the TUC and the Government. This issue too was to be another hot potato in the immediate years ahead.

We eventually accepted the engineering deal but we argued throughout the 1964-70 Wilson years that we could not be expected loyally to prop up the Labour administration if left-wing unions like the Transport and General Workers' Union could consistently oppose pay policy and were allowed to get away with it. In articles in the union's journal, I attacked the anti-incomes policy alliance of the left with right-wing critics like Tory MP Enoch Powell. But I also expressed hostility to the $3\frac{1}{2}$ per cent norm then operating for most workers, while MPs, judges, teachers and doctors got far greater rises. I was not against an incomes policy, but in practice, I became increasingly sceptical about this one.

In May 1965 we carried through a further vital restructuring of the union at our Douglas, Isle of Man, rules revision conference. The Communist Party organisation in the union had regrouped, and even with Les Cannon in the chair we had to fight for everything and lost some issues where political innocents were conned by the Reds into backing them.

The delegates did agree, by a tight majority, that the Executive Council should be full-time and elected for five-yearly terms. We also won backing for our proposals that industrial conferences of shop stewards should replace area committees, and that larger branches with full-time administrative officers to run them should be set up. There was a major political rumpus, however, over pay policy. George Brown, the Secretary of State for Economic Affairs and chief architect of the policy, was in the thick of his courageous – and sometimes outrageous – battle to win union support and he was our guest speaker. He delivered a rumbustious but powerful message. We had a motion on the agenda that was tantamount to a vote of confidence in George and the government. There was a bitter left-wing onslaught on him from the rostrum, with the Communists and their supporters in full cry. I wound up the debate, saying: 'The trade union movement has such power and strength that it can bring any government down. In this situation we have nothing to fear but our own strength.' The delegates voted by about five to one for the motion. George – working class, larger than life and the sort of character in regrettably short supply today – went off like a dog with two tails.

If the union was solid for the Government, we remained excluded from the movement's senior counsels. Respectability is relative: we were rid of the fraudsters; we adopted a vigorous anti-Red posture; the TUC and Labour Party were able to welcome us back to their ranks and to grab our affiliation fees and other contributions; but resentment lingered on. We had rocked the trade union establishment boat mightily and been a vast embarrassment for Congress House, the T.U.C. headquarters. The left-wing union bosses still hankered after their old Communist bedfellows, while some of the right-wing, timorous and slothful, saw us as a crowd of untrustworthy, renegade ex-Reds, turncoats to be kept at arm's length. Our nominees for the TUC General Council and the Labour NEC came in as also-rans in both 1962 and 1963; we got the lame excuse that our candidates were not well known enough.

Now that Les Cannon was our General President we put him forward in 1964 to join the senior union men on the TUC General Council, and I was nominated for the Labour Party NEC's twelve-seat union section. We were one of the biggest unions and we were clean. It was ludicrous that we should be unrepresented on these bodies. But neither of us were elected – a decided snub. I was well down the trade union list for the Labour NEC, though ahead of hopefuls like Clive Jenkins and Dick (now Lord) Marsh.

Relief was on the way. Early in 1965, the TUC General Council decided to increase its size by two seats, one to accommodate the newly-affiliated local government workers (NALGO) and the other for electrical workers; the autumn Congress in Brighton ratified the proposal.

It should have been plain sailing for Les, but the left mobilised against him and he just scraped home by 4,548,000 votes to 3,976,000. A lot of the smaller unions, resenting the horse-trading among their bigger brothers, must have rallied to him. I made it an autumn double for the ETU. Year after year, the moderates fumbled the trade union votes and delayed our representation on the Labour Party NEC; time after time, Bill Carron was elsewhere on union business and unable to guide his delegation on which candidates to support. Someone said he was like Jan Smuts who became a world statesman but lost South Africa. If we didn't get apologies from the AUEW, it was from some other union whose vote went wrong at the critical moment.

Years earlier, the union votes had been organised by a right-wing triumvirate that finally crumbled when Frank Cousins took over the TGWU. I admired many of his views and especially his firm belief in more rank-and-file involvement in decision-taking. But Cousins led from the front: not for him the approach of today's leaders, slavishly following behind their so-called activists. Cousins' successor, Jack Jones, did more to improve his union's organisation but he lacked the Cousins' will to fight against bad decisions.

Since the Cousins era, the messy, muddled and undemocratic system of electing Labour's NEC has meant that the moderates consistently lose out. The system is indefensible, but they have been unable to make the best of a bad job. As in TUC conference delegations, the only really organised group that can be relied upon to deliver, if not the vote, then a fight for their preferred candidates, is the Communist Party. Labour NEC members get elected or defeated by their efforts inside union delegations or executives and their more recent electoral college for choosing the Leader and Deputy Leader allows them a similar say – a development that is as scandalous as it is nonsensical. Our union has always regarded it as relevant that we were among the few unions to attend Labour's foundation, unlike some of the left-wing organisations that do so much of the shouting about their roots and birthright. We felt cheated throughout the early 1960s by the ganging up against us in our legitimate quest for that NEC place.

So, when I eventually squeaked home, it was quite an event for us, even though mine was the lowest vote of the successful union candidates. Like Les, I hardly did it in style, but we were both there. The TGWU and other left-wing unions tried to vote me off each year from then on, but they were unable to do so and it was not until the 1970 Labour Party conference that I was as low in the poll again. Since my departure from the NEC in 1971 to replace Les on the TUC General Council, we have put up senior members of our Executive Council each year for the Labour NEC – either Bill Blair or, more recently, Tom Breakell, our President. Despite the size and importance of our union and the life-long Party loyalty of the individuals, they have never recaptured the seat I held. The left have organised against us and the moderates have shambled on in their customary discordant fashion, trotting out the same old discredited excuses for their inability to deliver.

Membership of the Labour Party NEC, the Party's top policy-making body, should have been exciting and absorbing. Instead, it was a dreary and depressing experience, more like serving a gaol sentence. I had learnt a great deal from my Communist Party activities, whatever the ultimate bitter disillusionment, but I learned nothing of any consequence from my NEC role.

It was apparent from my very first meeting that the left made all the running and fought the same old battles over and over again. Ministers like Barbara Castle, Tony Greenwood and Tony Benn were brimming with criticism of their own Labour government and too few of their contemporaries were ready to take them on. George Brown did, he was always prepared to fight his corner. He had plenty of spirit and gave nothing away to his opponents, but support for him was tepid at best and he was a far less effective debater than Denis Healey, who joined the NEC towards the end of my term there. When the left tangled with Denis they knew they were in a punch-up that mattered. I had no hesitation in standing by him: he mixed intellect with verbal brutality and he was a powerful advocate whenever he chose to be – and he still is, though much more rarely these days.

I was a great fan of Harold Wilson's political skills, but I was most disappointed in him on the NEC. He seldom asserted himself or used his authority as Prime Minister, simply ruling himself out of disciplinary matters by saying that he didn't want to be an unfair influence. Harold played too much to the gallery, talked tough publicly when it only served to pre-arm the Party's left-wing. It would have been better if his language had been more temperate and his actions more determined. You never quite knew where you stood with him – he sometimes behaved like the left-winger he once purported to be, but was really sickened by the left and their stab-in-the-back exploits. He tried to outwit them and manoeuvre them out of their policy stances rather than confront them, fight them and defeat them. Labour's right-wing still play it that way. They cannot see that funk and fudge win nothing but contempt from friend and foe alike.

At the end of that first meeting I remonstrated with Jim Callaghan, the Chancellor of the Exchequer, that the moderates were not putting up any sort of a fight. He, for one, seemed to prefer to blur or bury disagreements in confusion or platitudes, which always seemed open to several interpretations. Jim's response was unhesitating: 'We don't want a return to the squabbles of the Bevanite period.' I came back swiftly and said: 'If we aren't going to have political arguments, then I have wasted my time coming onto this NEC.' It was a dismal start to my NEC penance. My presence gave the moderates a majority of one but it was seldom of any real value since, either through absences or lack of genuine debate, votes were rarely called for. That soon changed once the moderates lost that one-vote advantage for the left were much quicker to force divisions once they could muster a majority. They were usually helped by an appalling attendance record which inevitably handicapped the moderates still further.

There was never much cameraderie around – the politicians tended to sit on one side of the table and the trade unionists on the other. The trade union group did support each other fairly consistently and on industrial issues we frequently managed a left–right consensus, but the politicians were always sharpening their knives, mostly on each other. The Tories scarcely seemed to exist. It got far worse the nearer each annual conference came: they worried about their votes; they showed off, paraded all manner of disagreements over odd paragraphs in reports or over quite obscure resolutions; they pouted and preened until they secured the right to speak for the NEC from the conference platform.

The trade unionists were generally left to handle the most difficult and unglamorous conference issues. I was afforded very few chances to put the NEC case to conference in my five-year stint and one of my platform speeches was on Rhodesia of all things. I wasn't even on the NEC's international sub-committee and was hardly an appropriate choice, but the subject was regarded as a vote loser with the left at the time and none of the politicians wanted the job. Those left-wing politicians were a decidedly rum bunch. There was Ian Mikardo, a wily old MP who was always able to support the NEC in a way that would enhance his standing with the left-wing. Even as Party Chairman he played it that way, his skilful conference chairmanship making it impossible to nail him for the prejudice he clearly exercised within the rules of the debate. Frank Allaun, the waspish MP from Salford, would plead and whine to get his way, but never conceded a point to an opponent. He never seemed to differ from the Communist Party and I can't recall any criticism he ever made of the Soviet Union in meetings I attended. Barbara Castle, like Mikardo, was always probing for openings to knock her rivals, real and imaginary, and looked constantly for fashionable left causes to espouse. She numbered among the Party intellectuals who were generally anti-union, probably a hangover from their Bevanite days and their rough clashes with the old trade union right that controlled Labour's fortunes. Some of these left-wingers fairly oozed with dislike of the unions and I always thought that Barbara's subsequent White Paper, *In Place of Strife*, reflected this position. Not that Barbara was an orthodox left-winger. She was a snappy dresser, carefully coiffured and, for my money, as right-wing as they come in her attitudes and instincts, whatever her dubious policy pronouncements.

Those politicians spent much of their time at NEC meetings scoring points off each other – with the Tories absent, they needed their practice runs. Ministers would try to get matters raised that had already been dealt with in Cabinet, either in a bid to get a different decision from the NEC or simply to make things awkward for ministerial colleagues. NEC verdicts could be useful to quote inside ministerial meetings, but these NEC incidents often leaked out in the press with harmful consequences for the Labour government.

We had a lengthy row, for instance, over just how long Ministers who were not NEC members should be allowed to speak when they addressed the Party conference. Tony Crosland or Denis Healey would be expected to deal with vital matters for which they had Cabinet responsibility in far less time than any NEC spokesman, yet Greenwood, Castle and Benn jealously insisted on maintaining tight restrictions on their fellow Cabinet Ministers. I thought it was outrageous and said so: it was insulting to them and to the conference if they didn't get ample time to explain the difficulties they faced; but I was in the minority, as usual.

There were constant wrangles about press leaks and how it was that full accounts of NEC meetings appeared in the newspapers the day after they took place. The right usually got the blame. On one occasion, only Barbara Castle, Tony Greenwood and Transport House officials turned up to a sub-committee and still the press had all the details before the NEC could hear them. At the inquest, Barbara and Tony emphatically denied any press contact but the field was very limited; it all added to the perpetual suspicion with which the NEC was riddled.

Through all the squabbles, most of the trade unionists stayed friendly.

Some of them were dullards, but they were not concerned with the back-biting and carping, which was left to the politicians. The most capable of the trade unionists was Bill Simpson, of the foundry workers, who later became Chairman of the Health and Safety Commission. Bill was inclined to go for the easy option but he was able, likeable and humorous. There was Walter Padley, the shopworkers' MP, who regularly regurgitated old battles with the left. There was the steel-workers' Dai Davies, the Party Treasurer before Jim Callaghan, and a man who sounded as if he gargled with gravel. The TGWU's Jack Jones was a prominent figure whose trade union roots sometimes seemed to conflict with his left-wing political links.

Jones, and later Alex Kitson, also of the TGWU, tended to join with Castle, Benn, Mikardo, Allaun and Tom Driberg in applauding the sanctity of those Party conference decisions with which they agreed, particularly where they needed support for their criticisms of government policy. Whenever it suited them, though, they would adopt a very different position inside the NEC. They would do their utmost to overturn decisions and to push for different policies from those agreed by the Labour Cabinet, the Parliamentary Labour Party or even by past Party conferences. There was no let up in the feuding, even when I sat on the sub-committee to draft the manifesto prior to the 1970 General Election. What was of prime importance was would the document gain votes for us, not who got the last word about it, but Harold Wilson's ultimate say-so was fiercely challenged. The politicians were unworldly in their approach, not at all like practical people who were out to win an election.

Inevitably, I clashed pretty regularly with the left-wingers, pseudo or otherwise. There was a farewell lunch for Sir Len Williams, the Party's retiring General Secretary who was off to be the Governor-General of Mauritius. I made a jocular comment about titles and Barbara Castle turned to me and said scornfully: 'I know what title I would give you. It would be "the bastard of the NEC".' She certainly wasn't smiling. It was typically venomous and she meant every word of it. On another occasion, during a wave of student demonstrations around the country, Tony Benn waxed eloquent about giving youth its head. He said sagely: 'We must listen to all these new ideas.' I couldn't resist it. I told him: 'The one thing that the revolt of the students and the young hasn't done is to express a new idea. Their ideas are as old as Marx and Marcuse.' This would-be champion of youth was as out of touch with reality and real people then as he remains today.

Those Young Socialists, under the full control of the Trotskyites, were a permanent pain in the neck and a liability to the Party. I was asked to represent the NEC at one of their youth conferences at Malvern, Worcestershire and I was persuaded by one of my own staff, against my better judgement, to give them a spot of homely help and guidance. I spent a tiresome weekend with them and it was like fighting a monkey in a dustbin. They howled down Tony Benn and Roy Hattersley, the other guest speakers. Benn, a senior Minister, had travelled from London specially for the occasion and they murdered him. They were unbelievably vicious and only a political masochist like him could have gone on giving them aid and comfort. You had to be unhinged to accept their views and behaviour.

I plunged straight in with an attack on the Trots and the lunacy of the Young Socialists. My subject was youth training, but there was no point in pulling any punches and I left to a storm of booing. There was a somewhat surprising sprinkling of cheering, too, so perhaps the weekend was not entirely wasted. What's more, the vote on the training issue was the only one at the conference where moderate views prevailed.

I picked up another unpalatable and unwanted chore over the establishment of Labour's Greater London Regional Council to replace the old London Labour Party. There was a full weekend's consultative conference due at St Pancras Town Hall and the left were all out to block the NEC decision to set up the new body. Someone had to chair the conference and see to it that the NEC case got a fair hearing. Two union members of the NEC, Bill Simpson and Joe Gormley, met the London Labour Party for informal talks and got such a rough ride that they said it was time for the politicians to get their hands soiled. It was quite remarkable – not a single politician was available. Rashly, I volunteered for the job.

I let the conference know at the outset that the NEC decision was unalterable: they could like it or lump it. They could influence the details if they were constructive, but there would be a new single organisation representing Labour in Greater London. That got a raucous reception. The left were in full cry, with the Trots there in force and determined to thwart us. Sara Barker, the Party's National Agent, spelled out the situation, amid further hostilities. Soon, I had had my bellyfull of that unruly crew and I told them that unless they behaved and kept in order I would close the meeting. They knew they had gone too far and had alienated a number of the decent delegates who were there. It quietened down, so much so that the two-day meeting, scheduled to finish on Sunday afternoon, was over by three o'clock on Saturday afternoon and the new Labour organisation for London was virtually established.

Mostly though, the left advanced their cause during my NEC service and that was especially true in the constituencies. I complained to Peggy Herbison and Eirene White, two of the NEC's MPs, after we were hammered by the Tories at town hall elections. Too many of the local Labour Parties and Councils were run by tiny cliques of right-wing opportunists and incompetents. I said: 'The Tories have done us one favour. They have got rid of all those crabby old sods who did us no good at all. But we have to plug the gap. Otherwise the left will grab control.' My fear was that the extremists who were busily infiltrating Labour's ranks would fill the vacuum at local level and that was exactly what happened. The moderates were too few and too feeble; the leftward swing has accelerated over the succeeding years as the Party's membership and votes have declined.

One cardinal error I made was over the NEC's choice of a National Agent to replace the retiring Sara Barker. There was a strong right-wing lobby for her deputy, Reg Underhill (now Lord Underhill), but I assessed Reg as a total bureaucrat. The job was a stepping stone to the Party's General Secretary's post and I voted for Ron Hayward, then a regional organiser. The left were backing him, mainly for lack of a viable alternative, and were taken aback by my vote. It was a close-run thing and my vote was important, especially since I swayed at least one other NEC trade unionist to follow me. Hayward got the job and went on to become a disastrous Labour Party General Secretary. I worried at the time that I might have cocked it up and I have always regretted that vote.

There was no preconceived trade union line-up on that occasion as there was when it came to appointing a successor to Dai Davies as Party Treasurer. The moderates needed to get behind a single candidate so that he was sure of a big vote at the Party Conference. The union block votes were the key and the NEC's trade union members could mostly promise the support of their respective organisations. We union NEC members agreed that another trade unionist should get the job. After all, we held the Party purse strings through the affiliation fees our unions paid over. But we failed to hold our votes together. Harold Wilson sweet-talked Joe Gormley and cajoled one or two others into supporting Jim Callaghan, who emerged as the right-wing standard bearer. I supported him, but without any great enthusiasm, and he was elected by the Conference with a 3-1 majority over Michael Foot.

Early in 1966, and only a few months after my election to Labour's NEC, Jock Byrne announced his resignation as General Secretary. He had never fully recovered from his stroke and had been on sick leave for six months. Bernard Levin wrote a salute in the *Daily Mail* to 'a gallant Christian gentleman who for seventeen years – from 1944 to 1961 – fought the good fight on behalf of all of us, and won it, and got precious little thanks for doing so.' Whatever my differences with Jock, Levin was well justified in that tribute. I contributed one of my own in our union journal, underlining Jock's devotion to the struggle to achieve demo-cracy in the ETU.

I started clear favourite to take over, having effectively carried out the General Secretary's duties for several years. The main candidate against me was George Tilbury, one of our London area officials, whom the Communists supported and there were two other candidates who were similarly hostile to the anti-Red leadership. There was a hitch before the election got off the ground: some ballot papers were delayed by a combination of printing difficulties and because the Electoral Reform Society, which supervised our ballots, was moving office. Perhaps we were super-sensitive, but the Executive Council was ada-mant that the outcome should be above suspicion. They cancelled the election at a cost of several thousand pounds and ordered a new one. At the same time, we protested to the TUC about outside interference by pro-Communist AUEW officials who blatantly canvassed engineering workers from our union and urged them to vote for Tilbury. Not that they did me any harm. I romped home with 21,000 votes to 5,000 for Tilbury and about 6,500 for the other candidates between them.

My election as General Secretary overlapped with some important industrial developments. One was the Fairfields shipyard experiment, a tripartite scheme involving the Government, employers and unions in what looked like a brave new deal. It offered changes in 200-year-old working practices to see if we could build ships in a declining market against worldwide competition, particularly from Japan. George Brown was the Government's driving force and he screwed a private understanding out of Les Cannon that ETU money would be invested in the future of the yard.

Les put this proposal to the Executive Council, expecting no snags. I was full of scepticism, not because I was opposed to the general idea – there was a good management team ready, headed by Sir Iain Stewart, an industrialist for whom I had considerable respect – but because our union funds were none too healthy. It was a highly questionable use of our members' money in a depressed industry with a very uncertain future. We were not businessmen, entitled to back high-risk ventures in the hope of making fat profits. My view proved effective. Some unions did invest substantially, but we restricted our cash help to a £50,000 loan. We made our college in Esher available to the management and shop stewards so that they could hammer out details of their agreement. Our goodwill and active support were never in question, but financial prudence was necessary.

Les was unhappy and George Brown had to cool down. It was Tony Benn who, as Technology Minister, eventually wrecked the scheme by merging Fairfields with Upper Clyde Shipbuilders. If Fairfields had been allowed to carry on alone, it might well have pushed our ship-building industry to overseas levels of efficiency. As it turned out, my caution was justified: so far as I know, we were the only union to get all our money back from Fairfields and that was because our investment was only a loan.

Far more significant for me at this time were pay policy troubles which left me with a jaundiced view of Government efforts in this field. I was the chief union negotiator in a revolutionary deal for our 55,000 Electrical Contracting Industry members, giving them rises of about 33 per cent spread over three years in return for major changes in working methods. We set up a grading system which eliminated mates and provided a career structure for skilled men. We established a Joint Industry Board of employers and union representatives to regulate and control employment, to improve fringe benefits and allowances, to oversee the industry's productive capacity, to instil labour discipline and to deal with wage drift. The pay rises were the best ever achieved in the industry and, as I told our members, 'few parallels can be found'.

I beavered away to put the deal together for a very long time and was proud of it. The industry desperately needed decasualising. We were training our shop stewards for productivity bargaining, not futile class conflict, and here was a pace-setting national example that offered all-round advantages. To my chagrin, the Labour Government announced its pay freeze and the deal was caught: I sympathised with the Government's difficulties, but I warned that their action 'is likely to produce a disaster ... a setback of four years work for me and two years for our

111

members'. I reflected ruefully to myself that they wouldn't have dared do it to Jack Jones.

The industry's employers were not renowned for benevolence or throwing money around, but they recognised the need for reforms, not least to counter skill shortages. We were training apprentices and losing them because the pay rates were too low. Some firms operated bogus bonus arrangements to hang on to their workers. The employers joined with us in telling the Government that the agreement should be honoured.

If you want people to work harder and more effectively, you must pay them more. Incentive is unavoidable – it is a simple message which Labour has never understood. The 1964-70 Labour Government was reluctant to reward skill and productivity, largely because of the excessive influence of the big general workers' unions who wanted preference for the lower paid. Britain has a serious low pay problem, but it cannot be solved by penalising the contribution of other workers to much-needed higher output and greater efficiency. That is the route to the knacker's yard for everyone.

My simplistic thinking had been that it was our Labour Government and we should give it a go. Now I was kicked in the teeth and it meant a battle on two fronts – with the Government and with the left inside the union who maintained an onslaught on the grounds that our members were refused their entitlement. They managed to denounce the contracting agreement as a 'slaves' charter' while attacking the Government for stopping it and the union for letting ministers get away with it. George Brown asked Les Cannon and I to go and see him, knowing that I was the main obstacle to gaining union acquiescence. He wanted us to send the agreement voluntarily to the Prices and Incomes Board for examination. I told him bluntly: 'If you, as the Minister, want the Board to examine the agreement, you should instruct them to do so. We will co-operate but on the understanding that there is no way we will change that agreement.'

George was extremely put out by my truculent stand. He blamed me, with justification, for frustrating him over the ETU Fairfields investment, and I was at it again. Les was inclined to want to help him out but it was my agreement, my baby. I said: 'It's bloody ridiculous. If the PIB say it's a bad deal, we are stuck with an opinion we have sought ourselves. How could we disown it? It would cut the ground from under us.' I suspected that the PIB might not share my view of the benefits that would result, not just to the industry but to the nation, from the productivity element, because they would not be immediate.

My suspicions were well founded and there were heated exchanges. PIB chairman Aubrey Jones, the former Tory Cabinet Minister who is now a Liberal, made a remark on television, implying collusion between the union and employers over our evidence to his Board. That smacked of built-in prejudice against us and I said so, loudly and indignantly. The PIB inquiry was headed by Bob Willis, the ex-print union leader, and he, in turn, took umbrage at the suggestion of bias.

Yet the Board took evidence in camera from the Ministry of Works and from Imperial Chemical Industries, both of whom were alarmed by our agreement and keen to sabotage it. The craftsmen they employed customarily followed the electrical contracting industry pay rates and our new deal was too much for them to swallow. They were able to influence the PIB but we had no opportunity to know just what they said or to question them. It was grossly unfair.

I publicly accepted that the Government had little alternative to the deflationary package announced in mid-summer 1966 by Prime Minister Wilson. I repeated the ETU's strong support for what had been a voluntary prices and incomes policy, but I was careful to stress that we negotiated for agreements based on both higher productivity and higher take-home pay. Our contracting agreement should have been welcomed, not stifled. Eventually the PIB gave its reluctant approval to the deal but imposed a two-months delay in implementation and said the next stages should be renegotiated. It was highly critical of details of the agreement. My reaction was a mixture of relief that we could avoid a head-on clash with the Government and anger at the niggling criticisms. I denounced the report as a 'piece of jiggery-pokery'. My animosity towards Aubrey Jones for the shabby way the affair was handled was considerable.

George Brown had huffed off to the Foreign Office after another fracas with Harold Wilson to be replaced at the Economics Ministry by Michael Stewart. I protested strongly to Michael at the proposal to delay implementation. I was told that unless we accepted there would be a stand-still order against us in Parliament. We had no real choice and a two-months delay was not much more than a slap on the wrist.

We had survived the sorry business pretty well, but it certainly coloured my views back inside Labour's NEC. We met the Cabinet to discuss the Government's stringent economy measures, including the freeze, and Jack Jones harangued Ministers at some length, making no bones about the TGWU's non-co-operation. I warned Harold Wilson, George Brown and Jim Callaghan that unions like mine would be forced to defy the policy too, if 'rogue elephants' like the TGWU got away with it. I appreciated the Government's problems, but we were vulnerable to the charge of being insufficiently militant in defence of our members' living standards if the TGWU's muscle gave them advantages for their members. Jim Callaghan said tactlessly: 'You did well enough out of the contracting agreement.' That was a raw spot. I snapped back: 'No thanks to you and George.'

On the eve of the September 1966 TUC Conference, our Executive Council voted by six to five to oppose the TUC General Council's reluctant acquiescence in the freeze. There is no doubt that the Electrical Contracting rumpus swung the vote, though Les Cannon queried the potential productivity gains. We may have been against the freeze but we were equally anxious to distance ourselves from the ritual opposition of the left to Government policy, so we also agreed to reject the TGWU's all-out rejection of the freeze and accompanying Prices and Incomes Act. Les explained that we believed that the Government measures would freeze injustices and hit genuine productivity whereas a true incomes policy would redress imbalances, adding that despite our misgivings we could not associate with the left's 'unremitting campaign against the Government'.

Not long afterwards, he provided a more vivid illustration of the campaign we had in mind. Michael Foot wrote a *Tribune* article, accusing Harold Wilson of wanting 'devotion to the Führer' from Labour MPs. Les responded in our union journal by telling Foot and his Parliamentary supporters that they should back their Labour Government or resign. He said they sought 'reward without sacrifice'.

Britain moved from the freeze to a slightly less rigid incomes policy formula. Our campaigning over the contracting issue must have had some effect for the Government approved the next stage of the agreement without demanding renegotiation. That was a snub to the PIB, which thoroughly deserved it.

Government say-so for the deal to go ahead was, however, a signal to the Communists and Trotskyites to step up their virulent campaign against it. Some 200 demonstrators turned up at Hayes Court to have a go at the anti-Communist leadership. There was chaos when I met them in the canteen: I was punched, manhandled and had my hair pulled; fist fights broke out and the police had to be called; it was an ugly and violent occasion. We charged some of the hoodlums involved with breaking the union's rules. No self-respecting organisation could tamely ignore the riotous and intimidatory action from which we suffered.

Some months later the Red demonstrators were back again outside Hayes Court, about 300 of them this time, and their ringleaders were hooded. The masked men claimed that they wished to avoid identification and any subsequent victimisation by the union, but they covered up more than their faces: we had good reason to believe that a fair number of them were not even ETU members. They were out to discredit us and had donned their bizarre outfits to attract maximum publicity. The press had been carefully tipped off in advance, capitalist newspapers included, and the masked malcontents made good pictures. It was another example of the Reds exploiting an industrial situation for political ends.

Pay policy warfare continued unabated and every meeting of the NEC seemed to produce a fresh rumpus. On more than one occasion, I found myself alongside Jack Jones as a critic of the Government, though we got there by somewhat different routes. I always contended that low productivity and high unit labour costs were the big central problem which pay policy did nothing to resolve. Hard work and merit had to be promoted. Yet there were flaws in that argument, too, and it was as well to acknowledge them. Harold Wilson talked to the NEC about rewarding productivity, but I had to point out that there was no automatic link between high productivity and high pay. Farm output had soared but agricultural wages were still abysmally low.

At one meeting we had with Ministers, Dick Marsh, then at Transport, preached the high productivity, high wage economy theme, the same kind of typically left-wing speech we got from Clive Jenkins at TUC conferences. I said that it sounded simple and looked logical, but that pay and productivity didn't always march hand in hand. Why, I asked, are there so many places with high pay and low productivity? I referred to big building sites and the Fleet Street newspapers. Dick Marsh, now Lord Marsh and chairman of the Newspaper Publishers' Association, knows all about those problems now, even if he ignored them then.

I continued to hoist storm signals whenever possible about the ETU's position. I wrote in the union journal: 'The hand and word of a friend and partner has been mistaken for the fealty of the vassal and the plea of a suppliant. The credit of goodwill afforded the Labour Administration is not limitless and cannot extend to involving the union in self-destructive attitudes and actions.' I said that we were foremost in backing a prices and incomes policy 'to achieve and maintain a rapid increase in output and real incomes combined with full employment . . . to ensure that the benefits of faster growth are distributed in a way that satisfies the claims of social need and justice.' I added: 'Our support for this policy has been misunderstood and an acquiescence by trade unions to the perversion of this original policy, has been too readily assumed by the Government . . . Those policies and actions which are fair, efficient and productive, and in accord with our traditions, will continue to receive our support. We have no other commitment.'

What I went on to assert, however, in further articles, was that our criticisms should not delude us into vicious denigration of those burdened with the responsibilities of office. Militant sloganising could only lead to another inept and divisive Tory government; the bloody-minded attack on Labour really came from those who had contracted out of the battle to get a better deal for working people.

We had plenty of crisis meetings. At one of the sessions at 10 Downing Street between the Cabinet and the NEC, Harold Wilson lectured us on the need for the unions to give the Government more support. 'My union has backed you,' I told him, 'but it seems to me to be pushing your luck when you have so many of your MPs who vote and speak against the Government.' Some of those I had in mind were sitting around the table. They had been elected on a Labour ticket and should have been in the vanguard of the fight to preserve their own government. I went on: 'Trade unions have a different function to that of the Party. People don't join unions to have their pay reduced. You politicians must understand that when you call for our support.'

The wrangling over pay policy began to overlap with, and be overtaken by, the far more acrimonious conflict over proposals for trade union reform. The 1968 Labour Party Conference turned down legislative interference in industrial relations, but Barbara Castle persisted. Her personal stature as Employment Minister was at stake and in January 1969 she published her ill-fated White Paper, *In Place of Strife*. It proposed setting up a Commission for Industrial Relations to promote procedural agreements, investigate disputes over recognition of unions and generally to encourage trade union reform. It included provision for legally binding collective agreements, for a 'cooling off' period in certain strike situations, for strike ballots and for registration of trade unions. It was certainly not all bad but it promised endless trouble, political and industrial, for scant return. Too much of it was populist, rather than practical. Moreover, I smelled danger in it for the ETU, particularly over its recognition proposals which could have squeezed us out of many industries where we were not a major force in numerical terms.

The belligerent antagonism over Barbara's policy proposals often got overshadowed by the extraordinary clash of personalities that developed. Barbara rubbed the trade unionists up the wrong way. She carried her own irritation powder and the same old anti-unionism was evident, however petulantly she protested that she simply wanted to do us good. Jim Callaghan, now Home Secretary, began to pay her back for her earlier behaviour as a left-wing dissident and they played cat and mouse all over again; but this time the roles were reversed. It took Jim quite a while finally to come out against her, but there were enough judicious leaks and broad hints in the meantime to leave no room for doubt. I can't say that I approved of his tactics: they were no different to those deployed by left-wing Cabinet Ministers to undermine Harold Wilson at those earlier NEC meetings.

Even so, I was largely in agreement with Jim and with the rest of the NEC's trade union members. My position on legislation in this field was, and is, that it fails to tackle the right problem. Throughout the post-war years, low productivity and high unit labour costs, not the unions, have been all-important stumbling blocks to national prosperity. The unions may not have helped but there is no evidence to show that where you have weak unions, a strong economy follows; nor do governments introduce legislation of this kind with the intention of strengthening unions, whatever they pretend. If unions get a useful spin-off, they are lucky. Only dishonest politicians argue otherwise.

By now we were merged with the Plumbers' Union and had become the EETPU. Our Executive Council, enlarged to accommodate Plumbing members, held a special three-day meeting to discuss *In Place of Strife* and I relayed my fears. Les Cannon said that the campaign against the White Paper had quickly become hysterical, including calls for political strikes to bring down the Labour government. He was neither for nor against the White Paper's legislative ideas, but wanted negotiations with the Government over individual proposals. That, to me, was pussyfooting. I wanted straightforward opposition, without aligning myself with that 'massive left-wing hysteria'. I asked: 'What does the union get out of this document? I say nothing.' I branded it 'In Search of Strife'. I said that it weakened Labour and that if the Tories gained power they would keep the worst features. I attacked the constant desire for 'overlordship', this time through the CIR. I had our earlier troubles with the PIB very much in mind. I told the meeting: 'I am concerned with electricians. I do not want to take a chance. I do not want another body of nincompoops adjudicating on our affairs.'

Les Cannon took the greatest exception to my stance. It was probably the biggest feud we ever had – not such a bad testimony to our friendship over the years when you consider our respective volatility and political pugnacity. We went at it hammer and tongs. Les called my view 'reactionary' – I was only concerned with the ETU and 'damn the rest'. He knocked my cherished contracting agreement as phoney on productivity and only justified by the low wages we inherited in the industry from our Communist predecessors. He said that, despite extreme restraint and the strictures of the PIB, we had improved the real wages of our members at a faster rate than at any other period in the union's history. If we had to say that we were only concerned with the survival of the ETU then 'I want no part of such a role in this union because I can get out of it and do better for myself,' he declared.

That was a stark threat. Les had turned down offers of outside jobs before and could well have quit. For all that, I reckoned that his outburst was a mixture of bluff and anger, so I retorted: 'I get paid for working for this union. I don't get paid for working for anybody else. In fact, all I get is trouble from the Government and from the Labour Party.' I claimed that I did enough in the national interest, but, in the end, it was right to defend the union 'in all circumstances'. But Les wouldn't let go and he said that he worked for the union too and that was irrelevant to the argument. He asked the Executive Council pointedly: 'Do you agree then? Scrap the lot and so it is Heath?'

We needed our own cooling off period. Eventually, we went through the White Paper bit by bit, making decisions and comments on individual proposals so that they could be embodied in a document to go to the Government. It was a compromise – not what I wanted at all – but Les's wrath was considerable and the Executive Council was not prepared to buck him and toss out the whole Government case.

Back at the Labour NEC Jim Callaghan showed his hand. Harold Wilson and Barbara Castle were furious but he moved a resolution saying that the NEC could not 'accept legislation based on all of the proposals in the White Paper'. It watered down outright opposition, but nevertheless meant that Jim had carefully and openly distanced himself from a Government White Paper for which he had collective responsibility. It was a nifty piece of footwork, backed up by preliminary soundings to ensure that his formula would win the vote. It did – by sixteen votes to five.

We moved into prolonged and anguished negotiation between the Wilson Government and the TUC, after which the Government capitulated, wrapped up in the fragile 'solemn and binding' undertaking by the TUC to put its own house in order; Harold Wilson and Barbara Castle abandoned the package they had once claimed was so vital. A few months later came another White Paper, this time to recast pay policy more flexibly. In January 1970, there was at last a decision to scrap wage controls.

The forthcoming general election could still have seen a Labour victory – the Tories looked far from convincing and Roy Jenkins, the Chancellor of the Exchequer, appeared to have at last got the balance of payments right. I urged our members to vote Labour and to recognise, despite our misgivings, the achievements of the Wilson Government. There was, though, a price to pay for the years of economic strain and uncertainty and, most of all, for the destructive campaign by the left and the continued divisions in Labour's own ranks. That price was the Ted Heath Government.

## CHAPTER 10

# THE HEATH YEARS –
# BLINKERS ALL ROUND

Les Cannon had cancer. It was unthinkable that this dominant personality, who had so often driven us on with his fierce resolve and unflagging energy, had no more to give. The sudden loss of his leadership was an enormous blow to the union, to all of us. He quickly became far too ill to carry on, either at the TUC General Council or as Chairman of the electricity supply unions' negotiating team. We were shaping up for the annual pay talks and since we were by far the biggest union in the industry, I took over at short notice as leader of the supply negotiators. Despite Les's powerful past advocacy, the industry was illprepared for another round of realistic pay and productivity bargaining. Too many people at all levels, management and workforce alike, still cruised along in their jobs as a gentle way of life rather than actually earning their livings. It was a service industry with no apparent need to match manufacturing industry output targets and with insufficient enthusiasm for progress. That attitude wasn't – and still isn't – unusual in nationalised service industries.

It wasn't just a negative approach in supply; management at local level went out of their way to persuade our members that productivity would not be to their benefit. They didn't see much in it for themselves and didn't want the upheaval and disturbance to their relaxed operations. Some EETPU members were readily susceptible to these blandishments. I recall one early shop stewards' meeting at St Albans during which a member stood up and complained: 'You are interfering with our leisure.' I found it hard to follow and quizzed him. Quite unabashed, he said: 'Now when I book overtime, they want to know where I've been working.' In other words, his fiddle was over. It was too much, even for those hard-bitten shop stewards, and the meeting collapsed in laughter.

But it wasn't really funny. That deal was applied in a most haphazard fashion – some workers getting good bonuses from incentive schemes, others getting none at all. The national agreement failed to stick and local resistance to change on both sides of the industry left things in a mess. The 1970 negotiations were an attempt to pick up the pieces and produce a worthwhile bargain that wouldn't fall apart again, but the earlier muddle had left disunity among the unions and there was a marked reluctance on the part of some of their officials to pursue a fresh productivity agreement. There was rivalry between the unions for membership and everyone was looking over their shoulders, afraid of conceding something that could be a disadvantage when recruiting. An additional difficulty was the breakaway Electricity Supply Union, Yorkshire-based and originally set up by a group disillusioned with the Communists. Its organising secretary, although originally an area board employee, was now a market gardener.

I tried to overcome these difficulties. I am not usually credited with any skill as a conciliator, but I think that I can claim the achievement of greater unity among the four unions concerned. I was careful not to monopolise discussions and got the principal officers of the other unions much more involved in detailed negotiations than they had been before. It paid off. The Electricity Council offered 10 per cent, less than half our claim, and even that was condemned by the Government, which clamped down on any higher offer. That Tory interference exacerbated a very delicate situation; we decided on a go-slow and work-to-rule and there was full unity on the union side, a welcome change from previous years when we had been isolated in industrial action. The winter blackouts began. It was a grim and miserable business. Only the Engineers and Managers' Association, whose members worked on and went well beyond their normal functions, prevented a major national disaster.

The public was directly hurt and were encouraged to turn nasty by grossly irresponsible speeches by Tory Ministers. The Chancellor, Anthony Barber, accused us of 'blackmail' and on television the Industry Secretary, John Davies, urged the community to demonstrate its disapproval in a virtual incitement to violence. He declared open season on power workers. These remarks had a distinct effect: electricity workers and their wives were abused, assaulted, denied medical treatment, had their car tyres slashed and their windows broken; David Frost's provocation on a television show led to one of our shop stewards getting punched in the face; chicken farmers dumped dead battery hens and dung on area electricity board doorsteps. I was physically threatened and so was my family; the police took it very seriously. One night when I arrived home late, my wife, Joan, was worried about a car with two men in it which was parked near our house. It was still there next morning and I went out to see what it was all about. They were two well-meaning members of Moral Rearmament, one of them an EETPU man, who had come, quite unsolicited by anyone, to protect us.

The Electricity Council did its bit to stir up public feeling by deliberately ignoring emergency arrangements for covering essential services like hospitals and putting the blame for the resulting problems on the unions. It was a dirty fight. We were the first big test case for the Heath Government's de-escalation policy to curb the runaway rises of the latter days under Labour, but he picked the wrong bunch. The power workers were ready to show they had muscle. I reckon that our action put some steel in the miners in their later conflicts with Heath and showed that public sector industries were no pay pushover.

There was a brief moment of hilarity when Patrick Jenkin, the bumbling Energy Minister, advised the nation to save electricity by brushing its teeth in the dark. One enterprising newspaper promptly printed a shot of his home, ablaze with light from top to bottom.

My combative approach really wounded the establishment: Ministers were angered; the TUC, with Vic Feather now the General Secretary, stayed silent and offered no help – they weren't averse to seeing this upstart electricians' leader out in front and apparently struggling. I got a message to ring Jim Callaghan – I don't know why he couldn't ring me – and he told me that the go-slow was an embarrassment to Labour's Shadow Cabinet and that we would be well advised to end it. It wouldn't improve relations with the general public or the position of the Labour Party and the unions. I had had enough of Jim's soft-soap on the NEC; I told him, in effect and as politely as my strained feelings permitted, to mind his own business.

We had workers who accepted the need to step up productivity and that should have interested the politicians. If they had looked properly at the offer they would have realised that we were entitled to feel upset and insulted by the paltry amount on the table. If the rest of British industry had followed the electricity supply industry, then and in later deals, the nation would be in a far better condition today. We have shed thousands more workers over the years, yet serviced more and more customers and generated many more units of electricity. We have more job flexibility than most industries and the ratio of skilled and technical workers to the unskilled is greater than elsewhere, with only about 5,000 unskilled workers out of some 85,000 manual workers overall.

Each independent inquiry into the industry has praised its prod`
record and that productivity has more than met a higher pay `
1970 agreement was a breakthrough and it was absurd that we shou`
have to scrap for it against Government insistence that its arbitrary pay
ceiling should not be broken. Ted Heath had opposed the pay restrictions of the Wilson Government then, once elected, had swiftly imposed
his own. So much for politicians' promises. Even today the Conservative
Government doesn't seem fully to understand the importance to the
nation of realistic pay and productivity arrangements.

There was another little matter in the background during the 1970
dispute – I sought re-election as General Secretary. The Communists
were waiting eagerly to accuse me of a sell-out whatever happened, but
they found it very difficult in this instance and I eventually won with
65,000 votes to the 30,000 total shared by the Communist-backed and
Trotskyite candidates.

Public hostility grew increasingly acute. Escalation would have
risked life and limb and that wasn't on for me. Nor did I believe that our
members would want to black out, in any widespread way, vital services
like hospitals; they, like me, were dismayed at the Electricity Council's
tactics over emergency supplies. But few industrial battles give either
side total victory and some time there had to be a truce and settlement.
The Government proposed a court of inquiry under Lord Wilberforce,
but I was unhappy with the terms of reference which included the
'interests of the national economy'. That implied that the case would
not be dealt with on its merits. Nor did I or my union colleagues like the
composition of the court: Wilberforce was a known Tory, while the
employers' man, Sir Raymond Brookes, headed a company which
donated to Conservative Party funds and was in Ted Heath's first
Honours List. The unions' representative, Jim Mortimer, was about to
join London Transport's management where the workforce tended to
follow our agreements. It all looked loaded. However, we reluctantly
accepted and I announced that we would call off our action as 'an act of
faith'.

I expressed our fears about the court's vested interests at the opening
session, but I got into even more bad odour with the Government as the
inquiry progressed. We had expected Barber to give the Treasury evidence on the Government's behalf and I looked forward to questioning
him about the 'interests of the national economy'. But this was not to be,
for he sent two aides instead – Sir Douglas Allen and Sir Donald
Macdougall got the grilling I had reserved for Barber.

These Whitehall mandarins had just had a whopping pay rise of their own, so it was not inappropriate that Sir Douglas, Permanent Secretary to the Treasury, bore the brunt of my attack. How was it that he got 21.4 per cent extra at this time of restraint? Sir Douglas waffled on uncomfortably, arguing that the rises were fixed by an independent body and spread over three years. That was the sort of independent award power workers sought, I retorted. What was his pay in 1969? He couldn't remember. I told him: £9,800 a year. What would the pay deal give him? He admitted he would be on £15,000 a year by the end of 1971 and I probed him on the criteria used to justify this 'magnificent' increase. Why did the Government break that wages circle with permanent secretaries? What was their level of productivity?

I wouldn't let him off the hook. I asked how he reconciled a twenty to thirty per cent award to doctors with his evidence to the court against our claim. He stuttered and stammered and admitted that he didn't know why Ministers had allowed it through. I turned to judges. Some of them had just got £84 a week more and their average rise was £50 weekly. Sir Douglas refused to say whether he thought those rises were justified or what advice on them the Treasury gave to Ministers. He got no help from Sir Donald, the Treasury's Chief Economic Adviser, who maintained a tactful silence. It was like being back in the High Court, only this time I played the role of prosecuting counsel. I finished up with a blow at the inquiry team: I said that they were not competent or equipped to deal with the wider matter of the national interest and that the Government should do its own dirty work and not seek to hide behind the inquiry report. It was a pretty savage and sensational day and certainly hit the headlines.

The Wilberforce Report was a bit of a dog's breakfast but we didn't come out of it too badly. The Electricity Council got a slap in the face for the slow introduction of incentive bonus schemes and the resulting resentment by the workforce. They were told to speed them up. Rises in basic rates and allowances that would mean fair treatment for all staff were recommended, meaning a slight increase in the Electricity Council offer – a time-honoured court of inquiry style of compromise. More importantly, the full package paved the way for electricity supply workers to move up among the best paid groups in the country, a position they have maintained over the years.

I always reckoned, from my discussions with the management, that I could have negotiated that bit extra without all the disruption of a go-slow and court of inquiry award, but Ministers chose to muddy the waters. The union side and the workforce then had to prove that only industrial action could squeeze an improvement. One good thing that emerged was a new lease of life for the ailing mobile generator industry and for the candle-makers. It's an ill wind ...

The National Union of Mineworkers behaved in a curious way around this time. They decided on a strike ballot over their pay demand and Lawrence Daly, their General Secretary, came to see me at Hayes Court to seek our support. I gave him a prompt and unequivocal 'yes'. He seemed quite shocked. Maybe it was less a serious plea for help than an attempt to expose our expected lack of solidarity, in which case, the plan had misfired. In the event, the miners failed to get enough votes from their members to justify the stoppage.

That suspicion about the miners and their motives gained credence when they did strike, following our go-slow. They ignored all the supply unions and immediately picketed the power stations, causing resentment among the electricity unions and their members. The miners' leaders quickly understood that it would take a long time for a miners' strike to be effective, even after an initial overtime ban, but that if they could shut off supplies to the power stations the effect would be immediate, although this coal had been bought and paid for months before. They were prepared to go much further than we did in our limited, if highly effective go-slow. If they had come to us, we would have aided them and might well have organised further go-slow action, an overtime ban or partial shutdowns. But they didn't consult and went too far, dissipating much of their natural support among power workers.

After our own go-slow, the militancy of our supply industry members was aroused and they had an upsurge of enthusiasm for more direct action over the next pay claim. It wasn't easy to keep the lid on, but yearly threats or stoppages are debilitating for everyone concerned and you rarely do so much better from action that you can justify all the inevitable aggravation and perhaps hardship that it entails. You may get caught out, too, either by the employers or by your own members. You can cry wolf too often – it's the Arthur Scargill story.

We had our run in 1970 and showed what we could do if we had to. If we blacked out vast areas again, power workers would suffer the inconvenience with the rest of us and they would soon get fed up with leaders who regularly took them up that road. There was another good reason for keeping the peace: I have always had sympathy for the underground miners and recognise the onerous job that the face-workers do. They deserve high pay even though their leaders refuse to acknowledge that it is the electricity supply industry which burns their product and indirectly pays the miners' wages.

I went out of my way to avoid confrontation with the Electricity Council in the years after our go-slow, not least to help ease the pay situation for the miners. We usually found ourselves in pay talks around the same time and it was undesirable to have both groups involved in industrial action together. We would have masked anything that the miners could do and our impact, unlike theirs, would have been immediate. Moreover, such dual action would be seen as a challenge to the state, tantamount to a general strike. No government would tolerate it and there would be a straight battle between the unions and the Government. Industrial action for political ends is not for me and, so far, it is also alien to the TUC.

There was no respite from the tribulations of the industrial arena – Les Cannon's brave resistance was over. His death was a massive blow to the EETPU and to me personally. It left me, once again, in the chair at an important rules revision conference. It was in 1971 at Blackpool and lasted ten days. I was told in advance that the Reds were out to make me lose my temper, to bait me and to try to make me look incompetent. My primary task was to come out of that conference with a single rule book instead of the existing separate ones for electricians and plumbers that we had had since the merger. And if we tightened up the rules, it would make it more difficult for the Communists, aided by their tame lawyers, to exploit the loopholes.

I trod eggshells. Some of the left delegates who came to the rostrum pretended to be thoroughly objective, but I knew them of old and their histories flashed before me. Most of the conference, however, took them at face value and would have looked askance if I had leaned heavily on some 'innocent' doing his honest best. I had to hold back and argue things entirely on their merits. It meant mastering the minutiae and sweating over the details in my hotel room every night, but I did it. We won all the necessary votes, including a reaffirmation of the ban on Communist office-holders.

I kept my cool and avoided the rough and tumble, but I had to admit to one of my supporters: 'We've done it. But all this being nice to them ... there's no bloody fun in it. It's taken all the joy out of it for me.'

I finally established myself at that conference as the man in charge of the EETPU, subject only to the democratically expressed wishes of the membership. I had stepped from Les's formidable shadow and it was crucially important that I should do so. Les's untimely death left a vacuum. He showed his courage when, knowing that he only had a short time to live, he came to the Executive Council and said that our dual leadership had only worked because of our personal friendship. He argued that a single person should head the union, rather than risk it speaking with two voices as happens in some other organisations, and suggested merging the posts of General President and General Secretary or abolishing one of them. We had just had an independent consultant looking at our organisation and structure and he had reached a similar conclusion. There were other advantages: we would save a top salary and power would be spread more evenly within the Executive Council, which could elect a chairman-cum-president from its own ranks.

The Executive Council initially disagreed with Les and decided that an election for the post had better be held, but later considerations caused them to opt for a ballot of the membership seeking their approval to scrap the Presidency. In the meantime Les had died.

I was tipped off that there was to be a campaign inside the union to crush me. Mark Young, who had originally fought against Les for the job of President, was the main contender. There had been fierce antagonism between him and Les which had rubbed off on me: he was disenchanted with our leadership and frustrated in his own ambitions to run the show. He was no left-winger, but was a pal of ASTMS General Secretary, Clive Jenkins, who used his journalist contacts on Mark's behalf.

I was at a lunch hosted by National Economic Development Council Director-General Fred Catherwood (now Sir Fred) at which British Steel's Chairman, Lord Melchett, was guest speaker. The late Dick Crossman, then a backbench MP and *New Statesman* editor, was there and I gave him a lift from the lunch to his office. He didn't mention a piece of yellow journalism about me which appeared in his *New Statesman* column next day, fed to him by one of the reporters following a London hotel get-together with Young and Jenkins.

Part of the campaign was that the Presidency should be a senior union post, with the General Secretary taking a back seat. It had appeared, whilst Les was President, that it was indeed the senior post and I had not demurred because I had a high regard for Les, who was more ex-perienced than me. Not only had his leadership proved correct, but he was also a friend. An examination of the union's historical position confirms, however, that the General Secretaryship is the senior post. I had to make sure that this position would be restored. Les used to say: 'The workers don't deserve us, but they need us.' I didn't agree with him then, but I got round to it. I owed it to him to see things through; my work was far from done in keeping the anti-Communists firmly in control of the union.

There was another related event of major significance. The TUC was categorically against Heath's Industrial Relations Bill, calling it a threat to the unions, to working people, to orderly industrial relations and to the nation's well-being. The Bill required unions to register if they wanted limited legal protection and gave a registrar powers over union rule books; it provided for legally binding agreements, cooling-off periods and compulsory ballots in certain strike situations and for new machinery to define bargaining units; it proposed statutory rights to join or not to join unions which would weaken union authority over malcontents. It wasn't all bad – or so I thought – but the TUC held a Special Congress at Fairfield Hall, Croydon, to decide what to do once the Bill reached the statute book.

The TUC General Council recommended Congress to advise unions not to register, not to enter into legally binding agreements and to boycott the Industrial Relations Commission established by Labour and the new Tory National Industrial Relations Court. They nevertheless ruled out industrial action as futile and divisive. That didn't stop Jack Jones, for the TGWU, urging demonstrations in working hours and insisting that no union should register; Hugh Scanlon, the AUEW President, took the same line.

My view was very different: I warned that even the General Council recommendations, supported by the EETPU, contained the seeds of a final confrontation with the Government, challenging their right to govern and putting parliamentary democracy at risk. The unions, I declared, helped Labour from office and were largely responsible for the consequences. They should pause and realise that those who had already taken unilateral action against the Bill had given the Tories a weapon. I attacked Tory economic policy and the punitive aspects of the ill-conceived Bill, but then I really upset the union applecart by urging a new TUC initiative: 'Ought we not to challenge the Government's bad faith with our regard for the national interest? Could not the General Council, for example, in return for withdrawal of this legislation, give some guarantee of a strike free year?' There were angry cries of dissent. 'What's wrong with a year of honoured agreements to prove this Government's policies are wrong?' I asked. I stuck my neck out further: if the Bill was unworkable, we should prove it by over-co-operating. The jeers and howls were replaced by a slow handclap. Lord

Cooper, the Chairman, appealed for calm, but I doubt if anyone heard my ultimate rejection of the Bill in all the hubbub.

The General Council got the backing it wanted. I left the hall ahead of the voting announcement to confront the usual scrum of demonstrators waiting outside. One woman Communist whom I remembered from years back smacked me round the face. On the whole, though, I thought the Special Congress had been well worthwhile. I had chosen my words with care. I always consult close colleagues in the union on these occasions and did so this time. They wanted me to tone down the draft I showed them, thinking I was mad to go ahead and risk losing votes in that presidential election. I thought that I would gain and put out my election address with the same assertion that we should register under the new laws to get what benefits we could for the members.

No EETPU member should have been in the slightest doubt about my position. It was markedly different from that stated by any other senior union leader, whatever their private thoughts, but I considered that I knew our people. Most of them had no time for the kind of misplaced militancy which led them up blind alleys and did nothing for their living standards. There were five other candidates for the President's job and I won with a clearcut majority in the first ballot. The members came good, as they always have for me since I nailed my colours firmly to the anti-Communist mast and to common sense in their interests.

These were hectic times. I replaced Les on the TUC General Council in mid-term, but retained my Labour Party NEC seat until the autumn Party conference. I did wonder if wearing two hats was worth the bother. It meant two lots of committees to attend and I couldn't get to both the TUC General Council and NEC meetings since they were usually on the same day each month. The TUC took priority, unless I got a special call to arms at the NEC.

Labour was in disarray over Britain's pending entry into the Common Market: Roy Jenkins, the Deputy Leader, and other leading figures were set to defy the Party line and to support Ted Heath in taking us in; Harold Wilson and most of the Party chiefs were anxious to scupper left-wing demands for a special Party conference which they realised would expose the divisions more publicly than ever. I was persuaded to skip the TUC and to attend the all-day NEC gathering to discuss the issue. I was assured that heads had been counted and that my vote was vital, but at the meeting Shirley Williams, who was supposed to be firmly against a conference, voted for one. Once again the moderates had miscalculated and I felt I had wasted my time.

My own Executive Council favoured British entry. We agreed, however, that the members should decide for themselves on an issue of such major constitutional and political importance. We were the only union to consult the entire membership and we got a flea in our collective ear for doing so: they voted 'no'.

After five frustrating years on Labour's NEC, I couldn't wait to leave. I was far more at home at the TUC despite my own fierce disagreements there. Every active trade unionist probably wishes, at some time or another, to be a TUC General Council member in the belief that his or her contributions will have a mighty influence on its policies; I was no different.

There was one big difference in my membership of the two bodies: I did not have to worry about a so-called annual election at the TUC, since I was my union's only nominee in the Electricity Group of which, after minor restructuring, the EETPU became sole occupant. The way in which some General Council members had to go through an election procedure to get their places was a constant source of irritation throughout my TUC membership. They mostly needed the patronage of the big unions and my own union was thwarted when it made various suggestions over the years to end that unhealthy arrangement. One victim of the big battalions in my early General Council days was Jack Peel, of the dyers and bleachers, who offended Jack Jones and the left-wing hierarchy. Ken Gill, of TASS, got the job of fixing his eviction; the episode made my mind up for me that the General Council structure must be radically changed, though it took more than a decade to get there.

I had high hopes that my influence would begin where Les Cannon's had ended and I expected that debates would bear more fruit than those at Transport House; but I found almost as many frustrations. Labour's reckless withdrawal of its list of proscribed organisations – a green light for extremist infiltration – was matched by the TUC which forgot about the two pamphlets it had once issued on the same problem, called *Defend Democracy* and *The Tactics of Disruption*. This controversy was to be the subject of many of my interventions at the General Council and from the floor of Congress, as well as a constant source of bitterness, principally between me and the group of Soviet sympathisers whose main voice was Jack Jones.

The General Council took life very seriously. The competent Congress House staff tried to take positive and useful steps to see that policies were implemented, but they were all too often handicapped by the General Council's policy switches, sometimes over quite brief periods of time. My high regard for the staff didn't mean I wanted an insider to replace Vic Feather when he retired – I considered that their professionalism also meant that they lacked direct trade union experience and I preferred an outsider. So I voted against Len Murray to succeed Vic. It wasn't a personal thing but it didn't help my relations with Len. The only other opponent at the time was Jack Jones, who wanted the staff to be far more subservient to the General Council and thought Len was too identified with the existing system.

Much of the detailed and practical General Council work is carried on by its network of committees. There is a certain amount of horse-trading and no little jealousy about who gets on the more influential ones. I eventually became Chairman of the Fuel and Power Industries and the Nationalised Industries Committees. These were not TUC glamour jobs and my EETPU interests gave me a strong claim to lead here, which overcame the usual prejudice against me.

One very peculiar arrangement in the TUC's bureaucratic machinery was the Committee to Select Committees – the group of senior General Council members which met immediately after each year's Congress. Usually only a few of them turned up and their role was simple – to endorse the General Secretary's list of committee memberships allocated to each General Council member, including the newcomers. Just how Vic Feather, and later Len Murray, reached their conclusions was a mystery. Once the left was strengthened on the General Council, the list was challenged at every full General Council meeting following that of the Committee to Select Committees. Seniority and a balance of union interests were supposed to be the main reasons for selections, but there was much more to it than that. For many years, the pro-Soviet Alan Sapper and I both complained about being passed over for the International Committee. In the end, we both made it.

I even aspired to the Finance and General Purposes Committee – the TUC 'inner cabinet' – only to be removed, albeit for a short while, in 1980. There were four causes for my dismissal: my attack on a pending visit to Poland by the TUC Economic Committee; my outspoken views against the TUC Day of Action and the public services dispute; my union's stand in the Isle of Grain dispute; and the way I went 'public' on all these issues. The case against me at the meeting that threw me off was that I could speak out among my TUC colleagues, but to do so publicly

131

was unbrotherly. That sort of gagging attempt was rarely applied to left-wingers who kicked over the traces, but it was not more than I expected. Debates about who should go on overseas delegations were often full of pettiness and self-interest. There was a major row over a trip to China: I thought the International Committee settled it on a motion that the delegation of five would include the 'current Chairman'. Everyone believed that meant the Chairman in office at the time the delegation took place: not Alan Sapper, then occupant of the TUC chair. The visit was not to take place for nearly a year and Alan would clearly be excluded. I was likely to succeed him as Chairman in the meantime, on a 'Buggins Turn' seniority basis. His friends raised the issue at the full General Council and got a fresh interpretation – that 'current' meant the Chairman at the time the decision was taken. It was all part of the left-right manoeuvring, which took up needless time and trouble. Alan Sapper was to be included whoever else went. In the event, he had to attend a conference of his own union and didn't make the trip: all that hot air was for nothing.

You can't speak your mind and not hit trouble and I was always likely to explode at some TUC stupidity. There was personal antagonism too: shortly before joining the General Council, I wounded Jack Jones by offering an EETPU job to Les Kealey, a TGWU National Officer who was forced to resign from his post over a row with Jones about handling a Ford wage claim. Jack never forgave me for that and he showed it. I did, on the other hand, find a lot of common ground with Harry Urwin, the TGWU number two, who for some years was Chairman of the TUC's Employment Policy and Organisation Committee. On most practical issues, we reached the same conclusions and I had great respect for his capability, sagacity and judgement. Harry Urwin gave evidence to a House of Commons Select Committee and said that it was against the rules of the TGWU for the union to authorise actions in breach of the law. It is a curious contrast to the more recent attitude of Moss Evans and other TGWU leaders who seem prepared to flout their own rule book.

My early General Council days were constantly overshadowed by Heath's industrial relations and pay laws. Mostly, I thought that Tory Ministers were more prepared to listen and to enter into a dialogue with us than their Labour counterparts. Men like Robert Carr and Maurice Macmillan, the Employment Ministers of that period, were genuinely worried by industrial disputes. That said, we did get more out of Labour governments – sometimes far more than we deserved – and not all our meetings with the Tories were useful. I recall one very one-sided meeting with Ted Heath and his Cabinet colleagues at Downing Street when all we got was a lecture in economics and we felt that we made no impression whatsoever.

I did get one sympathetic hearing from Heath over those legislative changes which allowed an easy opt-out from union membership. He opened a Durham factory which employed a lot of our members and I hitched a lift back to London in his official plane. I used the opportunity to raise with him the breakaway Electricity Supply Union and the role of Tory Central Office in aiding these people. I told him that it was destabilising for the unions and for the industry and that it was a recipe for industrial anarchy which neither of us wanted. I think I made an impact, though without result. The issue wouldn't go away, even when Labour repealed the Heath laws and we virtually ended the ESU. The four power workers' unions wanted to consolidate their position, even though only a handful of ESU men – they worked at the Ferrybridge power station – were left. I preferred to leave them alone rather than press them to join us or be sacked under our closed shop agreement, but the union majority played it tough. The Ferrybridge Six, as they became known, went to a tribunal over their dismissals and got substantial compensation.

I had no time for them: they could have joined any of the four unions, offering a range of policies, but I believe they were simply anti-union. Even so, I kept away from the tribunal. I have too often been in the minority and subject to intimidation and I couldn't have spoken for the unions with conviction. Nevertheless, the support the Six got was wholly misplaced. The Tories cannot see that their approach is a gift to disgruntled and often malicious individuals – and to nut cases – who want to undermine sensible industrial relations and create disharmony. Sadly, the present Government's legislation in this area threatens to resurrect situations such as we faced with the ESU that could become a stalking horse for disruptive political extremists.

A regular TUC problem in our meetings with Ministers was persuading the General Council members to let the General Secretary and the relevant Committee Chairman do the talking. Jack Jones and Hugh Scanlon, and later Clive Jenkins, could never resist having their say. We had arguments, too, about allowing the TUC members on the National Economic Development Council, the Neddy Six, to represent us at talks with the Government. Jones and Scanlon were part of our Neddy team long before I became a member, but I argued: 'We can't all do it. We have to have some faith in them. No one can do serious business at a mass meeting.'

The consequences of that 1971 Special TUC Congress, which had voted not to register under the new Heath laws, rumbled on. The EETPU position over registration was rudely overtaken by events. We had contended that no one would end up in prison because of the Heath laws, but the dockers proved us wrong. The Pentonville Five refused to obey an order of the National Industrial Relations Court and were jailed. The crisis was tremendous. We could no longer sustain any co-operative gesture with the Government and told the TUC that we would deregister after all. No one could really doubt the Tory attack on free trade unionism, yet there is no doubt either that the TUC had not implemented that solemn and binding undertaking given to Labour in 1969 – it had not put its own house in order. Had it done so, the Tories would have been denied the public support that they enjoyed.

If the dockers brought an uneasy trade union unity, it was all thrown out of the window again by the September 1972 TUC Congress. The delegates voted to suspend a handful of unions which, for various reasons, had decided that their members' best interests would be served by registering under the Industrial Relations Act provisions. That happened on the opening day; I sought to speak but was not called. I had intended to protest about the inadequate time allowed to those defending their unions against the TUC axe – the EETPU was in the minority against the suspensions. By the Wednesday, I was raring to go again. Vic Feather wanted to keep the temperature down in the debate about the Act. He remembered the Special Congress at Croydon and persuaded George Smith, the Congress President, to shut me out once more. I was furious and our whole delegation upped and walked out in disgust.

Vic's behaviour was very counter-productive. The speech that was suppressed was used in full in three national newspapers. I was quoted all over the place and probably earned more attention than any other delegate. My speech said that the Monday TUC decision flouted natural justice and the TUC rules, that Congress policy had failed and that non-co-operation with the Government should now be reversed to prove that much of the Act was unworkable. I stressed that the Government now said it would change the Act and that we could bargain and I remarked of those who thought that unbending TUC opposition and demonstrations shook the citadels of capitalism: 'I don't know how the Government sees you, but by God you frighten me.'

I continued to nag away. Talks between the Government, the TUC and the Confederation of British Industry did take place, then foundered. I upbraided all of them and said the TUC should have grasped the opportunities for 'massive consultation' now on offer; a change of government would change the emphasis but not the problems. In fact, pay policy concerned me more than the Industrial Relations Act. The EETPU Executive Council told our members that we agreed with the TUC that the Government dealt very differently with wages and prices. It could not expect support from working people without guaranteeing essential price levels, rates and rents and it should reconsider its limits on productivity payments. But we had to keep talking.

In March 1973, the TUC held a hastily-conceived Special Conference to try to unify the movement. The delegates adopted a motion allowing ad hoc amendments to the General Council's report, including demands for a one-day general strike. We said that this violated Congress rules and the rights of individual unions. This was no way to do business and I led our delegation in another walk-out and announced our opposition to any fresh stoppages. Left vilification was stepped up: they always ignored my insistence that it takes two to make a bargain, that TUC vacillation was matched by Ted Heath's intransigence and the abject failure of his economic policy. The Government, the Labour Party and the TUC, between them, seemed to have little idea of how to fulfil the nation's needs and aspirations.

It was depressing enough for me to write in the union journal in December 1973: 'Five periods of Emergency Powers in four years. Today emergency is the norm. As for Labour in opposition – the sheer irrelevance of plans for mass nationalisation has had its effect in by-elections. No government – no opposition. How long can democracy survive at the centre?'

On pay, I was as vehement as ever in slating Ministers. I told Maurice Macmillan that my union's reasonable attitude angered some of our members. The latest counter-inflation laws and intervention by the Pay Board left little alternative to conflict in electrical contracting, where another agreement was vetoed. I accused the Board of 'ignorance and blinkered bureaucracy'; because of its 'crass irresponsibility' we would effectively have to tear up long-standing arrangements which had given the industry peace and productivity. The industry's unique disputes procedures had cut strikes dramatically, yet now the Board was wrecking a new national agreement, while allowing the inflationary scandal of 'lump' labour through sub-contractors to continue with impunity. I got nowhere fast. The squabble would drag on long after the forthcoming General Election.

There were many other pay problems which infuriated me and were the fault of the Government: the Treasury's treatment of the power workers; the Ministry of Health's attitude over hospital electricians; and the dispute at Chrysler's Stoke and Ryton car plants, where Government pay policy got in the way of a reasonable settlement for our electricians and cloaked bitter inter-union troubles. Just as in 1969, my primary aim was the best possible deal for our members, many of them the country's highest paid skilled workers. I firmly believed, and still do, that what's good for EETPU members is good for Britain. I have consistently beaten the drum for fair rewards for skill, hard work and initiative. Our members have delivered and will continue to do so, while governments and bureaucrats, however well-intentioned, have mostly just got in the way.

The Heath Government did so. Just before the first of the 1974 general elections, there was a major, if belated, change in the TUC approach. It emerged very clearly in the very last discussion they had with Heath at Downing Street during the coal industry crisis and the three-day week. The TUC asked Heath and his Chancellor, Anthony Barber: 'What can we do or say as a movement that would enable you to treat the miners as a special case?' It echoed my Croydon plea for a TUC initiative – the plea for which I had been booed and pilloried. Now the old TUC carthorse had lumbered into the race. But, incredibly, Heath and his Ministers offered no reply. The TUC opened a door and the Government slammed it shut. The Prime Minister was wrong in every way, politically, industrially, tactically, even morally.

My union sympathised with the miners, though we thought their leadership throughout the dispute was appalling. The power unions all said little, but there was resentment and dismay over the unjustifiable tactics – Arthur Scargill's flying pickets, for instance, and the prevention of oxygen from going into nuclear power stations, which created a serious physical hazard. None of this could be justified by any trade union principles that I know about.

The power unions were not asked for help. We agreed that our members would use no coal produced after the miners' strike began, but it was clear that the miners could not win a quick victory unless their power station blockading was highly successful. Even so, my Executive colleague Eric Hammond demonstrated that Ministers were out to heighten the sense of crisis. The Government claimed that coal stocks were dwindling rapidly and switched off power stations. Eric's EETPU survey showed that enough supplies remained to last for ten weeks, which embarrassed Ministers hugely. That disclosure was undoubtedly a factor in the 'Who governs?' election that followed.

Ted Heath's pig-headedness and his refusal to pick up the TUC olive branch in those Downing Street talks was his biggest error: it changed the atmosphere in which the election was held. I have no doubt that it made a substantial difference to the result and helped to give us another five years of Labour Government.

# CHAPTER 11

# RELUCTANT LOYALIST

Within weeks of Harold Wilson's triumphant return to 10 Downing Street, the far-left critics of his minority Government began to crawl out of the woodwork, including a fair sprinkling of trade unionists. The trade union movement has never had the power on its own to elect Labour governments but it has always been able to ensure that they are not re-elected. Labour's lack of an overall majority in Parliament meant that another general election couldn't be far away, and although disunity spelled certain defeat, that was of no consequence to the wreckers.

No government up to that time had mismanaged the union's affairs as badly as the Heath administration. Had the TUC been in its more constructive pre-election mood far sooner, Labour would have had a clear majority, and the Wilson Government now deserved assistance. It made a vigorous start, settling the miners' dispute, taking back Tory tax concessions to the well-to-do, putting in motion the repeal of the Industrial Relations Act and the Housing Finance Act, increasing old age pensions and subsidising vital foodstuffs to stabilise prices. It was honouring its promises.

Our union could claim some credit for helping it to power. We had consistently opposed moves for a head-on confrontation with Heath and sought instead to expose and exploit Tory weaknesses. We showed that there was some common sense inside the unions; we scanned the 'Kill the Bill' banners and said that the way forward was through the ballot box. The TUC grudgingly followed us in the end, though no one would admit it.

The need for our realism should have been obvious, at least to experienced trade union leaders. In a mature democracy, whatever the individual at the top of the heap thinks and wants, the great mass of people outside will make the real decisions. We had to convince the voters that Labour could do a job for them – they were well aware that it couldn't be done by passing esoteric conference resolutions. It should have been possible to assume that the politically active understood what was necessary, that politics is the art of the possible. Unfortunately, the Labour and trade union movement is full of political illiterates as well as dedicated mischief-makers and it has only got worse since the early 1970s.

My criticisms of the 1964-70 Wilson Government were hard-hitting, but I was always prepared to acknowledge their difficulties, too. Whatever the government, whatever its political colour, it often has to be helped in the nation's interests. It cannot aid the trade union movement either, if the TUC is permanently confrontational and divisive. In retrospect, it was a mistake for the 1974 Wilson Government to do so much, so quickly, for it earned little credit from the unions for keeping its word. Memories were very short. The extremists, whose objective is society's breakdown, steadily gained influence inside the Party. They fulminated against any concessions to maintain our own government and were aided and abetted by many who should have known better.

The Social Contract, agreed between the Government and unions, held the line effectively for a while, but it was handicapped both by the developing economic crisis and because the TUC could never fully deliver. The TUC General Council insisted on commitments from the Government, but could only make hopeful noises about making its part of the bargain stick. Nevertheless, Jack Jones is entitled to some praise for the early successes. After one Neddy Six negotiation with Ministers over the Social Contract, he sought General Council agreement to a deal. Glaring round the Congress House table he said: 'Those who don't support this view are enemies of the working class.' It was Orwellian phraseology, but those left-wingers who needed his block vote patronage to keep their TUC places hardly dare refuse him. I didn't care for the intimidation but Labour's survival was at stake.

For all that, much of the TUC co-operation was half-hearted. General Council members felt obliged to defer to what they thought the demands of their individual unions would be. Ministers wanted personal commitments and well understood that large democratic organisations could not be dragooned or taken for granted. Miserably, too few at the TUC were ready to go away and fight for the Government inside their own unions. They behaved as delegates, rather than representatives, scared to give a lead in case their organisations disowned them. I was sure that the bulk of my members would go along if it meant getting Labour re-elected or keeping it in power; most members of other unions were no different. British workers will not be hoodwinked, but will put up with a lot if they get a chance to understand the issues and what they are told is honest and credible.

Throughout the five years to the 1979 General Election, Labour balanced on a knife-edge. The Lib-Lab pact was a key factor: it was ironic that the Liberals supported Jim Callaghan when Harold Wilson resigned in 1976, while Labour MPs and trade unionists continually sniped at him and his backbenchers frequently voted against their own government in the Parliamentary lobbies. It was the same old story of betrayal from within that has faced every Labour leader; Neil Kinnock has it coming to him and won't have overlong to wait.

The twin problems of inflation and unemployment constantly plagued the administration. I made countless appeals for support from our members for the Social Contract, not just because it was TUC policy, but because there was no better alternative. The EETPU gave firm backing and our 1975 Policy Conference applauded the Social Contract as 'a positive step forward on the road to economic growth and social justice'. The far left were held in check: I heaped scorn on them at the 1975 TUC Congress, saying that neither the Government nor the TUC had any clear mandate to end the mixed economy. I added: 'It appears to me that we are being asked to believe that we can have capitalism without profit and socialism without discipline. I reject both those arguments as nonsense. It is a bit like those left-wing economists who condemn both the market system and the Communist bureaucracies without recognising the inconsistency, for if you destroy the market the only alternative is a bureaucracy and a large police force.'

It was a theme I returned to soon afterwards in a Newcastle University speech on 'Liberty, Equality and Democracy'. I picked up topical remarks by Shirley Williams, then the Education Secretary, who had said that if the choice was between socialism and democracy, we would have to choose democracy. I said: 'Whilst I go along with that view, I also believe that social democrats and all those who prefer freedom to dictatorship, should learn to defend the market system, for society has to have some discipline. It is better that that discipline should come in the loose and imperfect manner of the market place in a mixed economy, than the tight and imperfect manner of the state and its police. That state should hold the ring, not get into it.' That went a lot further than Labour politicians would go in those days, including those who later became SDP members.

As usual, everything I said was distorted and used against me by the Communists and their allies, still working feverishly to undermine, if not to oust, the EETPU's anti-Red Executive Council as part of their bid to turn the union against TUC and Government policy. They got some crumbs of comfort when, for the first time in many years, three Executive Council members were elected who were not Labour Party members and described themselves as 'independent socialists'. It showed that the far left could not be dismissed out of hand. More significantly though, I was re-elected as General Secretary in 1976 (after the membership voted to abolish the post of General President) with more members voting than ever before in the union's history – I polled 71 per cent of the votes cast. It was a massive rejection of the Reds and the candidates they were backing.

My long-standing doubts and anxieties about pay policy grew, but I swallowed hard and offered further solid support for the Social Contract. The original flat £6 rises were replaced by a deal allowing weekly increases ranging from £2.50 to £4. The TUC heard from a grim Jim Callaghan that unless the new limits were agreed, the Government would have to resign. Five General Council members spurned his appeal, voting against it and calling for a return to free collective bargaining. Union support couldn't prevent the Government from lurching from crisis to crisis, especially with resentment and frustration over pay policy bubbling away. I had a trenchant go at the unrepresentative and incompetent elite, the intellectuals and the bureaucrats, managing the nation's affairs: substantial pruning in public spending was possible at local authority and central government level and cuts in administrative and bureaucratic overheads would soften the effect on real public service.

The cutbacks and redundancies hit manual workers first. In the electricity supply, electronics and telecommunications industries there were first productivity bargains, then closures. I told one meeting: 'Universities are bursting at the seams with aspiring economic wizards, consultants and advisers – all hoping to join the wealth-consuming business when it is common ground that our problem is not how to consume wealth, but how to create it.' At one meeting between the TUC and Callaghan, now Prime Minister following Wilson's resignation, it dawned on me that the Government really needed the policy because it would otherwise be unable to resist the demands of its own employees. They always seemed to be well cushioned, compared with the skilled workers that I represented. I didn't get much change from Jim on that, though he did push me a note across the table: 'Do you need any barley?' I had previously bought some from his farm to feed my racing pigeons. I passed a note back: 'Yes, but how much?' My TUC colleagues were perplexed by all this – they doubtless suspected a fix, for Jim was, after all, a known intriguer. I did buy a ton of barley from him, but if it was a peace offering, it was certainly no bargain – I paid him the full market price.

There was a meeting with the Chancellor, Denis Healey, where I took another crack at the swollen bureaucracy. Denis was spouting about productivity needs and overmanning in British industry. I agreed, but I went on: 'I don't know how you justify your argument when there are five of us here from the TUC and about twenty civil servants.'

It wasn't easy to keep behind the Government and still satisfy our membership over their own pay settlements. If union leaders had stuck together, it would have helped a lot, but the backsliding was under way. I clashed with Jack Jones at the 1977 TUC Congress over his complaints about difficulties for his members under pay policy. My electrical contracting members had given up a £10 weekly rise on basic rates for a £6 flat-rate increase; we knew that anomalies were likely under the policy, but accepted it. I said: 'Now we are being asked to go back on our word. Jim Callaghan indicated that the Government accepts that it may be difficult to govern with TUC co-operation. He also understands that it is impossible to govern without it.'

That contracting industry situation, first cocked up by Tory pay policy, remained a very sore point. Michael Foot, Wilson's Employment Secretary, told us that although the Tory Pay Board would be scrapped, he could not vary its decisions meanwhile, other than for exceptional cases. He refused to treat us as an exception. Each successive year we ran into more pay policy trouble in implementing improvements to the industry's wide-ranging agreement. We tried to persuade Tony Benn, the Energy Secretary, to intervene and I supplied him with full details of escalating site bonus schemes, often bogus, for other trades which were not governed by our kind of nationwide agreement. I used the Isle of Grain power station site, years later the scene of fierce inter-union rivalry, as an example. Benn received conflicting advice, it all came to nothing and it took us until 1978 to get satisfaction. Our shabby treatment by successive governments was almost unbelievable. It was tantamount to deliberate sabotage of a model agreement.

By then the Government policy was for 10 per cent rises. Our latest negotiations were carefully tailored to fit and a deal was approved by the Department of Employment. Yet suddenly the Department changed its mind and threatened sanctions, under the pay laws, against employers who paid up. We were angered and horrified. We insisted that employers should honour the agreement and opted for selective strike action, though we did reject Communist-inspired demands for an all-out national stoppage and consequent full-scale confrontation with the Government. One employer took us to court and that was the Government's undoing. Sam Silkin, the Attorney General, had to confess in court that our unique, legally-binding agreement for the industry took precedence: the employers must pay and the Government must climb down. The agreement was sustained, but it was all a needless and bitter diversion. We suffered from pay policy simply because we had an orderly and progressive national arrangement which was easy to monitor and to restrict, while others, indisciplined and ill-organised, could get away with murder. These were the kind of anomalies that wrecked pay policy.

There were a range of other issues during this period where Government policy and the activities of Ministers aggravated and affronted me and my union's leadership. There was no greater political knave and double-dealer than Tony Benn. He gave the impression of great competence but his duplicity achieved nothing but trouble. He has never really sympathised with the unions and tailors his image of them to suit his prejudices. He appears to have no qualms about campaigning inside the Labour and trade union movement alongside the Communists, Trotskyites and any others on the far-left who might gain him a few more votes. He cannot accept, any more than Margaret Thatcher, that unions are groups of workers organised together to protect their interests.

His peculiar vision of the unions ignores our formal structures which is why, even as a Minister, he intervened unhelpfully behind the back of union officials who sought to resolve pay disputes. He did it by holding private talks with Windscale workers who later felt he had deceived them. He did it when power station workers took unofficial action – meeting the trade union side to tell them why certain negotiated fringe benefits could not be paid and, at the same time, allowing one of his aides to meet the unofficial shop stewards' movement and create the impression that union officials were dragging their feet over a settlement.

He was guilty of further deceit over the fast breeder reactor when he told the TUC that an early inquiry was impossible because design and cost estimates had not been finalised. Within a few days he said publicly that the proposal was delayed because he was not satisfied that the democratic machinery was strong enough to control the new development. He misled the TUC by assuring us of his support for Windscale expansion to process Japanese nuclear waste and then backtracked when it suited him. He bedevilled the whole nuclear power debate as Energy Minister by an unwillingness and inability to come to concrete decisions and by resorting to popular evasions.

I sat for a year as a member of the Plowden Inquiry into the electricity supply industry's structure. Benn disagreed with its conclusions, which were admittedly contentious, though they would have brought some justifiable centralisation to the industry when Labour's largely misguided policy was devolution. Any Minister would have had a tough time with the MPs if he or she had gone all the way with Plowden, but there was no action at all. All that time and the cost of the inquiry were wasted and Tony Benn was mainly to blame. He did establish the Energy Commission, a useful body which the Thatcher Government immediately abolished as part of its quango hunt. Even here though, Tony Benn gave them the excuse they sought, for under his chairmanship the Commission was largely a stage for him and a showcase for his views. It should have been recast and reduced in size, not scrapped, so that we retained a worthwhile national forum to discuss the energy policy which is so crucial to Britain's future.

Benn has an aristocratic disdain for British workers which he skilfully camouflages with empty rhetoric. He knows what's best for them and never tires of instructing them in what they ought to seek. He dismisses the views of the great bulk of workers and shop stewards and blames the media for brainwashing them. When he calls for a 'bigger role' for trade unionists, he means that it should go to those who have been taken in by the dangerous nonsense he peddles through that vast media coverage he carefully cultivates and pretends to scorn.

He is all things to all men. He has two images: one reserved for the private occasion and the other for the media and the impressionable. He has done more than any other single individual to devastate the Labour Party and to foster the atmosphere and produce the policies that have divided it and driven decent social democrats away. I was once at a dinner party with him where he referred to the socialist commonwealth.

'Do you mean Australia and New Zealand?', he was asked, since they had Labour Governments at the time. Benn said: 'No. I mean the Communist bloc.' It is a clear illustration of his alignment and thinking. He was never in any doubt as to my views of his gerrymandering and deviousness. I crossed swords with other Ministers, but there was no one for whom I felt such profound contempt over the years as I did for Benn.

Some just needed a hefty kick in the pants to get them moving. I aimed one at Edmund Dell, the Trade Minister who is now a Social Democrat and chairman of Channel Four Television. At a meeting with Jim Callaghan, I said to Dell: 'You roll over on your back so that the Japanese can rub your belly like a pet poodle.' It was a crude way of underlining my plea for action over Japanese car imports. I have never wanted protectionism, but the Japanese industry was heavily subsidised and competed unfairly. Selective import controls should defend those areas of our industry where we can produce the goods and where it is essential to ensure that our domestic products reign supreme. Most overseas countries protect their jobs and their trade balance that way – the French and West German telecommunications industries, for instance, use no foreign equipment. We often appear to think that it's all a game of cricket.

Eric Varley, as both Energy and Industry Minister, was likeable and able. At one TUC meeting with him to discuss a Government think tank report by Sir Kenneth Berrill about the car industry, the union men were steamed up over the report's attack on overmanning. I made myself unpopular with my TUC colleagues by agreeing with it. Varley should have taken my advice and enlisted the help of Jim Houston to rescue the ailing British shipbuilding industry. Houston, the long-standing independent chairman of the Electrical Contracting Industry Joint Industry Board, has the confidence of both the employers and union representatives and is also a former Fairfields shipyard man. I later discovered that Varley had been given contrary advice to mine from within his Department, but he was wrong to take it.

Two recurring themes within the TUC General Council were devolution and industrial democracy. Not unusually, I was in the minority on both issues. The Government's long-running political battle over Scottish and Welsh devolution coincided with the General Council's arguments over the need for regional TUCs. I was all for better consultation and for improving the existing regional advisory structure, but any large organisation like the TUC which devolves its central authority, sets up an area of conflict, almost calls it into being. The TUC didn't have so much authority that it could chuck any of it away, but it went ahead and gave the regions constitutional powers. There are times now when, as a consequence, the tail wags the dog.

Industrial democracy was forced along mainly by Jack Jones. Like devolution, it sounds fine in theory, but the practicalities of giving everyone a share in the decision-making process are against it. I considered that it would blur the purpose of trade unionism and could find no evidence of any widespread enthusiasm for it at shopfloor level. Nevertheless, it was necessary to respond to the Bullock Inquiry which the Government had set up. The EETPU entered its strong reservations and opposed the Bullock proposals for a statutory system when they emerged. My position was clear. It is vital that there should be much greater partnership in British industry, but not through enmeshing trade unions formally in a legally-binding structure.

British managers must abandon the class-based attitudes that have poisoned our industrial performance. They must begin to realise that there is no difference in status between management and working people, between white-collar and blue-collar. They must allow more job autonomy to individuals, provide more information, improve consultation and, most crucially, share the decision-making through joint working parties, training schemes or other participative arrangements. Workers don't have to sit on boards or be segregated from their peers to take part. Industrial democracy or participation will not be made easier by attempts to deflect trade unions from their major function of representing people in the labour market. If we do eventually tread the statutory path, through domestic or EEC legislation, it should be on the basis of flexibility and experimentation. We cannot simply graft overseas systems onto existing British industrial relations without the risk of unacceptable and unnecessary disruption.

There was another incident in this period which saw me out on my usual limb. Comrade Shelepin, chairman of the Russian 'TUC' and recent head of the KGB, was invited to Britain by some of the car industry unions. I was outraged that we should canoodle with this ex-boss of an oppressive killer squad who had now been down graded in Soviet terms to control his country's puppet unions. I recalled meeting Shelepin all those years before in Prague. Now I tried to stop the invitation and, when that failed, I urged a boycott. Clive Jenkins was the most vociferous defender of the visit. There was no way meeting with Shelepin could be helpful to us, but it could be useful propaganda for the Russians. He came to TUC headquarters, but I was sure that if anything went wrong with the trip, Shelepin would suffer politically when he got home. There were some hostile demonstrations against him in London and there was very little heard about him after that. Doubtless his record left him with plenty of enemies back home, ready to cash in on any embarrassment caused by his visit.

These matters were of secondary importance – the great pay policy row dominated. My misgivings mounted and I warned the Government yet again that the lot of the skilled worker had worsened unacceptably. I insisted that I could not back a further deal with the Government unless it permitted proper rewards for skill, effort and responsibility. That third, 10-per-cent stage of the pay policy didn't match up to those overriding requirements. The EETPU, loyal for so long, reluctantly opposed it. It was immensely difficult to reconcile our stand on this with our faithful support for this and other Labour Governments and we stressed that we would campaign as vigorously as ever for another Labour Government when the time came.

We felt convinced that the central bureaucracy applied pay policy unfairly and not in a way that resolved the basic ills of the economy. Inflexible pay norms failed to provide the stimulus which British industry desperately needed and despite growing unemployment, there were still serious skill shortages in some sectors of industry, which I felt resulted from a lack of incentives. I put it this way to our members: 'Nothing is more galling to those who contribute to the country's wealth through their productivity and skills, than to have their rewards determined by a group whose productivity contribution is nil.' Perhaps I blamed the tools rather than the workman, perhaps I should have given ministerial policy-makers more stick than their civil servants; but various pay boards and Ministry men had given me and my members the runaround for so long that I had a genuine sense of grievance.

Our dilemma – support for the Government and opposition to a vital plank of its policy – was heightened by the Prime Minister's refusal to call a general election in 1978; instead, he slapped a 5 per cent limit on wage rises. It is not being wise after the event to say that I always reckoned that Jim Callaghan would hang on in government in the forlorn hope that something would turn up – he liked it where he was and didn't believe he could win at the time. There was scant chance of a fresh agreement with the unions on pay, but it was his nature to cling on to what he had got. He was quite unable to judge the consequences of his shilly-shallying: the TUC was geared up for an election, not for another round of even more restrictive pay negotiations.

The TUC General Council were not prepared to throw the old sailor a life belt. They told Jim that his ceiling was far too low and, worse, that they had no intention of negotiating to raise it. Some of us, aware of the imminent political dangers, thought we should at least talk about it; indeed, Jim Callaghan challenged the 1978 Congress to produce its viable alternative. I didn't believe that Jim and Denis Healey had said their last words on the subject. I was ready to sacrifice my policy differences to help Labour stay in office and I was prepared to urge my members to do likewise, but the General Council majority thought differently. The expectations of trade unionists were worked on by those who wanted to see the Government defeated and, once again, Labour's leadership had to fight those within its own ranks, as well as the other political parties. All the major unions committed themselves to rejecting another dose of pay policy and negotiations were out.

I certainly claimed that my members deserved more than 5 per cent because of their contribution to the economy; on the other hand, the ceiling was really too high as a global percentage, measured against our lack of competitiveness and extremely high unit labour costs. Unflagging opposition on behalf of my craftsmen members might have been understandable, if undesirable, but I was not against pay policy in principle. My hostility was directed at the incompetent and unfair application of it. The narrowing of skill differentials, in particular, caused, and would continue to cause, major trouble on the shopfloor. Yet the most unrelenting opponents of the policy were those, like the National Union of Public Employees, whose lower paid members did far better under it than they had ever managed under free collective bargaining.

Both the TUC and the Labour Party Conferences in 1978 threw Jim Callaghan's 5 per cent back in his face. There was still a glimmer of hope when the TUC's Neddy Six met Cabinet Ministers to hammer out a new compromise formula to cool things down, but even their modest joint proposals were foolishly rejected by the full TUC General Council. There was one final unofficial effort to edge the unions back towards reality. Former Fleet Street industrial journalist, John Grant, was now a junior employment minister and one of the EETPU's sponsored MPs. He was a passionate prices and incomes policy man and inspired his own 'private enterprise' bid to trigger off a fresh union initiative. He thought that both the Government and the TUC had grossly mishandled the situation to overwhelming Tory advantage and he persuaded a dozen senior trade union leaders to sign a document called *A Better Way*. They included Alf Allen, the shopworkers' General Secretary and Chairman of the TUC Economic Committee, NALGO's Geoffrey Drain, Tom Jackson of the postmen's union, Tony Christopher of the taxmen, Terry Duffy, the AUEW President, Bill Sirs of the steelworkers, the NUR's Sidney Weighell and myself. He also cajoled one or two of the more reasonable left-wingers into backing the proposals.

It was hardly a blueprint for the future, but it offered the most coherent approach for a long while to the intractable pay policy problem, including a more flexible line on rewards for productivity. Regrettably, by the time it was printed and published, it was too late – we were already plunged into the horrors of the 'Winter of Discontent'. Callaghan, pressed to hang on by Michael Foot, had gravely misjudged the union mood and those of us who had feared the worst were proved correct. It took no great foresight – which made the Prime Minister's decision all the more remarkable.

The industrial chaos which peaked early in 1979 spelled the demise of that fragile Labour Government and caused immense damage to the already deeply unpopular trade union movement. MPs, including left-wing rebels, stripped the Government of sanctions to use against recalcitrant employers: our bitter experience with the contracting employers had left me with a jaundiced view of sanctions, but the Government was now left naked. Ford workers, bakers, railwaymen, British Oxygen workers, BBC staff, oil tanker drivers, all poured through the gaping hole in the Government's defences. Then came the really rough stuff. The TGWU confronted the Government in road haulage. Mrs Thatcher, rightly sniffing the heady scent of impending victory, began to enjoy herself at the Government's expense. Her speeches struck a sympathetic public chord as irresponsible pickets caused hardship, severe inconvenience and, in consequence, anger and disgust.

Soon, we were identified with the even more offensive behaviour of an uncaring and malicious minority in the front-line of the 'dirty jobs' dispute. Public service workers disrupted hospitals, refused to provide basic emergency services to the dangerously ill and even spited mourning relatives by impeding burials. There were ugly scenes on the picket lines. Whether the wildcat strikers in the vanguard were politically-motivated, misled, sick-minded or just plain stupid, it was all as far removed from trade unionism as anything I could remember. Prime Minister Callaghan called them 'vandals', though he prepared to run up the white flag in the face of their demands. In all my years as a trade unionist I have never seen such intense hostility from the general public and from most trade union members towards the unions. It made the public reaction to the power workers' go-slow seem like a picnic.

The Government and the TUC had a new concordat to see that vital public services were maintained, but it proved to be barely worth the paper it was written on. The TUC was its ineffective self: Alf Allen and I asked Len Murray to condemn the intimidation by pickets. Nothing happened. Someone had to show some concern and I minced no words. I said that some of the pickets were practising 'terrorism, not trade unionism'. My sights were trained on that fairly small but very vocal minority who clearly gloried in their harmful and obnoxious antics. Most union leaders privately agreed with me.

Saying it publicly, however, brought the inevitable storm of abuse. I expected it from the left, but I was disgusted when Len Murray strayed from the sidelines, not to rap the strikers, but to rebuke me for my remarks. He publicly deplored my 'uninformed and unhelpful' comments and said that my reference to terrorists was 'dangerous nonsense'. Trade unionists, it seemed, could do no wrong, even by flouting the law. It showed a strange sense of values.

There was a last vain and expedient bid by Jim Callaghan to pull things together in the aftermath of that calamitous spell and prior to the general election, which could no longer be held off. The TUC General Council met the Labour Cabinet at 10 Downing Street to help reshape Labour's programme to put to the country. Salvaging any credibility from the industrial wreckage was a prodigious task: the Prime Minister needed to say that he had a new deal, something, almost anything, to try to paper over the huge cracks between the political and industrial wings of the Labour movement. We put a series of questions to Ministers, but I felt a mounting despair: the unions had so much to answer for; the Government had no spunk left and were simply whining to us. Harold Wilson, whatever his faults, used to give us a tougher time and used to argue with us, but this subservience was miserable, degrading. Only Denis Healey retained a bit of dignity.

Jim Callaghan's last words to us were memorable: 'We are prostrate before you – but don't ask us to put it in writing.' Help him back to Downing Street again and whatever we wanted was ours for the asking.

He seemed to think we could forget the grim months behind us as if they had never happened. Had he learned nothing or didn't he care? I felt thoroughly sickened. It was truly one of the worst moments of my life.

## CHAPTER 12

# THE NUCLEAR NUTTERS

Soon after I joined the TUC General Council in 1971, a Fuel and Power Industries Committee was formed. I was a member from the outset. I have criticised Congress House shenanigans, but I exempt my TUC colleagues almost en bloc when dealing with fuel and power matters over the years. Apart from a brief and barmy late intervention from Arthur Scargill, our's was a team effort: we produced a sensible and coherent strategy which the nation would still be wise and prudent to follow.

Our first major job was to draw up an energy policy that would last. We involved all the TUC-affiliated unions and had lengthy discussions with the nationalised industries, oil companies and other relevant private sector people to produce our first study, in June 1973. Shortly after this I took over as the Committee's Chairman from Walter Anderson, who retired from his job as NALGO General Secretary and from the TUC. I stayed in the Committee chair until my own departure from the General Council ten years later.

There was a fair amount of agreement on energy policy from the start and two clear principles were established: the first was that our approach should be based primarily on coal because there were such large untapped stocks; the second was that North Sea oil and gas should be treated as primary fuels, should be used sparingly and should not be exploited so that they quickly ran out. We warned against over-reliance on any one energy source somewhat prophetically, since after our study was published, the oil producing nations raised oil prices by a massive 350 per cent in one year. We were not then to know the full scale of the energy crisis ahead, nor that it was to be followed by a recession which rapidly transformed an energy shortage into a relative surplus.

Certainly, prior to my Committee chairmanship, the major issue was how quickly could energy supply be expanded to keep pace with the continuous economic growth of the British economy since the Second

World War. Total UK consumption of primary fuels, for example, increased from about 260,000,000 tonnes of coal equivalent in 1960 to 325,000,000 tonnes by 1970.

The oil crisis brought the need for energy planning into sharp focus. We were inundated with energy forecasts of what future energy demands would be and how they could be met. We were confronted with a vast array of energy supply technologies, some exotic, like solar and geothermal energy, but all proffering solutions to the puzzle. Our complacency over energy supply was shattered for ever and long-term planning was suddenly the norm. Forecasting difficulties in an uncertain political and economic climate are enormous but there is no alternative to having a plan for energy if there are not to be shortages. In the depths of recession we too easily forget the power cuts of the 1950s and 1960s when demand for energy outstripped the electricity industry's ability to provide it. When there is an apparent surplus all the 'clever dicks' contend that money is being wasted by those who have planned and are responsible for energy investment. But, as a former Central Electricity Generating Board Chairman, Sir Stanley Brown, once said: 'The dearest unit of electricity there can be is the unit you don't have.'

The Fuel and Power Committee decided to update TUC policy with a review over three years and again we involved all those previously consulted, but this time there was an additional problem. The CEGB, chaired by Arthur Hawkins, wanted to start a nuclear power station construction programme, initially with eleven stations. Hawkins proposed to Energy Minister, Eric Varley, that they adopt the American-designed Pressurised Water Reactor (PWR), because the CEGB's own British-designed Advanced Gas Cooled Reactor (AGR) had proved very costly to construct, compared to earlier Magnox stations. The PWR design, more easily reproduced, would, the CEGB argued, overcome excessive construction costs.

The attempts by the CEGB and the General Electric Company to oversell the PWR on cost grounds heightened the suspicions of those of us who wanted to be convinced by detailed investigation about which type of station was best. The PWR lobby claimed it had great export potential, something I heaped scorn on as unrealistic. They had it all worked out between them, but they were too clever by half. My TUC Committee was very attracted by a Canadian system with a good safety record, but eventually supported the AGR. Our main challenge was on that vital cost issue: our evidence showed that, despite all the snags with the other power stations and despite the possibility of reduced construction time and costs, a unit of electricity generated by a PWR station offered scant advantage over that produced by its rivals.

Undoubtedly, one of the biggest problems our nuclear power programme has faced has been the dismal record of the engineering construction industry. At one time, it appeared quite incapable of building any power plant, oil, coal or nuclear, to time and cost. Construction delays on nuclear plant, with its very high capital cost, have been disastrous and I did not see that a change in reactor design could possibly help solve this underlying difficulty.

By the time our review was complete, Tony Benn had replaced Eric Varley as Energy Minister. Benn saw too much kudos in manipulating public concern with safety questions to commit himself behind any sort of nuclear programme. We warned him that by weakening the AGR programme, he would lay the basis for a return match by the PWR lobby – the CEGB and the engineering industry, led by the GEC. How right we were. Benn played a strange game, not only with our TUC policies, but also with the Plowden Committee which Varley had set up to look into the electricity supply industry's functions and structure and on which I served. Benn embarked on a series of consultations which led to the Energy Commission's formation, but which also seemed designed to frustrate and delay the options, rather than clarify them. It was a sorry tale of evasion and indecision.

Eight years on, the industry is still not reorganised; and the marathon Sizewell Inquiry is considering a PWR design programme – while apparently substantiating those original TUC anxieties about cost. My plain speaking and strictures on behalf of the TUC both embarrassed and irritated Benn. He was Machiavellian enough to try to get rid of me by the old device of kicking me upstairs: he offered me the Deputy Chairmanship of the Electricity Council, a well-paid job without clout. I told him: 'No thanks. My members would think I've betrayed them.' He understood that, but I would have plugged an awkward hole for him when, as always, there was some difficulty in appropriately filling a senior nationalised industry post. He also knew that if I took the job it would reflect badly on and would weaken the EETPU anti-Communists, so he had good cause to ease me out. I have had other Ministerial soundings since about such jobs but I have stuck to the same grounds for refusal.

Whatever the view of the TUC's long-term plans, the prolonged time-span needed to secure adequate energy supplies makes it strategically imperative to ensure that the nation doesn't run short. If an energy source doubles or trebles its prices overnight, or if that energy becomes scarce, we can't simply switch to some other source. It may take the individual householder, assuming he or she has the cash and the know-how, many months to change to another heating method. Many of our poorest households are lumbered with inefficient and expensive forms of space heating that are a throwback to the days of cheap energy.

For the economy as a whole, the time-scale is years, even decades. The development of a new coal face or construction of a new power station can take ten to fifteen years, given the jungle of planning decisions that must be taken in our democratic society. It is immensely difficult to plan for fifteen to twenty years ahead when the future is so uncertain, but the alternative is not to plan and to gamble instead. The risk of sabotage is far too great to leave our energy supplies to chance. The TUC plan took these factors into account and declared:

that we must keep up our coal supplies;

that there should be a regular nuclear power station construction programme;

that there should be modest research into renewable energy sources;

that North Sea oil and gas should be primary fuels;

that Britain should involve itself in the construction of a commercial fast breeder reactor;

that there should be an expanded energy conservation programme under a new Energy Conservation Agency.

I never doubted that we must be free from ransom by any foreign energy cartel if the security of supply was to be safeguarded. We had to maximise our indigenous resources and maintain self-sufficiency.

There were important lessons to be learned from the 1972-1973 oil crisis. Oil was cheap and convenient and the British economy, like all those in the West, was over-dependent on it. We were building very large oil-fired power stations and our domestic heating systems were tied to cheap oil. When the crisis came, we were trapped, pushed into runaway inflation and eventually into recession.

Opponents of TUC policy suggested that ours was a 'please every-body' approach with expansion for coal, nuclear power, renewables and conservation too. They failed to grasp the importance of diversity. The more energy options for the economy, the less likely is the prospect of a nation strangled by reliance on a single fuel source. I told one conference: 'I've always been against making ourselves captive to the oil sheiks. That's why I argued about early pit closures that took place twenty years ago. But I'm equally against making electricity supply totally captive to coal, without any guarantee that coal could be supplied and at the right price.' The TUC policy studiously avoided the single source position. Maybe there could be over-investment in energy, but if too much energy was economically embarrassing, too little would be economically disastrous.

The TUC continued to update its policy and, as part of another consultative exercise, again went to the affiliated unions for their views. I chaired a Congress House conference early in 1981, attended by some 140 delegates from thirty-nine unions. Most of them shared our view of the problems and possible solutions, but a vociferous left minority emerged and used the occasion as a platform for anti-nuclear outbursts. The National Union of Journalists, for example, was totally opposed to nuclear power. I did try pointing out to them that more people had died through exposure to printing ink than to radioactive materials. It was disquieting that the unions farthest from the nuclear power industry were the most vehement in their opposition to the nuclear option. Theirs was a predetermined opposition: their criticism was not constructive, but was the Luddite 'no technology' approach that has done so much to bring unions into disrepute.

I recalled my remarks at a conference five years earlier, when I had raised the prospect that coalmining might become unacceptable to a modern society: 'Are we not expecting too much in a modern community when people are really going down into the bowels of the earth and earning a living this way?' Yet here we were at a conference with trade unionists extolling the virtues of coalmining and rejecting nuclear fission. They seriously claimed that a centuries-old technique for producing energy at enormous social cost is preferable to developing a nuclear technology which offers potentially cheap electricity without immense environmental harm. They resorted to unfounded exaggeration and downright lies about nuclear power to bolster their case; their myths were hard to counter instantly in the heat of debate.

However, the satisfactory outcome of it all was the TUC's Review of Energy Policy, published in August 1981. The painstaking process of consultation and discussion had created a worthy end-product. The Review was unable to predict the extent of the current recession and alarming fall in energy demand, but the principles contained in it remain as relevant as ever.

One of my major personal tasks as Committee Chairman was to impress on the members the necessity for a broad outlook. This was largely reflected in the Review. The document plugged energy self-sufficiency and independence. That may appear superficially to be a somewhat insular, inward-looking policy, but energy independence for Britain and as many western economies as possible is of direct benefit to the world's poorest countries. It is predicted that world population will have doubled by the end of the century, along with a threefold increase in energy demand. When the developed economies emerge from recession, they will again have growing appetites for energy and it is therefore essential that the developed countries expand their indigenous energy sources and do not compete in world markets with the Third World, where the crying need is for precious fossil fuel. The EETPU made a point of this in its contribution to the TUC consultations.

The TUC still wants our existing AGR programme to be completed and accepts the need for the inquiry into the cost and safety involved in building a single PWR at Sizewell. The reasons are clear enough: since the 1981 review, there have been forecasts of declining energy consumption and energy-intensive industries have collapsed through recession. Delays in power station planning and construction may seem welcome at a time of over-capacity in electricity supply, but the problems will occur when power stations, currently operating economically, start to exceed economic production costs and break down more often as they come to the end of their working span. Magnox stations, which have served us so well, will have finished their economic lives by the 1990s. If their de-commissioning coincides with a leap in demand through expanded trade and manufacturing, then the nation will hit serious difficulties. I doubt whether those who constantly exhort the Government to cut energy investment because of a current energy surplus will be quite so vocal when the lights go out.

A useful by-product of the TUC Committee's work was that the miners' union, never very co-operative on issues beyond its immediate spheres of interest, was involved in drawing up our plans – until Arthur Scargill's election as the miners' President wrecked that joint effort. They had helped for some eight years, but Scargill went on the rampage. He denounced any sort of nuclear power project in irresponsible and lunatic terms. He turned up at one Committee meeting and launched a ludicrous attack; I told him bluntly that his propagandist rubbish might impress those who didn't fully understand the crucial issues, but it didn't wash with us. He didn't attend again.

We face an unlikely alliance between the miners' union and the no-growth or low-growth environmentalists – unlikely, because the miners and their industry are just as dependent on economic growth and an increased demand for electricity as the nuclear industry. The coal industry increasingly relies on the CEGB, following the fall-off in domestic use of coal. Power stations now burn 75 per cent of National Coal Board output, but instead of identifying common ground with the electricity unions, Scargill shares platforms with those way-out environmentalists who have little or nothing in common with the aspirations of his own members.

There is certainly no comfort for EETPU members, or for the general public, in the arguments of the 'greens', the no-growth or low-growth lobbyists. We cannot afford to dice with the political and technological uncertainties of low-energy options. My members have achieved decent living standards and they want further improvements. They want the convenience and even luxury that modern energy provides. They can identify with the advance of new technology and its benefits, not with the muesli-eaters, ecology freaks, loony leftists and other nutters who make up the anti-nuclear brigade. That is surely true of most of our citizens.

Scargill links arms with Tony Benn and his pro-Moscow men: unilateral nuclear disarmament and nuclear energy are thrust by them into the same pulsating package, to be rubbished together. They claim a monopoly of morality and posture self-righteously as the protectors of generations to come. If they achieved their dangerously ludicrous aims, I should certainly fear for the future of my four grandchildren in a Britain with grievously undermined defences and a potentially disastrous energy deficiency. Scargill's perpetual assaults on nuclear power could easily lead to the breakdown of commonly accepted TUC policy. He reneges on the work of his own union, as well as the TUC position, but Len Murray has yet to even murmur a reproach.

Ironically and unwittingly, the miners' union has given much comfort to the nuclear industry. The miners resist change and refuse to let uneconomic pits shut, so that the price of coal to the CEGB stays higher than it would if it came from the largest and most economic mines. Nuclear power would have far more trouble competing with large coal-fired stations sited next to the major pits. The miners ensure that there are sound economic reasons for continuing with nuclear power, quite apart from the strategic ones.

I remain firmly committed to the importance of both coal and nuclear power. Oil and gas are finite and far too valuable to burn in power stations. That doesn't mean that we should maintain clapped-out or hopelessly uneconomic pits, but we must phase out lame, obsolete or superfluous industries, or their useless parts, and the nation must bear the social cost. It is certainly not enough to tell workers concerned, who have done their best, to get on their bikes, but blinkered refusal to square up to the situation will leave Britain like a banana republic – but without the bananas. We shall all be worse off that way.

We must carry on doing the things we do well and scrap those that don't work in favour of new developments. That is not a call to use Britain as a laboratory for oddball theories, industrial or economic; it is a demand for practical solutions that will work, will halt our decline and will put people back into jobs. We have often led the world in technological development – antibiotics, radar, the jet engine, atomic reactors, computers, the hovercraft, even the silicon chip – but we have not always reaped the benefits of our own inventiveness.

We need more public investment in projects like rail electrification, in better training and retraining, in new technology for industry and schools and in new sources of energy, although we should also conserve those we already have. We must invest in coal and nuclear power. We must not allow our nuclear programme to be stifled by a mixture of political cowardice, administrative incompetence, bureaucratic inertia and political infighting in the power plant industry.

There are overwhelming dangers along the route of the militant Hampstead doomwatchers and those self-interested miners' leaders whose scare tactics grab public attention. Fear must not swamp rationality. If the energy gap arrives, there would be a headlong rush to complete new nuclear stations to make up the shortfall. That would present the most perilous situation of all. It would force a crash building programme with much of the existing nuclear expertise no longer available. That kind of misconceived scramble is made for mistakes – those that could spell a nuclear catastrophy.

My union, primarily skills-based, is vitally committed to the health and safety of its members and of the wider public. We reject the simplistic and emotive reactions which link nuclear power to nuclear warfare as a wildly unrealistic and inaccurate scenario. The risks in generating energy from convention sources almost certainly greatly exceed those from nuclear systems. That is why we favour a steady, carefully planned and controlled nuclear power programme in which nothing is left to chance and any risk is minimised.

The other great energy centre, the Middle East, is still aflame with both industrial and political turmoil. Who knows what new wars of conquest are likely as the quarrels over finite oil supplies increase? It would be a grave folly and criminally capricious to rely on imported energy. I sincerely hope that through the continued pursuit of energy self-sufficiency and independence and a firm rejection of the wild men in the wings, our country can isolate itself from the overseas conflicts which will threaten us during the coming decades.

## CHAPTER 13

# STORM AFTER STORM

Labour's 1979 General Election defeat became unavoidable: Callaghan's mistaken timing, the vicious Party infighting, the 'Winter of Discontent', all had taken a heavy toll and Labour had its lowest share of the polls since 1931. Its vote among skilled workers especially plunged disastrously. A lot of my EETPU members undoubtedly withdrew their support.

According to the lunatic left, the devious British voters kicked out Jim Callaghan because they wanted a more left-wing government, which makes it odd that they put in the most right-wing Conservative administration since the war. The reality was that doctrinaire socialist dogma was overwhelmingly rejected. Labour's post mortem threw up the need for a thorough re-examination of the Party's organisation, policy and structure – that was my union's clear-cut point of view. Many working class voters now shunned Labour, membership continued to decline and the finances were in a sorry state. The NEC's role had become negative and destructive: many of its leading lights ranted and raved at the Callaghan Government, supported it for the three weeks of the election, then returned promptly to the fray. If they kidded anyone with their temporary truce, it wasn't the electorate.

I called for drastic changes: MPs should be selected by the whole Party membership in the constituencies on a one-person, one-vote basis; the NEC should concentrate on organisation, rather than harmful politicking; parties within the Party, like Militant, must get their marching orders; and the unions would have to take their political role more seriously; otherwise, I warned, Labour would be an electoral dinosaur, limping towards extinction.

The necessary re-examination took place. There was a special commission of inquiry, but it led, not to common sense reform, but to still greater disaster. The lemming-like will for self-destruction prevailed and, once again, Jim Callaghan was much to blame for the slide. At the

Party's Bishops Stortford summit conference with the unions in August 1980, he went along tamely with those who sought to remove from Labour MPs the exclusive right to choose the Party leader. A leadership election giving every Party member a vote was worth backing, but short of that it was best to leave it to the MPs. We ended up with the worst of all systems, an arbitrary and undemocratic division of votes between MPs, unions and constituency parties within a trumped-up electoral college. On the matter of re-selection of sitting MPs, I favoured a change, in principle, but the proposal to force constituency parties to hold a contest when they were fully satisfied with their MP was a total absurdity. A one person, one vote system for all the members concerned was again my real preference. I could see that, in practice, the only likely switch would lead to a nest of warring factions and a recipe for further strife.

The third major issue was over who should have the final word in drawing up the election manifesto. I had sat on the NEC sub-committee charged with that task. It was the electorate that must be convinced and it was logical that the leader, who must have conviction in the case he presented, should be entrusted to put the finishing touches. The left wanted a leader in handcuffs. In themselves, the proposed changes might have seeemed innocuous, but they were, of course, subtly designed to strengthen the position of the left and they tore the Party apart. The issue could have been easily resolved in a Party at peace with itself, but not within the Labour Party, always fractious and now introducing these proposals on top of deep divisions of policy and principle between the revolutionary wing and those seeking to retain the old reformist social democratic outlook.

The 1980 Labour Party conference voted for both the electoral college to elect a leader and for compulsory re-selection of MPs, the Bennite left and their motley bedfellows capturing enough union votes to see them home. It was their triumph, but it was a tragedy for the Party. It was followed by the special Party conference at Wembley in January 1981, to decide on the exact composition of the electoral college – a carve-up that proved to be the last straw for a good many Labour moderates, who quit soon afterwards to set up the fledgeling Social Democratic Party.

Between the two fateful conferences, Jim Callaghan resigned as Party leader. Our Executive Council was overwhelmingly in favour of Denis Healey, rather than Michael Foot, to be the new leader. We had a lot of respect for Denis: he thumped the left with gusto and relish and invariably won the arguments against them. His one blemish was his switch from a pro to anti-EEC position for pure expediency. Still, our own union, contrary to the Executive's wishes, had balloted against entry and Denis's EEC antics were not something we held against him now. The left, however, were determined to stop him, since they couldn't afford to have a right-wing toughie of his undoubted calibre leading the Party. Michael Foot was their natural choice – intellectual, indecisive, full of windy rhetoric and still the darling of the left-wing, despite his spell in government.

Labour MPs were under a lot of pressure and many of them were threatened by the re-selection issue. Nevertheless, it was time to stand up and be counted, which was not a habit that came easily to them. I was not surprised to learn that out of our four sponsored MPs only John Grant could be relied upon to support the union's choice and openly to advocate a vote for Healey. The EETPU never sought to impose union policy on our MPs in the manner of some other unions, which did mean that on occasion we paid for their opposition to policies that the union supported. We had no wish to dictate to them, but we might have hoped for a greater sense of responsibility to us at such a crucial time. But MPs looked over their left shoulders, glimpsed those constituency re-selections, and funked it.

It was that attitude, so widespread among Labour MPs, that gave the election to Foot. It is no exaggeration to declare that with Healey in command those who went off to form the Social Democrats may well have stayed inside the Labour Party. Only the hard-liners say 'good riddance' and mean it; most people realise that the split has deprived Labour of power for a very long time and possibly for ever. If Callaghan had got that election timing right ... if Healey had become leader ... the political map today might have looked markedly different.

The special Wembley conference saw a further decisive advance by the left, as the Bennite Rank and File Mobilising Committee, the broad left grouping, did its worst. The conference decided to give 40 per cent of the electoral college votes to the unions, with 30 per cent each for the MPs and constituencies. Shirley Williams, David Owen and Bill Rodgers stomped off to link with Roy Jenkins, now back from his post as President of the EEC Commission, forming the Council for Social Democracy and issuing the Limehouse Declaration. I signed it. I anticipated forthright allies at last in the fierce campaign inside the Party to alter both its face and its policies. If the end product had been our expulsions, I wouldn't have worried, for it would have given us a legitimacy in forming a new party that a walkout didn't really confer. We would then have had no alternative way of presenting our views.

I had slogged it out with the left when some of these latterday assault troops had their heads down in the trenches. Some of them had criticised my stand as too belligerent: Shirley Williams, for instance, admired Jim Callaghan and couldn't understand my caustic appraisal of his weaknesses. I had lunched with Roy Jenkins during his EEC days and, like him, I abhorred the unfairness of Britain's first-past-the-post electoral system. I had long considered that proportional representation would give our people the non-extremist political balance in Parliament which their votes properly demanded. That is why I back the present campaign for proportional representation and electoral reform.

Roy was uncertain at that lunch about his political intentions, but hinted that he might leave Labour. I urged him to come back to fight a Labour seat and said that he could count on EETPU support. But Roy, Shirley and most of the others never had the killer instinct, possessed in abundance by the far left, which is so essential to achieve any kind of victory in Labour's rough-house politics. Of the SDP leaders, David Owen, who I know the least, seems best equipped to come through.

It was easy to put my name to the Limehouse Declaration. The majority of Labour Party members and supporters almost certainly favoured its moderation and common sense; all the more reason to stay inside the Party to punch it out in a war that could still be won. I appreciated the moral and tactical reasons of those who departed and believed that the charge of treachery could better be applied to many of those who stayed and cowered. I contended, though, that if a Labour split was inevitable then it should be the left, not those who truly represented millions of working people, who should be forced to quit. The Labour Party was not the property of the quasi-Marxists and they, not us, were the trespassers. Many of the Party moderates were craven and ingratiating before the left; they were too concerned with their own careers and ambitions to combat the takeover.

There was another overriding consideration for me – my obligation to my own union. We were a bulwark against the left and my deviation would create a new battleground within the EETPU, which would be an invaluable gift to the extremists who never ceased in their efforts to recapture the one-time jewel in their industrial crown. I wanted to help to mobilise trade union moderates to oust the unrepresentative left-wing majority on Labour's NEC; I wanted us to intervene where we could in local Labour Parties. I was concerned, too, because Roy Jenkins declared that a trade union based rescue of Labour was unacceptable. I could see the virtue of that detached position, but it was unreal and utopian. The best prospect for halting the leftward drift lay within the unions and not in the confusion of a new fourth party.

Yet I qualified my position by saying that if the Labour hard-liners eventually emerged rampantly triumphant and the moderates continued to appease the Marxists, while disassociating themselves from social democracy, then the necessity for a new party might become overwhelming. My views were not enough to prevent the now fast-rolling Social Democratic bandwagon. The SDP was established with ruinous consequences for Labour and I am bound to say that the progress of the new party has far exceeded my early expectations and has undoubtedly thrown Britain's political future into the melting pot. Those who gambled courageously to launch it could yet have the last laugh.

Labour's moderates still show few signs of kicking the hard-liners into touch, but the hard left has tightened its grip. Beneath Labour's more acceptable image, the 'Kinnock Look', the same bewhiskered and dangerous policies are largely intact. The unpalatable and undemocratic constitutional changes are on tablets of stone and the right-wing remain on the defensive, unharmonious, unwilling, and unable to carry the fight to the extremist enemy. It is no longer enough to whine that the SDP Gang of Four should have stayed to fight on, for that stable door is shut and the horse has long since bolted. They chose a different option and by any objective yardstick their party offers social democrats a viable alternative, whatever its faults. The perfect party has yet to appear.

These were grim years for Labour and much of its turmoil was reflected inside the TUC. We were in poor shape to handle the jubilant and aggressive Margaret Thatcher following her May 1979 election success. I was soon in TUC action on a familiar theme – the need for constant dialogue with the new Government. I told the TUC Congress that September: 'This is the most doctrinaire of all post-war governments. They seem intent on conducting an onslaught against the organised working class, unparalleled since Taff Vale.' I warned, though, against joining in wrecking the economy and attacked the 'socialism through misery brigade'. Any initial inclination to endorse my lead was short-lived.

The Tories were elected on a pledge to tackle what they, and much of the electorate, saw as abuses of trade union power and the new Employment Secretary, Jim Prior, moved quickly with his Employment Bill. His package was ill thought out, but I stuck to my plea for us to talk to him about it. Blanket opposition and refusal to negotiate would be a cardinal error of judgement. I mistook a tactic for a principle, so often a fault in the Labour and trade union movement.

Prior's closed shop changes would create problems for us, but I said firmly that we couldn't be happy with a system that allowed non-unionists to be sacked out-of-hand after working for an employer for many years. What of the disgraceful way in which craft unions, including mine, found their members dragooned into closed shops implemented by other unions with more members at their place of work? That was not in accord with the spirit of trade unionism. We grew strong as a movement without the closed shop, which often made the unions less socially acceptable. We were foolish to reject all change.

On picketing, the proposals capitalised on the public outrage about the disputes of the previous winter. I cautioned that this issue could be a time bomb, ticking away beneath the Government. Some secondary picketing was difficult to justify, but there were many occasions when a dispute could not be fairly conducted, quite apart from won, without it, particularly when work was physically transferred elsewhere during a stoppage. As for Prior's plans to fund union ballots, we had no hesitation – the EETPU was all for it and our elections were already in line with Government requirements. Democracy is not cheap, though: adherence to the TUC boycott of this government funding has lost us £250,000 over the past five years, cash we could have used to good effect on behalf of our members.

The TUC should, I believed, make concessions over the closed shop and in its attitude to ballot funding in exchange for concessions in our favour on picketing, where we faced far greater danger. The easiest compromise of all could have come on ballots, were it not for the gesture politics of the General Council. David Basnett, by now the TUC Economic Committee chairman, wrote to me on behalf of his General and Municipal Workers' Union to say that they wanted the TUC to advise all unions to ignore the Government money for ballots. The offer was, he claimed, divisive and designed to attract credibility to the bill. It would give the Government's Certification Officer control over the conduct and content of ballots and, if accepted, would encourage the Tories to make them mandatory.

I replied that the row over this would distract everyone from the 'far more pernicious sections relating to picketing'. The TUC would alienate the public by throwing out the ballot proposals; using public funds for ballots was no different from the TUC's use of state money for trade union education. Those arguments were repeated inside the General Council, but only the AUEW leaders voted with me.

There were some fruitless meetings with Prior. I met him back in the days of the Heath Government and he was a decent enough cove. He was not really anti-union but he now had a manifesto obligation to fulfil. I stayed away from TUC meetings with him about the new legislation, telling my TUC colleagues that I didn't agree with them and didn't want to embarrass them by saying so if Prior sought my view. There was inevitable deadlock. The total disagreement over the Bill and the more general TUC hostility to Government economic policies fuelled demands for the half-baked Day of Action, called by the TUC for 14 May 1980. It was to prove among the most tempestuous of my many defiant TUC offensives.

The proposed stoppage was an absurd and irresponsible way to show our disapproval. My Executive Council denounced it in advance as 'untimely and unwise' and we told our members to make up their own minds whether to work or not. They were left in no doubt about what we thought they should do. My own publicly-expressed advice to them pulled no punches: I said that this kind of protest called into question the seriousness of the TUC's concern about the nation's economic plight. In one newspaper article I wrote: 'It is a sad day for democracy. It takes us nearer to a different political system than the one we have now. Democracy cannot function if Government policies are to be changed, not through the ballot box, but through the disruption of industry through political strikes. If that happens, a real can of worms will be opened up and the way paved for either a right or left-wing dictatorship.'

If the demonstration succeeded, it would weaken democracy; if it failed, it would weaken the TUC and the unions. It was a no-win situation. As it turned out, the Day of Action flopped and far fewer workers than expected took any time off at all. Len Murray put the best face on it: he actually called it a success but added, at a General Council meeting, that it was no weakness that the TUC was more advanced in its views than the union membership and public opinion generally. It was tantamount to a confession that the TUC was out of touch, that most of the union rank and file spurned the whole pointless fiasco.

The left branded me a saboteur and inside the General Council I was said to be 'culpable of causing confusion'. I simply repeated the need to forget the belligerent rhetoric and to get back to representing members' views in a renewed dialogue with the Government. The fury was not entirely confined to the left, but not only was I unrepentant, I was proved right. That really hurt.

There was another running battle which upset quite a few General Council members: I accused them of being 'inconsistent and hypo-critical' over human rights and I argued my case at the full General Council, in the International Committee and in correspondence with Len Murray. The TUC protested about infringements in non-Com-munist states but protests were rare and muted where Communist governments were involved. The TUC, I pointed out, had refused to talk to the fascist puppet unions in Spain and Portugal and assisted their strikers and underground trade union movements, yet they behaved very differently towards people imprisoned in the Soviet Union for trying to establish independent trade unions. I declared that those who 'refused to become tools of Soviet oppression' were met by character assassination, smears and ridicule at TUC conferences.

The highly unsatisfactory upshot of my assault was that the General Council timidly approved a 7,000-word document acquitting itself on all charges. It reiterated its policy of judging every issue concerning the defence of specific trade union freedoms on its merits and being circumspect and sparing in taking stands on issues involving general human rights, which could better be dealt with by Amnesty Inter-national. I labelled this lamentable response: 'doublespeak behaviour which betrayed the worldwide struggle for human rights'.

This rumpus was barely over when another started: the TUC Economic Committee arranged a visit to Poland to discuss trade and economic affairs, and my Executive Council took strong exception to the proposed visit. We presented a list of pointed questions for the TUC to pose if they insisted on going. We urged a probe over cheap labour, which was unable to strike or form independent trade unions and was being used to make products which were dumped on the United Kingdom market. We expressed concern about Western capital in-vested in Poland which should have been used to update our own industries. The planned trip was overtaken by events in Poland – strikes, brutal repression by the authorities, internment for trade unionists and the suppression of Solidarity, the independent union headed by Lech Walesa, the courageous shipyard electrician. I argued that the TUC should only go to Poland if the delegation could meet Walesa and other Solidarity people.

There was a fierce debate at the General Council. Jim Slater, of the seamen's union, said it was only worth talking to the state-run unions! More surprisingly, Geoffrey Drain, the moderate NALGO man, said that he wouldn't give any support to a Catholic organisation like Solidarity. I got pretty heated and said that religion should have nothing to do with it, we were talking about freedom. I toughened my stance and demanded that the visit should be scrubbed. As the whole sordid business came out into the open, the shamefaced General Council slowly backed down. They decided that they wanted to meet representatives of workers' committees at the plants they visited and others concerned in 'recent trade union developments'.

At the 1980 TUC Congress, David Basnett, very much on the defensive, put the General Council's case for making the visit. He explained that the Polish TUC said that it would do its best to meet the wishes of our delegation and appealed to me to withdraw an emergency motion from my union to avoid division. I refused and said the General Council seemed to be expressing embarrassment and almost irritation that the Polish workers' actions would create unnecessary difficulties for 'this cosy delegation trip'. I took a sideswipe at Lord Carrington, the Foreign Secretary, who had merely said that it was all an internal affair of the Polish Government. I called for full support and solidarity with the Polish workers.

David Basnett tried a last platform ploy. He invited me to join him on the 'cosy' trip which I had adamantly turned down. There was some laughter when I retorted: 'Let me say to David that if he could guarantee I would be coming back, I wouldn't mind going.' Our motion didn't win the Congress vote but I reckoned that the growing public pressure would bring a Polish Government veto anyway. My stand forced the TUC to hedge the trip with conditions and to say things publicly which indicated that it would all turn sour and be bad propaganda for the Polish Communists.

I continued my attacks and, sure enough, the Polish Government cancelled the visit, much to David Basnett's annoyance. I urged Len Murray to wind up TUC relations with the old state-controlled General Council of Trade Unions in Poland, their TUC, and to forge links with Solidarity. I pressed the Labour Party to sever all contacts with East European Communist parties that were deeply involved in repression of Polish workers and to stop inviting them to Labour Party conferences.

There was continuing trouble in Poland and the General Council did express its revulsion at events there to the Polish Ambassador, calling on East European trade union centres to influence their governments on behalf of Polish workers. It was progress.

The TUC International Committee met Lord Carrington at the Foreign Office over the shooting of Polish workers by their police and the internment of trade unionists. Carrington was sympathetic but then astonished me: he told us that what he was saying was 'against my political creed' but much of the unrest arose because the Polish peasant farmers were not collectivised fast enough to produce the goods the nation needed. I nearly fell off my chair. I remonstrated with him so strongly that Tom Jackson, leading our delegation, stressed that I was speaking for myself and not for the International Committee. Carrington must have swallowed a Foreign Office brief for breakfast.

More than a year later our diplomatic apologists for the Polish Government were still at it. I spoke at a British 'Solidarity with Poland' meeting at the Royal Albert Hall and my message was short, sharp and thunderously applauded. I called on British unions to break all ties with East European puppet unions; to campaign for the release of Polish political and trade union prisoners; to demand an end to military rule and to restrictions on Solidarity; and to 'black' Polish and other Communist bloc goods. I said that western banks should refuse to reschedule existing loans to Poland and I called for the east-west Yalta agreement, which divided Europe, to be re-negotiated or renounced. Geoffrey Rippon, MP, was on the same platform for the Tories and Denis Healey was there for Labour. They must have been using the same lousy Foreign Office brief, for both appeared to be more preoccupied with protecting bankers' money on loan to Poland than with trying to give democracy there a chance.

1980 was a turbulent year for me – human rights, the Day of Action, Poland – and the menacing Isle of Grain dispute produced some of its worst moments. The completion of the Isle of Grain power station was now some six years behind schedule and the cost had soared from an estimated £350,000,000 to more than £800,000,000. The Central Electricity Generating Board, far from blameless in allowing the site chaos, finally got fed up with escalating earnings and pay strikes and tightened up agreements. The General and Municipal Workers' Union laggers were among those asked to take a cutback; they heaved out three settlements negotiated by their own officials and struck. The CEGB got tough. It threatened to close the site and the other unions agreed to provide alternative labour. I had tried to get David Basnett, the GMWU leader, to take an interest months before it all blew up; the inter-union dangers loomed, but he did nothing that helped.

The laggers formed a violent picket line and there were some ugly incidents: stones were thrown; workers were bussed in with police protection, amid jeers and attempted harrassment. We never had more than one of our members directly concerned in the lagging operation, but my EETPU colleague, Eric Hammond, joined John Baldwin, the AUEW construction workers official, in one of the buses that crossed the picket lines. It was a show of solidarity with the men trying to keep the site open. While the trouble dragged on, Eric and I were at a conference in Brighton. We were cornered after a meeting in the back room of a seafront hotel by half a dozen burly laggers who threatened us with a beating. We managed to get into the hotel lobby before there were any fisticuffs, but it was a nasty moment.

The bitterness between the unions gave the TUC dreadful trouble when its 'inner cabinet', the Finance and General Purposes Committee, tried to resolve the dispute. It produced a peace formula which it said was equitable. If the individual unions then rejected their advice, they could be carpeted by the General Council, reported to Congress and suspended. Both the AUEW and ourselves did reject it. It was a tense situation. The full General Council discussed it and Len Murray blamed the CEGB for refusing terms to the GMWU laggers and making the work available to members of other unions. The TUC proposals favoured the laggers and David Basnett had no difficulty in accepting them.

The AUEW's Terry Duffy said that the TUC advice would only harden attitudes and called for a meeting of the General Secretaries of all the unions concerned to try to work out a solution. I said bluntly that the GMWU was wholly to blame, not the unions working to keep the site open and save some 1,600 jobs; the laggers prevented an expansion of the workforce and their greed and lack of regard for other workers had nothing to do with trade unionism. It was ludicrous for the TUC to support the laggers when the overwhelming majority of union members on the site were against them. Nevertheless, the General Council backed the formula by 27 votes to 4. I denounced the laggers publicly and said that they had 'hijacked' the job. Eventually, the AUEW backed down. We were ready to stand by the engineers but our direct interest was peripheral. Moreover, we realised that the TUC formula would never be implemented by the men at the site, whatever we did, and in fact the existing arrangements, which kept out the laggers, were simply maintained until that part of the site was complete. Len Murray knew all along that it would almost certainly end that way, but he had scored the technical victory he wanted.

I had blotted my copybook all over the place. My attacks on union misdemeanours during the 'Winter of Discontent', on the misguided Day of Action, on the hypocrisy over Poland and now on the TUC's cockeyed Isle of Grain peace formula, added up to a thumping indictment of my behaviour – or so the left, always out to do me, reckoned. They seized their chance. TGWU leader Moss Evans was pushed into the vanguard of hostilities, but he is a decent enough fellow and it wasn't personal. Moss is the least offensive man ever to be General Secretary of his union – that was his trouble. Some of us used to call him 'Mouse' because he was such a pliant creature in the hands of his left-dominated union Executive Council and of conspiring TUC figures like Clive Jenkins and Ken Gill.

As a senior General Council member, I was now one of the Committee to Select Committees. It met straight after the 1980 Congress and I was the quarry: without any advance warning, the left pushed through a proposal to kick me off the TUC 'inner cabinet'. David Basnett, embittered by our clashes over Poland and the Isle of Grain, backed them. He was doubtless also influenced by the close relationship he then enjoyed with Clive Jenkins. Len Murray warned the Committee not to play into my hands by making a martyr of me, but he got nowhere. I decided to let them get on with it and didn't vote.

By the time the General Council met, some support had mustered and, somewhat surprisingly, Lawrence Daly of the miners was first off the mark. He said that we frequently disagreed, but removing members from committees in this way was wrong and divisive. Moss Evans was clearly carrying the left-wing banner: the unions, he complained, were ridiculed by my public criticisms. David Basnett said that I embarrassed and undermined the TUC and hid behind the General Council's tolerance of dissent. Terry Duffy and Sid Weighell jumped in for me, the latter saying that the General Council was undermining its own credibility. 'Who's next?' he remarked, prophetically. He wasn't to know that it would be him – shortly to be unceremoniously dumped as chairman of the TUC Transport Committee in another left coup. Tom Jackson backed me and Sir John Boyd, the AUEW General Secretary, said that the suggestion that I helped to sabotage the Day of Action ignored the fact that few unions could mobilise their members for it.

I told them: 'For being more frank about my views than some other members, who sometimes privately agree with me, an example is being made of me.' The General Council, I said, could only damage itself by going ahead. Len Murray had the last word: the General Council, he said, should let the movement judge if I had brought it into ridicule. He warned against setting a dangerous precedent, but a mixed variety of members allied to endorse the Committee verdict by twenty-one votes to twelve.

It was no skin off my nose; outside, the decision was seen as mean and spiteful. A year later, I was not only restored to the 'inner cabinet', but found myself on more major TUC committees than all but two of the other General Council members. That was in addition to the Neddy Six, the TUC–Labour Party Liaison Committee and a host of other bodies requiring TUC nominees. I would cheerfully have dropped any one of them to lighten the workload.

There was a movement at last over the reform of TUC structure and David Basnett, so often weak and vacillating, was prepared to have a go at it. He pointed out to the General Council that the 1979 Congress told us to consider fully the so-called automaticity plan and we hadn't carried out that duty. He met counter-arguments and action was shelved – by twenty votes to ten – but Basnett, Terry Duffy and some other leaders of major unions, of whom I was one, were groping their way forward. The signs were hopeful and the issue certainly couldn't be allowed to go away.

There were often occasions when I could have joined in the TUC scrum, but refrained. My position was well enough known and I recognised that my intervention could sometimes have been counter-productive. There were times, though, when I stressed that my silence must not be taken as agreement. That was mostly the case as we moved to the next Government industrial relations package – the Tebbit Bill. There were renewed shouts from the left for withdrawal of all TUC co-operation from the Government and for the removal of all our people. from all governmental bodies and agencies, but I believed that such action would be self-defeating and could only prevent us from defending our members' interests; it was a view Len Murray shared. He told the General Council: 'We shouldn't threaten what we can't deliver.'

Nor was the TUC likely to frighten Norman Tebbit, who had replaced Jim Prior as Employment Secretary. I quickly formed the impression that Tebbit was not only very ambitious for political promotion, but also that his own trade union background in the airline pilots' union, admittedly pretty limited, nevertheless gave him a 'feel' for the job. He understood the weaknesses of the TUC leadership. He was no typical Tory and would be a mean and worthy opponent. He did reach some wrong conclusions, though: he might have been a bit less enthusiastic to quote my anti-Red speeches to the House of Commons, a certain kiss of death for me; but he thought a great deal about the issues and I stick by my early impression of his capability.

The argument over the Tebbit Bill rumbled on into 1982, with the left still pushing for withdrawal from Government agencies, including Neddy. There was not much pro-Neddy affection among Ministers – the Prime Minister's scepticism was well known – but the outcry if she had axed it was not worth having. If the TUC were to destroy it, unwittingly doing the Government's dirty work for it, we would get the odium. I have my reservations about Neddy, but if we didn't have it we would have to invent it, or something very like it. True, government, unions and employers try to use it for their own propaganda ends and tangible results are scarce, though last year's energy price discussions there had some effect on Ministers' decisions.

Neddy does, however, provide a forum for tripartite talks on the national economy between the main parties involved. People do let their hair down from time to time and Michael Heseltine, whose golden locks are legendary in Tory circles at least, was one. It was in the aftermath of the Toxteth riots, when he was Environment Secretary, and he offered a long and agonising appraisal of the lessons to be drawn from what happened and of the grave dangers of ignoring unemployment. It was a quite remarkable performance from a member of a Cabinet presiding over three million-plus out of work. He shook other Ministers as much as he did the TUC team, to judge by their expressions.

The Prime Minister occasionally chaired Neddy meetings, mainly, it seemed, to give us a lecture. I said to a TUC colleague at one meeting: 'You'd think we were a lot of bloody schoolkids.' For all that, I respect her as someone who appears to stick to her guns. I have met her personally at functions and she seems much nicer than her abrasive public image would suggest. Not that trade union leaders are supposed to hobnob with Tory Prime Ministers. There was one amusing occasion when David Basnett, Moss Evans and I were at meetings together for much of the day, including one with Sir Keith Joseph, then Industry Secretary. That evening we all turned up at a Downing Street cocktail party with our wives. None of us had told the others in advance that we were going and we were all suitably surprised when we met there.

Neddy members sometimes met for working dinners and I clashed at one of them with Norman Tebbit. I said to him: 'If you are right about the unions and high pay and pricing men out of jobs, then those countries with no unions or only state-controlled ones, should be flourishing. It's just not happening. Look at the South American dictatorships or at Eastern Europe. If you carry your argument to its limit, a slave society is best where there's no pay at all.' 'I don't believe that,' he replied, but he didn't say what he did believe.

Right-wing economists usually fail to answer that case. High pay is not a major problem in Britain; poor management and lack of investment are far more responsible for our difficulties. Trade unions may not have helped overmuch and their antagonism towards management, rather than co-operation with it, has sometimes made a bad situation worse, but the situation is not of union making: the movement is simply a handy scapegoat. If the TUC would accept its own shortcomings, if General Council members were not stuffed full of their socialist society pipe-dreams, then our criticisms of unacceptable Government policies would merit more attention and would carry more weight.

The Tebbit Bill was bad law, likely to bring more chaos than clarity to industrial relations and doing nothing to raise productivity or to lower unit labour costs. I see no reason to modify that view now that the legislation has been in operation for some two years. Substantial changes are needed if it is not to cause more outbreaks of disruption; the Government should have the sense to be flexible in the light of experience, if their prejudices will let them. The Tories contend that trade unions interfere with the efficiency of the labour market – but so does the flu, bad communications, difficult travelling facilities or housing needs. Removing union immunities has not aided Britain's economic recovery and the risk of disgruntled individuals making life difficult for their unions through repetitious court actions continues.

The TUC fell into a trap: it failed to avoid giving justification to the unwanted and undesirable changes the Government was set on introducing. Public opinion polls could not be brushed aside and they told us that trade union members dislike many of the decisions taken by their unions on their behalf, that many of them favoured reforms, Tory-style or not. By indiscriminate resistance, we played into the Government's hands. I doubt if we could have got much out of Tebbit, but we would have got some marks for trying. As it was, he made us look obdurate and his package was enacted virtually intact.

The left argued that it was all a bid to destroy union power and that argument was not without some validity, but many of those who pressed most strongly for industrial action, boycotts and so on, were no defenders of trade union freedom. Nor are they now. They believe that once the trade unions have served their purpose of demolishing capitalism, then they themselves must be demolished or else brought under the complete control of the party in power.

## CHAPTER 14

# MR CHAIRMAN DEVIATES

'I am reliably informed that I have to watch what I say this week because it may affect my promotion.' Those were my opening words from the rostrum when I spoke for the EETPU at the 1982 TUC Congress in Brighton. The air was heavy with rumours of an unprecedented breach in the hallowed TUC tradition of Buggins' turn, which should have seen me elected as TUC Chairman by the incoming General Council. People sidled up to me to whisper that my past transgressions seemed bound to scupper my chances and the left certainly discussed the possibility of opposing me and how best to do it. They hoped for a topical excuse, prayed that I would put my foot in it during the conference week: I was the TUC's stormy petrel and anything could happen.

Len Murray, on the other hand, told me that so far as he was concerned it was all beyond argument and I think that he let that be known to my critics. It was important to him that the framework within which the TUC operates should not be upset while it still served its purpose. Precedents are very important at the TUC and preventing my chairmanship might lead to further consequences than could be foreseen. The same tactic could be used against a left-wing contender on some future occasion and, moreover, I would have been a danger, running loose and feeling cheated. I decided to play it all low key to give the left the least possible excuse to vote me down.

Even so, as I told Congress in that speech, there were things that had to be said and principles to stand by. The debate was the familiar one – the clash between pay policy and unfettered free collective bargaining. The left was fiercely determined to adhere to the latter position and to reject a more orderly approach, even under another Labour Government. I stressed that past pay policies had helped the lower paid. I didn't like pay restraint and nor did my union, but ordinary workers, I claimed, look for a sensible policy on pay and prices. A decision against incomes policy would be used 'to sink the next Labour government's economic policies'.

It was an argument we had been having privately inside the TUC-Labour Party Liaison Committee and other meetings where Shadow Cabinet members like Peter Shore and Eric Varley did their best to instil economic common sense. It was pretty hopeless: Moss Evans rounded on Terry Duffy and me for pressing him to help. He was trussed up by TGWU policy and unwilling to even try to move it along. Those meetings were full of politicians' gas and irrelevant soul-searching. There was no advance at the Congress either and I was on the losing side again in the debate. However, mine was a temperate contribution and I presented no stick for the left to beat me with.

The General Council met briefly before we all went home from Brighton and the only real business was to pick the next Chairman. Alan Sapper, the previous year's Chairman, presided. Mick McGahey, the miners' Communist vice-president, caused a momentary flutter. It was his first-ever General Council meeting, but he was cocky enough to suggest that I might be asked to give an undertaking that I would carry out TUC policy if I was elected. McGahey had over-reached himself. There were some hostile reactions around the table and cries of 'it's never been done before' and 'rubbish'. Len Murray formally nominated me, I was elected unopposed and took over the chair for the rest of the meeting. My first job was to welcome the new General Council members: 'I want to reassure the General Council that when acting on their behalf I will do no differently to what I have always done and will support their policies. I reserve the right, like all previous chairmen, to my own opinions and to expressing them whenever I feel it necessary to do so. I now have to welcome Michael McGahey as a new member and we will not require any undertakings from him.'

One of the earliest misfortunes during my TUC Chairmanship was the shock resignation of Sid Weighell from his post as NUR General Secretary. Sid had pluck as well as skill and was a tiger against the far left, who witch-hunted him for years. He was a great loss to the General Council and my sorrow at his departure was only matched by the hard-liners' delight. They knew that the union moderates were now without one of their most formidable and one of their few outspoken champions. Sid argued strenuously for a different TUC structure, seeking more central authority so that the unions could keep their bargains – could deliver as well as demand.

I had backed him strongly only a few months earlier in the acrimonious flexible rostering dispute with ASLEF, the loco' men's union. The long-running row was dropped in the lap of the TUC 'inner cabinet' to sort out and we gathered at Congress House. Clive Jenkins thought he had things lined up for his friend Ray Buckton, the ASLEF General Secretary, but he was quite wrong. As soon as the meeting began, I said: 'I want to make it clear that, if we sit here until next week, I will not endorse the ASLEF position.' 'Next week' looked like no idle threat as the meeting crawled on. There was no shortage of information or views, but much of it conflicted. I said that we should advise the train drivers to call off the stoppage in their own interests, as much as those of the trade union movement, and there was a one-vote Committee majority against backing them at that stage. ASLEF's supporters were led by Moss Evans, with Clive Jenkins pulling the strings, and they talked on, trying to inch more support. Alan Sapper, in the chair, didn't realise that he could vote – something I later put him right on when I took over as Chairman.

We wrangled on and on into the night and through it, either at Congress House or at the London headquarters of the Advisory Conciliation and Arbitration Service. It was twenty-seven hours from the start before I left for home. The left finally acknowledged that their case was shallow and caved in; it was a near-disaster, but ASLEF was told to call off the strike and to accept flexible rostering. Of course, we were accused of a sell-out, the tired old cry that goes up whenever the TUC refuses to send the unions on a suicidal course. Our decision allowed Ray Buckton to save face and duck behind the TUC in a strike which threatened to collapse under him.

Sid Weighell emerged with credit, but it was one more black mark against him in the far left book. They intensified their efforts to get him and pounced on the Labour Party Conference rumpus over the way he cast the NUR block vote. His departure has meant that a customarily moderate union has moved rapidly to the left, hardly a reflection of what the ordinary railwayman wants.

This was the year of automaticity, of TUC structural reform. The issue was predominant and the fierce controversy made it a most difficult year for me as Chairman. Opinion on the General Council was fairly evenly divided and on a number of occasions, in addition to voting as the EETPU representative, I used my casting vote to break a deadlock. It was even more rare for the TUC General Secretary to vote, but Len Murray did so on this key matter. The row over structure ran on all the way to the 1983 Congress. The 'inner cabinet' made re-commendations, but a poor turnout of moderates at the full General Council saw proposals tossed back for further consideration. The left refused to give up and brought up a range of side-issues to prolong the squabble in the hope that they might ultimately win.

The General Council's pro-Soviet faction often met beforehand to line up their votes and their contributions at the meetings. They could be relied on to vote as a group for any left-wing cause unless it gave credit to the Trotskyites. There were various attempts to counter this by the moderates, but they never worked out and I gave up hope for them. That TGWU block vote was always in the background and moderates who didn't want to alienate the TGWU often took the easy way out and deliberately stayed away from meetings.

There was an extraordinary unworldliness about many of these left–right struggles, like so much of what goes on at Congress House. It was not in the same crackpot class as Labour's NEC, but decisions are represented as the legitimate TUC view, influence the Labour Party and then reflect back again onto the wider trade union movement. They have little or nothing to do with what goes on in the plants, the factories and the offices, or with the practical everyday problems of industrial survival. What is legitimate? If a resolution goes through at Congress, are those who refuse to argue for it traitors, acting against the movement's best interests? The right-wing try to deflect unreasonable demands which they know are not truly representative, but they are democrats and are wrong-footed.

There is a peculiar illusion that the Communists are nicer than the Trotskyites, that they are more logical, that you can make a bargain with them. Their simple logic is to get you in a position where they can cut your throat. Theirs is a singular approach – power at any price – and they are far more sinister than the Trots, despite the latter's disruptive and damaging Labour entryism. If the Communists and their sup-porters are in the minority, they show no squeamishness, but only contempt for the majority. They will intimidate or outwit the majority so that they can direct and control the situation and this happens wherever they have a foothold, just as it does on the TUC General Council where their hold is rather more substantial.

There are those who know all this but seldom act and those who don't want to know. The key figure among the TUC moderates is David Basnett, who wanted to 'lead' the General Council and remains best placed to do so. He is the senior and most experienced General Council

180

member and also heads the third biggest union. Unfortunately, he is a great disappointment. He too often falters, has second thoughts, and he appears to believe in unity even if it buries him. Even now he could do much to bring the movement back to sanity, to save it, before he retires. Basnett is a moderate, even conservative, man; my appeal to him is to stop trimming and to stand up for what he really believes in.

I did my best to behave with restraint and impartiality in chairing the General Council and various TUC committees throughout the year, but it was often a tricky task in the face of some of the left-wing tricks and antics. Still, I managed to keep my naturally rumbustious temperament in check. Despite that, I was involved in perhaps the most remarkable incident to happen to any TUC Chairman in office. I found myself inadvertently on the verge of exploding a huge bombshell in the middle of Labour's faltering General Election campaign. I earned headlines, the vitriolic anger and abuse of the left and the deep displeasure of the entire Labour establishment. My crime: to publicly endorse ex-Labour Minister John Grant as an SDP Parliamentary candidate.

It was an independent act of loyalty towards an old friend. I said on his behalf: 'He is a man of integrity who can be relied on to keep his promises and stand by the principles on which he fights the election. If you elect him, it will be a wise choice and one you will not regret.' I made it clear that this was personal backing for someone I had known for more than twenty years, but those few lines were political dynamite and the outcry was immediate. Arthur Scargill and the Communist Mick McGahey fired the first salvoes. Scargill is a big-mouth and a raging egomaniac who ceaselessly plays to the gallery of the far left and spends much of his time manipulating the media he professes to despise. He called my statement 'outrageous' and demanded my resignation as TUC Chairman, making it plain that he would raise the matter at the next General Council meeting. My critics were out in force too, at one or two union conferences that were in session, including that of SOGAT, the print union.

I determined to get in first and make my own statement to the General Council. I saw Len Murray and told him what I mentioned to no one else: that I had agreed to sponsor John Grant at a time when it was expected that the election would be in October, by which time I would have left the General Council. When the early election was announced John phoned to free me from my promise, but I said: 'No. I'll do it. I want to do it.' That, I told Len, was not for the General

181

Council's ears. I had never intended to embarrass them, but I was offering no excuses. Len was both astonished and angered when I insisted that I would seek a vote of confidence and would resign if I didn't get it.

I was clear as a bell on this: if Scargill and his gang were spoiling for a fight, they could have one. If I went, the onus would be on them for provoking a major crisis and they would collect the brickbats in the quite stupendous public brawl that was sure to follow. I refused to be contrite and not only was I prepared to resign, but my statement to the General Council was in my pocket – along with a second statement, in anticipation of my losing the vote. It was ready for the press, waiting eagerly below in the Congress House lobby. If I went, it would free me completely from my obligation to support TUC policy and the Labour Party, a thought that certainly occurred to David Basnett, Chairman of the Trade Unions for a Labour Victory set-up, and to Len Murray.

Just before I opened the meeting, there was one crumb of comfort: I felt pretty isolated, but one senior General Council member said to me quite openly: 'If the truth is known there are a large number of people around this table who would have to say that John Grant was the most helpful junior Minister we ever had at the Department of Employment.' That was right. Even now, the General Council still gets Government funds for a scheme started on John's initiative when he was in the Labour Government.

I told the General Council that I wanted to make a statement and that took most of them by surprise. I said I wouldn't fudge the issue, but that I was taken aback by the remarks of some colleagues who usually claimed, on their own behalf, the right to do and say as they pleased. I added: 'I have no doubt that a detailed examination of what has happened inside union conferences would reveal the clamour to have been orchestrated by the usual cabal of Communists and fellow travellers.' Then I shook them: since there was a resignation demand, I wanted a vote of confidence, otherwise 'I shall resign from the chair forthwith'. David Basnett was quick off the mark and moved 'next business'. Len Murray emphasised that mine was a personal statement. Scargill and McGahey jumped up and down, muttering and spluttering, dubbing me 'traitor' and 'turncoat', but there was no debate and Basnett's motion was carried by nineteen votes to ten.

It was not what I had sought, but I could hardly quit in the circumstances: the majority were, in effect, telling Scargill to belt up.

He complained bitterly of a gag and Jim Slater, of the seamen, stalked out in synthetic protest. I was as piqued as they were – that second statement was burning a hole in my pocket. I had fully expected to make it and was mentally tuned up to do so. In it, I said that since I didn't get the confidence vote I was honour bound to resign and I continued: 'I have done so with great regret for, after forty-six years as an active trade unionist, being Chairman of the TUC was a great accolade which has been diminished by petty vindictiveness and politically orchestrated intimidation. Those who have supported, as well as those who have led, such attacks are a disgrace to the movement. Rank and file trade unionists everywhere should take note of the fact that the General Council has not condemned its Communist members who support candidates standing against Labour all around the country: neither have they condemned Arthur Scargill who is seeking to set up a Communist front "Miners' International".'

My statement said that those in the forefront of the attacks on me also backed Soviet actions in Afghanistan and Poland and supported links with East European puppet unions. They were the people who found my three sentences of support for a Social Democrat 'such a great crime'. I recorded that John had been a personal friend for twenty-three years and was formerly sponsored by the EETPU, and that although his party allegiance had changed his politics remained the same. The EETPU backed Labour and had just given the Party £130,000. I concluded: 'I think that ordinary decent men and women will understand that I was not prepared to compromise an honourable friendship for the sake of political expediency. I have never been prepared to be intimidated into doing damage to what I really believe.'

I wasn't seeking martyrdom, but I had no real heart for Labour's lost election cause and no time for its reckless policies. I was utterly dismayed by the extremists who gripped so much of the Party and by the gutlessness of the moderates. Enforced resignation, with all this on my mind, would be no great punishment. I admit that I was disappointed and frustrated by the outcome at the time, though in retrospect it was probably just as well that I stayed on. I still had a further sizeable contribution to make at the TUC, particularly as President of the forthcoming Congress.

My fears and misgivings about Labour were in keeping with those of the electorate: on 9 June 1983, they sent Margaret Thatcher to 10 Downing Street with a massive majority; Labour was routed with 119 lost deposits and the lowest average vote per candidate since 1900. A vote for Labour, not one for the SDP/Liberal Alliance, was a wasted vote in half the country. It all added up to more unemployment and fresh attacks on trade union organisation; another Tory victory in 1988 could leave the trade unions as crippled as the Labour Party and that grim prospect had to be faced.

Once again I aired my thoughts publicly, this time in *The Times*. I called for hard thinking, not sentimentality, and declared: 'The greatest problem we face can be summed up as Socialism or Survival. So long as trade union leaders elevate the idea of socialism above all else, the greater the risk to the future of the trade union movement.' There was plenty more, including a call for proportional representation which might veto socialism but would also veto rampant anti-unionism. I said too, that if the unions were not so completely tied to Labour's coat-tails, they could have urged their members to vote SDP or Liberal where they had a better chance of winning. 'Over and over again,' I said, 'our loyalty to Labour let the Tories in on June 9th.' I warned that if Labour couldn't save itself, the unions had to consider their own survival: 'Anything less would be a betrayal of working people.'

It was hardly heresy now the election was over, but Len Murray, sensitive as ever, said publicly that I spoke for myself. That was self-evident but Mick McGahey told the next General Council meeting that the article was 'a campaign against the policy of the TUC'. Len's statement was endorsed, but it was all pretty feeble. They were licking their wounds. There were various unofficial pamphlets circulated by the left to draw attention to my inactivity on behalf of Labour during the election. They were right, I was inactive, and I couldn't speak with conviction for Labour's key policies. I kept quiet about them rather than damage the Party and now I was condemned for that.

The lessons of the election debacle certainly took time to sink in for some trade unionists. Union conferences held after the election, including that of the TGWU, endorsed and even applauded the same discredited policies that had brought defeat – and dishonestly blamed the presentation of the manifesto for its failure at the polls. That reaction said far more about the unrepresentative composition of union conferences than it did about the views of rank and file trade unionists.

Mick McGahey told the Scottish miners that it was Callaghan, Chapple, Hattersley and Healey who were responsible for Labour's hiding. He omitted to mention that the Communist Party – of which he is a prominent member – put up thirty-six Parliamentary candidates and that even their derisory votes were at the expense of Labour candidates.

## CHAPTER 15

# 'CHAPPLE'S CONGRESS'

The intensive politicking in the run-up to the TUC's 115th Annual Congress ensured that two issues were predominant when we got to brash and breezy Blackpool, both of them massively important to the TUC's future. They would shape the way we conducted ourselves in the difficult period ahead and would consequently dictate the degree of influence we could hope to have elsewhere on behalf of our 10,500,000 members.

The first of those issues was that whole vexed question of automaticity – a word now established as part of the TUC's gruesome vocabulary, but necessarily coined to sum up the rights of individual unions to gain automatic representation on the incoming General Council. Automaticity had certainly brought out the ugliest side of my trade union brothers as they jockeyed and intrigued for power and places throughout my year of chairmanship. The way that Congress handled that hottest of hot potatoes could dramatically affect the General Council's balance and hence its attitude to the fast-changing world around it. The second, even more emotive, issue was whether we could any longer sustain our thoroughly indecent heads-in-the-sands posture of refusing to talk to the nation's legitimately elected Government.

We met against a grim backcloth: TUC membership had slumped by 500,000 in a year; the cash coffers of many individual unions were in a parlous state and our overall power was unquestionably at a post-war low. Industrially stricken, we were politically even more impotent: we had thrown in our lot with Labour and the nation unmistakably intended us to share in the general election rebuff it so rudely delivered. Labour's internal strife had cost us dear, yet the unions had created, or failed abysmally to prevent, so much of the trouble. It was *our* crackpot policies which Labour had peddled: the TUC-Labour Party Liaison Committee could not be wished away, nor could those undemocratic block votes used maladroitly to enshrine the still more undemocratic constitutional absurdities of Labour's recent past. Labour's leaders, as always, kow-towed to their union paymasters and we got what we asked for whenever we asked for it.

The British people aren't daft. They saw it all and didn't like it. We remained Labour's albatross – not as blatant in our unhelpful interventions as in 1979, but nonetheless seen to be unhealthily in charge of what was probably the most divided and least relevant political team the Party has ever fielded for any general election. If the unions had cleaned up the Party, we would have had a fighting chance, but, all the way from 1979, we funked the tough action that was so urgently needed. What could we expect? Our top people were at odds with each other and our policies were wrong. Margaret Thatcher had little to beat: a few more days of electioneering could well have seen Labour trailing the SDP/Liberal Alliance in a disastrous third place. The unions were not simply the crippled victims of an economic slump beyond our control; they were also guilty of a chronic inertia, clouded perception and poverty of intellect for which the blame could not be blithely shifted to others.

There was a crisis of TUC leadership and perhaps that was the real root of the trouble. Time was when big men sat at the General Council table and looked beyond narrow party dogma and self-interest, to wider concerns. I have referred to my admiration for Frank Cousins before I became a member of the General Council and, indeed, one of the few accolades in the early years of our leadership had been a telegram from him to our conference at Scarborough, thanking us for our union's support at the Ford Motor Company, Dagenham, for their ten sacked TGWU shop stewards. We were, I might add, the only union to show solidarity.

I managed no such rapport with Jack Jones, with whom I frequently clashed, yet he was at least a heavyweight. George Woodcock had the intellect, but seemed to disdain both the movement and those for whom it spoke – hardly my kind of trade union leader. Like them or loathe them though, all these men had stature; today's TUC is submerged in mediocrity. Terry Duffy battles on and a handful of the younger newcomers offer hope, but they are all too few in number. Union power peaked in the 1970s and stayed on that plateau all the way to the 1979 'winter of discontent'; then we threw it away. That same power sabotaged the return of Callaghan and his Labour Government and

187

every union leader is uncomfortably aware of it, whatever their more public blatherings.

By 1983, we posed no threat at all to Mrs Thatcher, defused as we were by our own behaviour and by four years of Tory rule, during which we had been largely ignored. We humiliated Callaghan, just as we had humiliated Wilson and Heath before him, but now the humiliation was ours. We could man illusory picket lines, but the British people walked straight through them. All this washed over the General Council in a slowly lapping wave of uncomfortable realisation. The mood was pessimistic and troubled when I arrived in Blackpool on Thursday 1 September to chair the preliminary General Council meetings ahead of the following week's conference.

It should have been a proud and gratifying climax to my year of chairmanship and I was proud. There can be no greater honour for a life-long trade unionist than to preside over what, for all its glaring faults, is still the greatest trade union movement in the world. But gratified? I knew I had to ram home some unpalatable truths and I certainly wasn't going to disappoint my raucous opponents, lying in wait to bombard me. I was sure that they would try to provoke me, too: I suffer neither fools nor villains gladly so they had more than a sporting chance, but I was determined to give them as little opportunity as possible – in so far as my nature would allow.

The General Council kicked off with a lengthy meeting that Thursday to sort out, as always prior to Congress, what our attitude should be to the sizeable crop of resolutions and amendments on the conference agenda. It was not hard to guess that automaticity would produce the most protracted and heated wrangle, for the left had battled for months to scupper the proposed new scheme, reckoning it was odds-on that it would bring extra moderates on to the General Council. Whereas the big battalions would have automatic representation according to size, those unions with less than 100,000 members must fight it out for eleven seats set aside for them.

The pro-Soviet group continued to spearhead the outright opposition, but by the time we reached Blackpool they had scant hope of stopping the scheme and they adopted a fall-back position. They fixed their 'slate' of candidates, so the moderates, better organised than usual, matched them with a 'slate' of their own. The left wing had another ploy: they tried to overturn a General Council ruling which prevented their patrons in the Transport and General Workers' Union from topping up its automatic five General Council seats by also casting the extra 130,000 votes of its agricultural and textile workers' groups in the small unions' section. They wanted to have their cake and eat it. The far left always have one thing going for them – sheer persistence. They had been beaten before on the same matter, yet they kept the struggle going to the very last. Once again they were thwarted: the General Council ratified its previous decision, though the margin of victory was narrow.

There was more contentious business to transact that day – how to respond to a resolution from the Communication Workers' Union calling for a review by the General Council of problems arising from Common Market membership. The left smelled it out as a back-door bid to shift the TUC from continued support for unconditional withdrawal, Labour Party style, and of course they were right. The CWU was simply recognising that by the time the next general election arrived, probably in 1987, Britain would have been inside the European Economic Community for around sixteen years and that withdrawal was becoming less and less of an option as time marched by. There was always a chance that the resounding thumping in the general election for Labour, with its anti-EEC line, might have jolted the union leadership from its political stupor. The General Council split into three camps: those who favoured the resolution; the fence-sitters who wanted to back it, but didn't dare, so opted to leave it to Congress with no recommendation on how to vote; and the outright opponents.

You can count on someone going missing when the General Council chips are down and this time several moderates were absent. In particular, three of the four engineering workers' members had hopped it, reasonably enough to try to prevent a railways workshop closure. So when I put it to the vote, the left and their witless or wilful allies won by 23 to 19. One consolation was that it proved to be the last really cockeyed decision of the old General Council – reform was on the way.

Friday morning's General Council meeting took an hour, largely devoted to discussing the horrifying shooting down by the Russians of the Korean civil airliner. Len Murray adopted a righteous, if traditional, TUC position: 'We aren't completely aware of the facts,' he said. 'Until we have them, we shouldn't make any statement.' Len was technically correct, but this was more than a technical situation and what he said was sweet music to the ears of the pro-Soviet mob. These creeps immediately supported him and went on to argue hypocritically that the incident should not be allowed to threaten world peace. I swallowed hard, restrained myself and Mr Chairman stayed impartial, if ingloriously so.

I had, though, spoken to Terry Duffy before the meeting and he, like me, was incensed. Terry may not be one of nature's great tacticians, but he doesn't lack courage, and he moved in with an emergency motion condemning the Soviet Union unequivocally. That would have gone to Congress as a General Council view, if approved, but Len Murray was on his best bureaucratic behaviour and ruled it out of order, saying that the conference arrangements committee must be sounded out before we did anything. Once again, self-restraint was not easy, but I managed it. Not that I was silent outside the meeting: I told the press frankly what I thought of the Soviet murderers and added, for good measure, that 'it would be a damned good thing to tell the Russian Ambassador and his staff to stay away from Congress'. I wanted to kick the TUC welcome mat from under their blood-stained feet.

Before the day was over I was plunged into the making of a far more personal controversy, though it was the Sunday before it all broke around my ears. What transpired has since been attributed to Machiavellian motives or to some grand design on my part to interfere in Labour's deputy leadership contest, but the truth of the matter was cock-up, not conspiracy. It was early evening and the phone rang in the Imperial Hotel's Westminster Suite, allocated as usual to the TUC President for the conference week. It was David Roxon, of the *News of the World*, calling. He asked if the Sunday newspaper industrial reporters could have a pre-conference chat with me. I said: 'By all means. Come up now.'

What I didn't realise, until they all trooped in shortly afterwards, was that they needed to check a story with me – or so they said. For all I know they could have made it up, spurred on by hope not accuracy, but it gave them a good excuse to see me and, in fairness, it was the kind of mischievous tale that could have been true. They told me that there was a rumour going the rounds that my presidential address to Congress was not yet printed. The suggestion was that it was held up because of a row I was having with Len Murray who wanted to censor four controversial paragraphs. It was pure baloney and I laughed it off. I said: 'It's very unlikely. The speech isn't even in Blackpool yet.' It was still being drafted by one of my headquarters staff who was due to bring it to Blackpool; he knew what I was intent on telling the delegates, but no one else did, including Len Murray.

That was that. It was clear that the journalists were stuck for a story to file next day and I unwittingly filled their gap, admirably so, from their point of view. I can't make excuses, I've been around long enough to know better. Newspapers later described the occasion as a briefing and made it all appear predetermined, though it most certainly wasn't that. Having scotched that ill-founded rumour about my speech, I relaxed and indulged in some banter with the reporters. They got round to my own union's decision to boycott Labour's farcical leadership and deputy leadership elections. Might we yet change our minds? I didn't think through my reply. I was only really repeating remarks I had made publicly three weeks earlier, when opening the EETPU's new leisure complex at Esher in Surrey – a fact they did not see fit to report.

It was already apparent that Neil Kinnock had the Leader's job in the bag and that our abstention would make no difference to him, but Roy Hattersley was far from home and dry against the Bennite Michael Meacher's challenge for the deputy leadership. I have never thought much of Hattersley: he is able, of course, but I am among the many who see him as an opportunist, always ready to use a pledge of over-riding loyalty to the Party as a cloak to hide a lack of basic principle. It is a valuable expedient to fling about in a power struggle and excuses many sins, as any good Communist will admit: if the end is what you want, to hell with the means. I recall the sorry affair of Reg Prentice: whatever that former Labour Cabinet Minister's suicidal political tendencies and misjudgements, he got no help from the Hattersleys of this world when his back was against the wall. That's when people need friends and I told Hattersley so at the time, when he was privately sneering at his political colleague's anguish. Prentice's subsequent move to the Conservative Party doesn't clear the record of those who idly stood by.

All this doubtless conditioned my Blackpool outburst. The pens were scrawling away furiously as I said: 'I wouldn't vote for Hattersley at any price, not if he was the only candidate.' I called him a disaster whose compromises with the left embarrassed those who wanted to fight for moderation in the Party. I said he harmed the Party by giving in to the left and added: 'If you deal with a shark then all you do is keep losing your limbs.' I gave a bit of a plug to Neil Kinnock: I wasn't to be wildly enthusiastic about him, but I said: 'It is possible that Kinnock can put the Party right. He's got balls.' Picturesque, but provocative to ardent feminists, as I was to learn. I referred to Kinnock's defiance of the Labour Government's devolution plans and his opposition to Tony

Benn's deputy leadership election campaign two years earlier. I made it plain, however, that Peter Shore was my personal choice for leader.

It was the timing even more than the content which pitchforked my comments into the Sunday newspaper headlines. They may have been largely repetition, but right on the brink of the TUC's gathering, they were variously described as 'astonishing' and 'remarkable' and were made all the more piquant by the sharp warning from Len Murray to all the Labour leadership contenders to kindly leave the Blackpool stage to the TUC. Hands off, he told them, it's our show and we've had quite enough of politicians for one year. It was not my intention to cause a further rumpus, but it must have seemed that I was embarking on a calculated campaign against Roy Hattersley.

It naturally brought a swift return of fire. Hattersley thought that I was out to spoil his chances, though I might well have done him more good than harm: some left-wingers might see him in a new light and say: 'If Chapple's against him, we're for him after all.', but I couldn't expect Hattersley to see it that way. He retorted: 'Mr Chapple and I have disagreed over a number of policies for many years – private medicine and civil liberties among them. I was, of course, profoundly opposed to his endorsement of a Social Democrat candidate during the General Election. He is entitled to interpret these disagreements in whatever way he chooses. My concern now is that Mr Chapple and I disagree over a more fundamental question. I want to see Labour succeed as a Party which embraces all forms of democratic socialism. That seems no longer to be what Mr Chapple is seeking.'

I daresay that there have been plenty of policy issues on which Roy Hattersley and I disagreed – and even more where we were in agreement – but I don't recall any first-hand discussion with him over civil liberties or private medicine, or, for that matter, race relations, which some papers reported that he also mentioned. But then he regularly parades his 'progressive' approach on race and civil liberties to help allay left hostility to his pro-EEC and multilateral disarmament views, and he didn't miss a trick on this occasion. His reference to my support for Social Democrat John Grant was not surprising. Grant had been a friend of Hattersley's before he quit Labour and his defection undoubtedly cost Hattersley a firm supporter. Hattersley's inability to place principle above party is matched by an inability to see people as more important than personal power. He screws all he can out of assaulting his one-time mates who are now in the SDP. It is one more way to ingratiate himself with the left. My Blackpool comments gave him a chance to take a smack at one of them and to reduce any impact my remarks might have in the Labour Party by stressing my SDP link, tenuous and personal though it was.

Still, I couldn't blame him. I touched it all off and I suppose it was typically me. I certainly shouldn't have relaxed while all those reporters were there, pens at the ready. There was an amusing sequel; well, I found it amusing. I upset the doughty Ms Anna Coote of the *New Statesman*, by talking of Mr Kinnock's balls. She was quite unable to relate his anatomical attributes to political courage. 'They simply would not turn themselves into a metaphor for me,' she wrote in her tart and prissy fashion. Laugh-along-with-Anna devoted a column and a half of the *New Stateman*'s precious space to proving what a sexist beast I am. The editor must have been mightily pleased that a member of his staff could fill so much blank space so adroitly from so little. After all, he might otherwise have had to pay some expensive outside scribbler like Roy Hattersley a lot of money to plug the gap. For my part, Anna, I freely admit it. I boobed.

While all this bubbled on, the union delegations met around Blackpool to decide how to vote on Congress resolutions and to horse-trade their votes for those precious General Council seats. The EETPU, along with the AUEW and CPSA, unanimously agreed to slap in an emergency motion condemning the Soviet Union over the Korean airliner atrocity. They shared my view that talk of US spyplanes was largely irrelevant. Even in war-time to shoot down an unarmed plane would have earned censure as an act of barbarous inhumanity.

The General Council meets briefly each morning before Congress begins, giving a last minute opportunity for review of the business to come. On that first Monday, we were soon occupied with the airliner affair once again. The pro-Soviet group still questioned whether all the facts were known and suggested that the Russians were merely protecting their territory. They wanted to spin out the evasion to the end of the week so that we took no decision at all. As always, ideological commitment prevailed over any concern for the innocent victims, but the TUC majority had heard enough. They agreed on a tough anti-Soviet statement so that unions, including my own, could be asked to withdraw their motions in favour of the General Council line. The statement said: 'There can be no justification for this callous act which showed a shocking disregard for human life,' and called for 'a speedy explanation and apology'. There was no vote inside the General Council – the pro-Soviet group knew when they were finally beaten.

They had done their obstructive best and certainly earned their sponsored trips to Communist paradise.

Now it was almost time to open Congress and my presidential address was ready for the test. I had spent hours working it over with my union colleagues and there were seven drafts before it got the final polish. I knew that if I made it into a blatantly overt confrontation with the left it was unlikely to be heard at all in the din they would kick up and it was certainly not my objective to have the unions portrayed in a worse light than ever on this show-piece occasion. I would not mince my words, but I tried to design the speech so that my opponents would have to think before they began shouting the odds. The record shows that I succeeded in getting my message over positively, but without arousing the real beast in my Blackpool audience.

Len Murray, doubtless nervous that I might go over the top, did ask to see the speech in advance. It was my swansong, I had nothing to lose in purely personal terms and he was well aware of my frustration during the year, which he shared more than he would care to admit. But there was no question of censorship – that would have caused an explosion and wouldn't have worked. He knew it, I knew it and it never arose. He said tactfully: 'If I see it, I shall know whether I can defend it or not.' When he got it, he had no hesitation in saying that he could defend it, if necessary; indeed, it was very much in tune with an article he had just contributed to a Sunday newspaper – even though my approach was somewhat more trenchant. Len suggested one or two slight changes which I agreed to because they improved the speech in phraseology, not in substance.

We trooped onto the Congress platform to start the week's long haul. It was up to me to get things under way and I went through the usual niceties, introducing the town's Lady Mayor and a rather wild and woolly local Trades Council representative, whose choice of sweatshirt slogans was later to cause a rumpus. I don't think I kidded myself in sensing a certain air of expectation: muscles were being flexed and they weren't just mine. If I chose my words with more than usual care, I still left no room for doubt as to my meaning: can anyone seriously challenge my contention that I spoke comprehensively for the British trade union movement when I lambasted left union leaders for junketing off to hobnob in Moscow while refusing to talk to our own elected Government at home? Or when I ridiculed those who thought we should take to the streets to drive Mrs Thatcher from office?

It was this part of my speech that caught the headlines. I said: 'Our duty is clear. We have to argue with the Government and build a partnership that can revitalise Britain. We cannot contract out of this responsibility or behave like some obscure religious sect that insists on not talking to unbelievers.' There was a mixture of jeers and cheers when I added: 'I am sure that the majority of our members are as baffled as I am that some trade union leaders will travel half-way across the world to sympathise with Communist dictatorships, yet seek to prevent the TUC from talking to the elected Government of Britain.' Yes, I had Arthur Scargill and his Moscow jaunt in mind when I spoke, but that part of the speech was actually drafted before his visit and I could have thrown in a good few more names of union leaders who treat Eastern Europe as a second home. I said: 'If we equivocate between freedom and totalitarianism we will injure ourselves and the values which founded our movement.'

I warned that threats to destroy elected Governments were not only infantile but they were also a dangerous boomerang, 'alienating us from our members as well as threatening the only type of society that guarantees our own freedom'. I called on the movement to refashion itself in order to strengthen its appeal and said that sometimes unions appeared to act as though they were the mouthpiece of the few. I went on: 'We must never treat our members with contempt or distrust their judgement. We will have to understand that solidarity is not just the majority supporting the few but the few supporting the majority. We cannot claim to protect the weak if we ourselves endorse actions which inflict harm upon them.'

I disassociated myself clearly from the Government's 'free market extravaganza', saying that it would learn eventually that such policies were just as irrelevant as the inefficiencies of state planning bureaucracies and warning that in the meantime unemployment and its social consequences would remain intolerable. 'Together with the labour pains of a new industrial revolution and those politicians who seem to believe in either total state planning or absolutely no planning, it is a wonder that we are not in an even worse state. We need a range of policies to reduce unemployment. We have to encourage a greater industrial consensus and stop using our factories and services as political footballs. We need stability, better management, greater co-operation at work and radically improved training.'

Congress had to provide leadership and be brave enough to face difficult decisions, and it had to be far-sighted enough to see where members had not even begun to look. 'Crucial to these qualities is the willingness, indeed the determination, to look reality in the face; to confront the truth; to assess where we are. There is no doubt that our movement has suffered in the past few years. Membership has fallen from a high of twelve million in 1980 to 10,500,000 by the latest count.'

I dealt with the political setbacks: the new employment laws and the June re-election of the Government when Labour had been humiliated. I said some pundits thought it extremely unlikely that Labour could win in 1988 and that brought inevitable booing, but I asserted that the trade union movement was neither defeated nor finished as some commentators wistfully pretended. We still organised more than fifty per cent of the employed population and millions of members appreciated the value of the contributions that they paid.

'No one can pretend that these millions have not spoken. For more than twenty years our popularity has been sliding – at the same time too many of our members have been expressing their unease. This unease has not all been simply whipped up by right-wing newspapers or manufactured by opinion pollsters. It has also reflected itself in the mass desertion of Labour votes and the support which this Government's industrial relations legislation has attracted. Accepting that we ourselves have to make necessary reforms will not only give us a fighting chance of regaining the trust we have allowed to wilt, it will also blunt the attacks made upon us and put an end to some of the self-inflicted absurdities we stumble into and strengthen our appeal in the final part of the twentieth century.

'We have to broaden our base, not narrow it. We have to concentrate on finding the common ground that can unite our members rather than dividing them by party politics or prejudices. We will have to appeal to the new working class and not cling to old-fashioned definitions of fifty years ago. We will have to perform the job that working people pay us to provide and stop involving ourselves in problems that we cannot solve but often only make worse.

'We will have to improve further our internal democracy and reputation for fairness. We need to encourage positively mass participation, guarantee that every member not only has the right but also the easiest opportunity to vote and decide matters which affect them.' That seemed to some like a blessing for the so-called Tebbit Bill, later taken over by new Employment Secretary Tom King. It was hardly that, since Tebbit failed to insist on postal ballots among his reforms and there can be no security from the fraudsters without them.

I finished with a plea to Congress to reaffirm the qualities which built the movement – 'fighting for what is right: mass democracy, generosity, and self-sacrifice'. The applause when I sat down was polite rather than rapturous, but that in itself was quite a minor triumph for me. It indicated the sober state of Congress and inability of the left to whip up its customary hate campaign among the delegates.

The retiring president gets a vote of thanks straightaway – fortunately, I do have friends. Gavin Laird, General Secretary of the Amalgamated Union of Engineering Workers, moved the vote, saying of me: 'He may be controversial, but he is courageous and a first class chairman of the General Council of the TUC.' Leif Mills, leader of the Banking, Insurance and Finance Union, was about to join the General Council: his background is very different to mine – he claims to be the first Balliol and Leander man to get there. He seconded in witty style, then turned to me from the rostrum to say: 'Many people say many things about Frank Chapple and if I were you I would take that as a compliment because I know you do not get many of them.'

Sam McCluskie, of the seamen's union, only did marginally better than me in terms of applause when he delivered fraternal greetings from the Labour Party of which he was then the Chairman. He called for unity, no panic, no U-turns or policy changes, which should have been a lot easier than my hard gruel for the delegates to swallow, but they seemed subdued rather than impressed. Maybe they were still recovering from what I had chucked at them.

We moved on to the debate on automaticity and the day continued to go well. The card vote was three to one in favour of the new system for electing the General Council and Arthur Scargill failed to hang on to a second General Council seat for the miners. His union only retained the one seat which he had agreed in advance should go to Mick McGahey. Exit King Arthur from the General Council, after a one-year stint of self-imposed idleness and non-appearance. Alan Sapper, fearing his own come-uppance, complained bitterly about 'a coup spread over three years'. His real grouse was that it was a coup against him, not by him – he and his pals know all about 'hit lists' – and he got nowhere. It all looked pretty good for the next day's election for those eleven seats for the small unions.

My speech got a good press next day – it was sure to be praised by papers like the *Sun* and *Daily Express*. The *Sun* called it 'wonderful – the REAL voice of organised labour in Britain today.' It wept at my pending retirement and declared: 'Frank, your country NEEDS you!'

The *Express* said it was 'the very stuff of commonsense'. There were headlines like 'Another Win for Big Frank' (*Daily Telegraph*) and 'The TUC takes its reform medicine quietly' (*Guardian*). Paul Johnson, in the *Daily Mail*, said that Chapple gave Congress 'a robust piece of his mind'.

The *Daily Mirror*'s Industrial Editor, Geoffrey Goodman, is now the doyen of his trade and is, I suppose, soft-left to centre in today's Labour Party terms. He said I commanded special authority in ending a memorable year as TUC Chairman and wrote: 'He has been an outstandingly good chairman and it seems that he is going to have a good, if difficult week as president of this Congress, judging by his opening performance. The impact of his speech will certainly be felt in every debate at Blackpool this week ... it was a courageous, controversial collection of home truths which even those who were audibly hostile to the electricians' leader probably secretly admired for its nerve if not for its content.' Who am I to argue with such a wide-ranging and distinguished opinion? I safely left that to the *Morning Star* which took a more jaundiced view. The personality stuff was good for a laugh: the *Guardian*'s Michael White claimed that my only serious rival as the left-wing activists' hate figure was Norman Tebbit. Geoffrey Goodman thought I looked unnervingly like the Godfather, 'short but heavily built, powerfully shaped inside a swarthy Italianate appearance'. *Daily Telegraph* sketch-writer, Edward Pearce, was even more imaginitive: he saw me as 'something between a medieval Franconian monarch and a man about to carve the beef. Mr Chapple's enemies, their passionate opposition to racialism briefly suspended, see in his Italianate handsomeness the features of a man as big in Chicago as in Palermo – Big Frank and the Capella mob. Mr Chapple, who is winning a lot of battles presently, responds to this like a slim-line rhinoceros. This is his conference.'

It was knockabout and friendly enough, but what was far more significant was the feedback I got from ordinary delegates at the TUC and later from those elsewhere who read my remarks or picked up extracts from television and radio. They were saying: 'Thank God someone is talking sense at last. They're not all mad at the TUC after all.' The left kept pretty quiet, but I was told that a lot of the delegations were pleased. Tony Christopher, of the Inland Revenue Staff Federation, said his delegation were delighted and light-heartedly suggested that I might like to chair a special conference of his union. I said 'I'll do it – and for nothing – if your lot will pass by tax forms on the nod.' I'm often told by my members that 'my wife thinks you're the only trade union leader who really understands what is needed'. My post-bag arising from the presidential speech bears that out – a lot of the letters were from women. It was apparent though, that my appeal was only political; still Ms Coote could probably make something out of it.

There were a few problems as the week trundled by, but I was told that my opening salvo had not only set a realistic tone for the entire Congress, but also allowed me to dominate from the chair. I wouldn't go that far, though some left-wingers alleged a Chapple *diktat*. I certainly made it plain early on that I would root out any troublemakers and, contrary to my own forebodings, I found very little cause for anxiety. There was a ripple here and there, inside and outside the conference. A prime selection of Labour leadership candidates turned up, ostensibly as observers or to attend fringe meetings, and 'I'm for Roy' Hattersley was one of them. He tactfully said no more about me in Blackpool, but travelled on to nearby Lancaster to deliver a public denunciation of me for intolerance, defeatism and, by implication, that most heinous of crimes – preparing to desert to the Social Democrats. I was invited to react, but declined. I had started it, he could have the last word; otherwise we could go on playing this political ping-pong match indefinitely.

I was less reticent over Arthur Scargill's next extraordinary gaffe. *News Line*, the Trotskyite Workers' Revolutionary Party's newspaper, published a letter from Scargill in which he described the banned Polish trade union, Solidarity, as 'an anti-socialist organisation which desires the overthrow of a socialist state'. The Trots took full advantage of him by dropping their bombshell story in the middle of TUC week. It came on top of his one-sided Moscow speech, blaming Margaret Thatcher and Reagan for being the main threat to world peace. I thought that I had belted him hard enough, if not by name, in that presidential foray of mine, but here we were again. Not surprisingly, my views were avidly canvassed and I said: 'I regard these sort of remarks as the ravings of an idiot.' There was a consensus of like opinion among the moderates and even his left pals were embarrassed by his outburst. They shared his sentiments but abhorred his tactlessness. In some people that perverse behaviour might be endearing, but in his case, it was another exhibition of supreme egotism.

Kate Losinska, that spirited little president of the Civil and Public Services Association, took him on. She has battered the left in her union for many years and though she has had reverses, she has never packed it

199

in. She went to the Congress rostrum to give a stark illustration of just how the Soviet Union makes crude propaganda use of such claptrap. She read out a transcript of a Moscow Radio English broadcast on what Scargill had said. It read: 'Arthur Scargill, leader of one of the leading trade union federations of Great Britain – the National Union of Mineworkers – condemned a Polish trade union organisation, Solidarity. This organisation, although it has been disbanded, is still continuing its subversive activities, which are now illegal.' The transcript quoted Scargill and said that his letter had 'aroused the fury of the right-wing activists of the British Congress of trade unions'.

Kate said: 'Those who care about the fate of Solidarity, in defence of our trade union brothers and sisters in Poland, should be glad that Arthur Scargill's strange letter has reminded us all of the existence of Solidarity – that's really all I want to say to Arthur... General Jaruzelski and his repressive government will take such views as representative of the British trade union movement as a whole – and I do not believe that. If they were aiming to publicly use them, they will further punish and diminish a free trade union which we are supposed to be supporting.' My sentiments entirely. Throughout TUC week Scargill did maximum damage to free trade unionists, at home and abroad; the letter to the Trots was only part of it.

He proposed defiance of any laws imposed by Norman Tebbit, but his rabble-rousing was voted down. He bounced back, self-importantly, to make a useful, if emotive, speech on energy: he began to the mixture of boos and clapping that is not unusual for me, but might have jolted him into some recognition that he isn't universally popular with trade unionists. Still, he finished to repeated applause and a standing ovation from a few left-wing delegates, out to offset the persecution he always claims to suffer from the capitalist media which pays him so many lucrative appearance fees. Then his mixture of vanity and sheer stupidity took over. Up he got, Soviet-style, and applauded back. I heard someone behind say: 'You'd think it was the bloody Bolshoi.' I called out from the chair: 'This sort of demonstration doesn't do us any good.' Nor did it: the more the public see of TUC delegates back-slapping Scargill, the more they'll be convinced that we're all a bunch of loopy militants.

There were one or two occasions when I did act the Godfather – in the interests of free speech. During the debate on nuclear weapons, for example, the heckling was getting out of hand and I threatened to have those responsible ejected, telling one agitator: 'I know you're trying to irritate me and you're succeeding.' Alistair Graham, the CPSA General Secretary, upset the left by reminding them that it was a Russian missile, not an American one, that blasted that Korean airliner out of the sky. They didn't like it one bit and gave him a rough ride. I told them to stop 'this damned hooliganism', or else.

There was even greater uproar when Eric Hammond, my General Council successor for the EETPU, blitzed Ken Livingstone's Greater London Council lunacies. He counselled against TUC support for backers of 'terrorist groupies, lesbians and other queer people'. If he wanted to prove that the electricians won't go soft without me, he did it. The language was unduly rosy and earned him a rebuke from Len Murray, but the sentiments were justified, especially when he accused the GLC Leader of 'giving comfort to Sinn Fein and, through them, to IRA terrorists'. It summed up Livingstone's irresponsibility and the left howled their outrage. They chanted 'off... off... off' just like a bunch of soccer vandals and I had a struggle to drum home the authority of the chair.

Mind you, we had our own nutter on the platform: that local Trades Council man must have looked to the TV watchers like the Raving Loony Party's punk-rocker delegate. He wore a sweatshirt each day with differing slogans prominently displayed on his chest. At one point there was a scuffle behind me as he was firmly ushered out to the wings. He had a 'Troops Out' slogan on show and was told that unless he changed his garb he was out. It was a disgrace that he was there at all. Trades councils shouldn't pick representatives who will bring us into disrepute. We've troubles enough with our public image as it is. As for the General Council, they were all dressed up as respectably as a conference of bookies.

I took no time off from the chair and my only break was to face a vote of no confidence. It stemmed from a barney I had with Tony Dubbins, of the National Graphical Association, over whether there should be a time-consuming card vote on a motion I reckoned was already carried on a show of hands. Len Murray advised me to let the conference decide and I was persuaded by what he said; perhaps I should have ruled on it, but I announced that I would put it to Congress. The calls for a card vote became louder and more persistent as the militants realised that they could use the occasion to attack me personally. Another NGA man came to the rostrum and moved the no confidence vote. I stepped down and Alan Sapper, the Vice-Chairman, took over while the left did their best to rustle up the necessary two-thirds majority against me. Their motion was overwhelmingly defeated and I resumed the chair.

Congress went on to opt for the card vote which, in turn, carried the original motion. If they had accepted my initial interpretation, all that bother could have been avoided, but the chance to score off me was too good for them to miss. Later the NGA sanctimoniously complained to the conference arrangements committee that I should have made the card vote decision and not asked for a Congress view. If I'd done that, ignoring Len, you can bet I'd have been branded as a dictator; you can't win with these people.

It fell to Alan Sapper on the final morning to thank me for my chairmanship and to present me with the silver bell of Congress. He must have swallowed hard, I know I did. It was another of those moments for delegates to relish – anything could have happened. Common sense, if not brotherly love, prevailed and he got through his remarks with some humour and caused no offence. I replied with a final message. I recalled an East European ex-Communist who said that where Communist leaders feel their policies to be unpopular with the public – they simply changed the public. I said that for us, 'it's easier to change the policies than to change the people'. I had presided over a Congress that had belatedly and cautiously started that vital process of change.

My own passage could so easily have been a violent one. I had expected the left to bait me and try to show me as incompetent and they certainly lost no opportunity to deride me and to barrack. Down there, at the front of the hall, Barbara Switzer, Communist number two to Ken Gill in TASS, glared up at me throughout, or so it seemed to me. Those who might have lent support mostly stayed silent, but I was determined that the left would gain no advantage from my role. The key to it all was that general election result. It was not so much the Tory victory – after all, they only managed 42 per cent of the poll – it was rather the huge public hostility to Labour and the bleak fact that only 39 per cent of trade unionists backed policies which were TUC policies too.

Those TUC delegates realised glumly that they are stuck with Thatcherism for a long time to come. They realised that she can ride roughshod in Parliament and use her massive majority to push through still more legislation to clip the unions' wings. They realised that full employment, as they once knew it, is a goner, probably for good, and that much of their bargaining power has vanished with it. They realised that three to four million out of work may well be with us for the rest of the century and beyond and that their own trade unions had helped to enshrine that very situation.

Yet this enforced collision with the truth offered some encouragement. The demoralising years during which the Transport and General Workers' Union had dominated the General Council through its patronage was busted at last by the new procedures for electing Council members. Scargill, with his anti-Parliamentary, anti-democratic tub-thumping had taken a good kick in the teeth. The much needed decision to get back round the table with the Government so that we can seek to defend our members' interests at first hand again had been taken. We had subtly loosened our links with Labour – not a breakaway but a decisive return to the notion that our industrial interests are paramount. All of this was a severely damaging blow to the trade union left and to their political counterparts too.

It was the week when Len Murray emerged from the shadows, to be his own man in that restructured TUC. My speech must have helped – I had stuck my neck out ahead of him and helped clear the pathway – but he picked up from where I left off with zest and with finesse. He fully understood the desperate economic situation and the equally desperate need to try to influence the Government to act and he managed to convey those feelings to Congress. His speech in the major economic debate was a model of casual, yet persuasive, command and it was good to hear his firm emphasis on the requirement to reflect our members' views. Or, as he put it succinctly: 'We are representative organisations. Being representative means knowing and respecting what our members want and expect from their unions. Not the Government's unions, not the Labour Party's unions. Not even our unions. The members' unions.' That kind of bite, clarity and assertiveness from Len was long overdue, but events had removed his shackles and he had responded.

Even the left heard him out with sullen respect and the vote which followed was a clear-cut endorsement of his view. He got a virtually un-qualified go-ahead for the General Council to talk to the Government and any other political parties that might gain power. He secured the rejection of industrial action for political purposes and agreement to a full-scale reappraisal of TUC economic policies. He said: 'We cannot talk as if the trade union movement is an alternative government.' That, at last, established the unvarnished truth and paved the way for a painful acceptance that the unions must distance themselves from Labour if they are to genuinely represent their politically diverse and fragmented membership and avoid what could otherwise lead to a far deeper and more permanent rupture.

All that said, there remains a very long way to go to bring the TUC right back into the real world. It stuck to unilateral nuclear disarmament and to its outdated commitment to quit the European Economic Community; it wasn't easy to rouse the delegates against that Soviet airliner atrocity – anti-Americanism was a far smoother option. Scargill managed his adulation as though he was some kind of heroic victor rather than a big-headed, loud-mouthed bigot who has all too frequently led his members like a drunken driver who burst the breathalyser bag and pleaded not guilty through lack of police evidence. The real world is one in which the Tory government can ram its policies down the throats of our members and yet ignore the General Council as and when it pleases.

The new younger breed of General Council members must beware of seeking to counter this by playing political footsy; they must argue their own case, press and persuade on merit, not in the hope that some future government will eventually gain office and do their bidding. That could be a dangerous delusion and our members need to be represented today. At least one commentator called it 'Chapple's Congress'. Perhaps that went a bit far. I had helped to establish the new mood but the Government, the economic situation and Labour's suicidal short-comings were the major factors which brought limited change.

I fear for the permanency of what happened in Blackpool and the willpower of the right and moderates to stay on the offensive. They must not relax, they must press the arguments home. The Communists can be beaten at their own game, but no concessions must be made to a spurious unity, for those who buy this argument end in the political and industrial graveyard. Never mind about repetitiveness: all speeches should be as challenging to Communism as to capitalism; votes must be organised, not left to chance; no one must bend to intimidation, for when the Reds get vicious then it means they are being hit where it hurts. The newcomers to the General Council – Alistair Graham, Alan Tuffin, Eric Hammond, John Lyons, Leif Mills – should be up to it, but they cannot rest on their laurels. The 1984 Congress is crucial and it will be there that the 1983 Congress may yet prove to have been less of a watershed than a temporary hiccup in the continuing leftward lurch of the Labour and trade union movement.

There was one remaining duty from my TUC chairmanship which still had to be dealt with and it posed a problem. I was due to take the

TUC's fraternal greetings to the 1983 Labour Party Conference at Brighton in October and Sam McCluskie, the Labour Party chairman, urged me to keep the date despite that general election row over my backing for my SDP friend. I was sorely tempted to do so and to play the hell-raiser again. There were a number of motions on the Labour agenda calling for my expulsion, but I couldn't see them going through. Such victimisation would only have led to further contemptuous public reaction which the Party could ill afford.

It was pretty clear, though, that the left would orchestrate fervently against me. Party conferences in recent years have tended to degenerate into shouting and slanging matches – the clenched-fist brigade has been unduly prominent. I would be howled down and I had no wish to add to Labour's difficulties by provoking another damaging scene. Nor could I necessarily put the view of the TUC General Council: some represented unions not affiliated to Labour and others would bitterly disagree if I spoke my mind. It all pointed to a tactful withdrawal, yet the truth needed to be told and I did so in a newspaper article which was, in effect, the speech I didn't make. Most of the delegates undoubtedly got the message.

I said that four years looked woefully short to fashion Labour into a shape that could win the next general election and that, given the Party's in-built divisions, it would take a miracle to save it. I called for the expulsion of the Trotskyite infiltrators and for the election of a leadership team that was legitimate and credible and I derided the current leadership contests in which union payola decided the size of their vote and in which Communists and other non-Labour people could play a vital role. I attacked the scandalous way in which so many constituency party members were prevented from voting, explaining that the EETPU would not take part in this so-called election, that we would not sully ourselves or legitimise a procedure that disgraced democracy. I said: 'One member, one vote, has been our slogan since the whole argument about the election of the Labour leadership began. It still is.'

Credible policies were vital and 'extremist rubbish' should be jettisoned; there must be a commitment to Parliamentary democracy and a preparedness to listen to the voters. I said: 'Such a goal is totally incompatible with shrieking harpies, police bashers, Trotskyites and those who care more about not upsetting the Russians than for the fate of Polish trade unionists.'

Imagine offering that little lot to the Labour Party conference, with shrieking harpies, police bashers, Trotskyites and Soviet apologists galore among the delegates. It would have lifted the roof and brought the kind of uproar that could only gratify the revolutionaries. I preferred to deny them that pleasure.

## CHAPTER 16

# FREEDOM'S ROAD
# TO PROGRESS

Our trade unions must advance or decay. They have yet to choose. It looked very much as if the belated TUC demonstration of common sense at the 1983 Congress was to be no more than a temporary advance when it was so swiftly followed by the National Graphical Association's perverse and misjudged *Stockport Messenger* dispute. Fortunately that perilous affair concluded not only with union capitulation, but with an important reaffirmation by the TUC General Council that the unions must abide by the laws of the land and change them through the ballot box. We could breathe on.

That decision reflected an impassioned plea that I had sustained for decades, though I was no longer there to bless it. The situation remains potentially explosive, however. How fragile is the peace? How permanent that scurry to safely? The left is determined to wage war to reverse the TUC verdict. They were savagely rocked by Len Murray's unprecedented public repudiation of a wild pledge by the Employment Policy Committee to support the NGA strike action in deliberate defiance of a High Court ruling. The pipsqueak Clive Jenkins petulantly called for Murray's resignation. Len beat him off, but the twenty-nine to twenty-one vote was hardly that convincing.

The NGA's Joe Wade accused Murray and the TUC majority not only of selling his union down the river, but of sending the rest of the movement with them. It was the familiar lament of the union loser, anxious to shift the blame for defeat. But Murray had shown much-needed steel and heaved the whole trade union movement back from the edge of the precipice. It was a blow for moderation, struck while the Labour Leader, Neil Kinnock, maintained an embarrassing silence in the face of inexcusable violence on the picket line. His was an unpromising response and a let-down for me after my Congress comments about his potential courage – it was all too reminiscent of Callaghan and Foot, fudging on to disaster.

The issue was plain enough. Should decisions arrived at by democratic elections be overturned by force? Trade union action which aids law-breakers is a comfort for the IRA bombers and those other extremist groups which seek to destabilise society. The bomb and the barricade are the same in principle and theirs is a dark and dangerous route. Any step in that direction by trade unions may lead to the removal of the very freedoms their action is said to protect.

Len Murray's new-found confidence came through again in a TUC document in which he candidly admitted that the ailing unions must 'prove their fitness' if they are to recover their role in Britain's future. He argued that unions have a duty to deal with governments of different political colours. He underlined the gulf between members and their unions and the need for a rethink on internal democracy, pointing out that strikes not only hurt business and the community, but also the workers involved. It gave cause for renewed hope that we could yet produce a modernised, democratic and responsible trade union move-ment fit to meet the challenges of the next century effectively, efficiently and in the interests of working people.

There is, though, a very long way to go – the unions in recent years have taken two steps backwards for each step ahead. The bid to thwart Len Murray and those who back him will be vehemently promoted by the broad left – Communists, Trots, fellow travellers and malcontents of all kinds. They hide their hostility to progress and reform behind a loud-mouthed and indiscriminate opposition to the Tory Government. Murray's moderates must not only support him, but see that he does not waver, does not retreat at the sound of gunfire to the bad old habits of pliancy and compromise which he appears to have renounced. They must prove themselves a more reliable prop against the TUC's pro-Soviet gang than in the past.

I have been an active trade unionist for more than forty-six years and have held nearly every post possible, from shop steward to TUC President. I have felt so many disappointments along the way. Some-times, I have been ashamed of what has happened within individual unions and of the way certain trade unionists have behaved. Notwith-standing these events, I have always remained a committed trade unionist and the EETPU has been my life: if I had to lead my life again, I wouldn't choose any other path.

It is fashionable to suggest that the practice of trade unionism is sordid and shabby. Sometimes it is, as this book discloses, but it is far more than back-door wheeling and dealing and the cynical exercise of power. On the contrary, for all its faults trade unionism has significantly improved the status of labour, has successfully overcome the notion that a worker is no more than a commodity and finally has been, and still is, a powerful force for democracy. Unions remain an essential bulwark in the defence of working people and an irreplacable part of our democratic society.

But that same society has changed drastically, dramatically, since the days of the Combination Acts and the Tolpuddle Martyrs, and today's unions have mostly failed to keep pace with that change. Their pace must be ever quickening to match the greater prospects and opportunities ahead and to combat the threats to trade unionism, too.

I have tried to keep the EETPU in the vanguard of that essential trade union advance. I never had a master plan, a grand design, for the sort of union I wanted, but there were three main tests against which our structural changes could be measured: they can well be applied to the wider movement. Firstly, the union had to be given back to its members. We made a genuine and successful attempt to apply that principle long before the politicians pinched it for their slogans. It meant complete reform of our discredited election system, of the union's conferences and of the internal discipline and appeals machinery. Secondly, I had to use the General Secretary's powers to ensure that there would be no further corruption. Thirdly, the union's administrative machine needed overhauling and modernising in support of that enhanced democracy.

All that has happened. The Communists and their allies beaver away to recapture the union and even now seek to reverse our changes, but they will not succeed. Secret postal ballots have been our most farreaching reform: the old union rule book gave undue influence to pathetically-attended branch meetings, easily manipulated by Red elitists, but now there is genuinely representative democracy. I have told our shop stewards often enough not to fool themselves into thinking that they represent the membership. They must recognise that, like me, they are part of a tiny neurotic band of activists. Our members are not like that and if the activists forget it, they lose touch with those members and they with the union.

The self-same case can be made about conferences. Our switch from a fifty-delegate affair to conferences of 700-800 delegates, one from each branch, lately topped up with elected shop stewards, has eliminated caucus control and contributed enormously to rank and file participation and open debate. These union-wide conferences are supplemented by industry-based shop stewards' conferences where specific industrial problems are dealt with. The industrial conferences, in turn, are supported by a nationwide network of national and local shop stewards' committees for each industry. They involve thousands of stewards discussing things that concern their local members and those bread-and-butter issues that make the union real to its members. I believe that we have done more than any other union to achieve mass participation.

The left has opposed every extension of democracy, including secret postal ballots, increasing the size of the conferences and allowing shop stewards to attend. They have resisted the convening of the national industrial conferences and have tried to sabotage the formation of industrial branches that are relevant to the members' places of work. We still face constant fabrication and smears and I am still presented as some kind of authoritarian ogre. The Reds use their sycophantic media hangers-on, often paid-up members of the broad left masquerading as objective commentators, to allege that those who buck our anti-Communist leadership live in fear of the chop. It is the big lie technique, peddled whenever and wherever possible, and not surprisingly, some of those who know no differently accept it.

The left carefully ignore our unique disciplinary appeals system: unlike other unions, which supervise their own arrangements, our tribunal is appointed by the TUC General Secretary and usually consists of members of other unions and independents; we have always complied with its decisions. No one is expelled on trumped-up charges now and our last disciplinary expulsion was more than fourteen years ago. Yet the Communists opposed this system, too. They denounce our growth, our educational facilities and every effort to widen the basis of membership participation; they seek to blacken our name beyond the confines of the union; whenever someone from the EETPU speaks at any Labour Movement conference, the organised left shriek, stamp and hiss; their behaviour owes more to national socialism than to democratic socialism.

Theirs is a deplorable record, but ours is a proud one that is the undoubted envy of many of our trade union contemporaries who frequently approach us for help and advice. The administrative bedrock of our participative democracy is our headquarters' computer set-up, the most advanced that any union can boast. It produces a central register of members that is updated twice weekly and our records are estimated to be 96 per cent accurate. It facilitates our postal ballots, votes on national or local negotiations, delivery of the union newspaper to every member and of our financial report to them as well.

It has revolutionised our financial system, with major savings to us.

Our services to the members are second to none. We run residential education and training centres at Esher, Surrey, and Cudham, Kent, and have spent £900,000 in the past three years on redevelopment there. We have recently become the first union in Europe to develop our own new technology training and we have highly efficient research, legal and work-study departments. We provide full-time officials to run our large branches and we have a network of twenty-eight local area offices. We increasingly cater for managerial and technical membership, a major growth area of the future. All these services owe nothing to the idea that trade unions are there to smash capitalism. They are designed to uphold the rights and dignity of our members in their reasonable demands for a fair deal at work and for improved living standards.

Employers know that we negotiate for real. We are never out for trouble and we keep our bargains, but we expect others to do the same when they deal with us. No union has more industrial muscle, with so many members in key places, but we know that we are failing if we need to use it. There is good reason to suppose that the bulk of our membership does appreciate, even applauds, our streamlining, despite the perpetual stream of misleading propaganda from the left.

Our most recent biennial conference at Blackpool last November threatened a left revival that would wreck all that I and my Executive Council have achieved. The broad left alliance presented amendments to the rule book, some of them clearly drafted by their lawyers, that would have thrust us right back to 1961. Communist leaflets circulated amongst the delegates, urging our defeat; inevitably, their demands included an end to the ban on Communists. Our backs, it seemed, were to the wall.

The outcome was a great and gratifying surprise: all the pro-Communist amendments were thrown out and the left were reduced to a rump of sixty or seventy delegates – less than a tenth of the conference. Even on controversial policy votes, like unilateral nuclear disarmament, the campaign of the left flopped and we had big majorities against them. A large number of new young delegates let me know that their eyes were opened by the arrogance and machinations of the Communists. It augers well for the union's future and was especially pleasing to me.

I made my valedictory speech there. I said that our critics could not intimidate an EETPU leadership whose authority is based upon the legitimacy afforded by mass elections and 'not political obedience'. Later, I was presented with the union's gold medal and the delegates

211

gave me a standing ovation, the only one I can ever recall receiving. A sprinkling of hard-liners stayed in their seats, arms folded, unsmiling. I should have thought they would have been up and cheering at my pending retirement.

It might seem presumptuous to claim that ours is a model union. There is much more to be done by my successors, but we have worked with considerable success to remove the union's inadequacies and faults, to innovate and to create a union for today and tomorrow. The rest of the movement might do worse than follow our example.

The former Editor of the *Daily Herald*, Francis Williams, once described the history of the trade union movement as a 'magnificent journey'. So it has been and although some employers glibly say that if they didn't have unions they would have to create them, the unions' battles on behalf of working people throw up little evidence of employers helping to form unions. Mostly, they have hampered their formation and even now refuse justifiable claims for recognition rights. The real debt is to the character of ordinary British working people who have always been prepared to toil against the odds and stand up for what they believe.

The unions *are* at a watershed. They organised most of the major sectors of the economy to a point where their membership peaked at twelve million and where governments, Labour and Conservative, found it necessary to consult the TUC on most major matters concerning the economy. Today it is not just society and the attitude of government that has altered; almost unnoticed by the unions, the expectations of the members have changed. Trade union rules, structures and policies have remained almost the same throughout two centuries of growth and unless the movement recognises what is happening all around it, decline is inevitable. The failure of trade union leadership to anticipate the demands of the next century will accelerate that decline far more rapidly than any government laws.

The political and economic right refuse the unions any credit and blame them for the nation's incapacity to compete, seeing their sole purpose as disruption of the market price of labour. They claim that the unions are too harmful and too powerful: their evidence is imprecise and ill-founded, but the unions are wheeled out as a convenient excuse whenever right-wing policies fail as abysmally as those of the left. Few of these critics distinguish between importance and influence, and power.

The left-wing see the unions as their battering ram for fundamental political change, their means to full-scale state control; once achieved, the unions can be discarded or turned into Soviet-style tools of government. Today's unions, they contend, are managers of discontent who sidetrack and obstruct an otherwise unstoppable movement towards revolution. They must be fully motivated in that cause. Those beliefs arrogantly defy our whole tradition.

The unions, though limited in real power, do have great reserves of strength: there is institutional loyalty from their members; there is the instinctive feeling of workers in large production plants that they are vulnerable to management and must band together for mutual protection. Unions are large trading organisations and employers in their own right and they have a significant financial standing. But their strength has been dissipated through a zest to fight the battles of yesterday, through tokenism and through debates that are largely irrelevant to their members' everyday concerns. The movement has unthinkingly forfeited its central role in society to become little more than a ginger group.

Trade union power has never been excessive; in so far as the unions try to exercise an influence, it is open and above board, we protest by march, demonstration and deputation. Even under Labour Governments, our every move in the Whitehall corridors, overt or covert, is daily exposed and reported. The multi-national corporations and the great financial institutions conduct their business in a far more closed manner, almost by stealth. Their power over successive Governments has been far greater than anything the unions could muster.

Measure the actual impact of the TUC over the years: Congress passes resolutions on issues of worldwide significance, but our influence on foreign affairs is minimal; our representations on budgetary policy have had little effect; levels of unemployment have remained intolerably high, notwithstanding persistent TUC protests; we have failed to persuade governments to reinflate; incomes policies have been imposed against our will; import controls have not been adopted; our opposition to social service cuts has been ignored.

Many trade unions can put pressure on the Labour Party because they provide so much of its cash and because of their voting strength at Labour Party conferences. Even so, our overall political influence is more negative than positive – more illusory than real. It is almost entirely confined to industrial relations and labour market matters and even that degree of influence has largely disappeared since 1979, shattered by the combination of spiralling unemployment and government disdain. Excessive union power is a myth: the cause of working

people has been advanced, inch by inch, through application and dedication and in the teeth of forces far more powerful than ours. The plight
and weakness of the individual worker in the market economy has fired
the cause of trade unionism in every continent. Millions of working
people have learned that the free market is imperfect and have combined
together, irrespective of repressive laws or different social systems.

Despite my own fears, anxieties and censures, I emphatically reject
the oft-repeated charge that the trade unions have outlived or exceeded
their original purpose. Much the same was said one hundred years ago.
Likewise, I reject that other populist, if hypocritical, view that strikes
are necessarily wrong. It was once summed up like this: whilst all admit
that it is the right of men in a free society to withdraw their labour, the
line must, of course, be drawn at strikes; the day that we become strike-
free will be the day that the totalitarian state is in place.

The political and economic right seems to believe that trade unions
should act as a kind of social policeman, keeping the workers in line,
knocking some sense into them. We must agree with governments,
moderate pay demands, stop strikes, encourage harder work and not
oppose the decisions of employers or politicians. These critics have
much in common with the left: both reckon that they know more about
what we are for than we do, and both believe that they know more
about what is good for us than we do.

In fact, they misunderstand our purpose. Our job is not to struggle for
a Soviet-type state which would militarise us or convert us into
instruments of forced labour, neither is it to comply with a concept of
trade union responsibility which insists that we should be responsible to
everyone but our members. That is not to say that the role of trade union
leaders is to be servants of whoever shouts loudest, or that we should
ignore the effects of our policy on the economy and general public: the
first would be abdication, the second suicide, and I cannot be accused of
preaching or practising either. We must neither abandon responsibility
nor fail to properly represent those who enter our ranks. Leadership and
representation is a difficult balance to achieve: we must resolutely
defend our members' interests while, at the same time, being aware of
the wider implications of what we do.

What is disappointing is that the movement has not been as successful
as it might have been: the unions cannot avoid responsibility for that
but the fault is not entirely ours. Trade unions are primarily defensive,
reactive bodies, others initiate, we respond. We are at the receiving end
of the economic system and of the shocks that accompany it and mostly

we have to cope with the effects of the decisions of those who have positive economic power and command over resources and technology. We are told that new technology creates more jobs than it destroys, but that is of little immediate comfort to the ageing worker who suddenly finds that he is jobless, to the redundant man who sees his skills obsolete, to the father who worries about his son's future, to the family who must make ends meet without the wife's earnings.

Trade unions articulate these concerns and are attacked, but the critics are rarely those who offer constructive alternatives rather than platitudes. Without trade union resistance, would workers always have been consulted about, say, change, paid compensation or retraining? This is not to say that our traditional defensive response is enough: we must adapt to new technology, embrace it, or fall further behind in the new industrial revolution. That means a fresh dimension of commitment from everyone: companies, government, unions, as well as the individual. The shorter working day and week will mean cultural changes if costs are to be contained and our goods are to remain competitive. Seven-day shift working must be envisaged and a tremendous development of leisure activities and pursuits is needed.

There is, as yet, little indication of a will for progress, but on the contrary a remarkable complacency about the scandal of mass unemployment – ours, that of our children and of their children – prevails. This is all the more reason for the trade unions to act positively, to provide a constructive offensive. They must be prepared to negotiate with the Government, to work for a deal that would guarantee to cut that appalling unemployment total, create new jobs, improve our industrial performance, encourage the growth of technologically-orientated industries and remove the worst features of recent industrial relations legislation.

Of course, the Government would need an assurance that we could keep our side of the bargain. The present atmosphere of hostility, distrust and suspicion between the Government and the TUC cannot be banished overnight but must be overcome. The TUC requires a new and greater authority, based on the genuinely representative democracy of its affiliates. In parallel, then, with a new attempt at meaningful and wide-ranging talks with the Government, the trade unions must reform themselves, must stop pretending that only they, in an imperfect world, remain near-perfect. Trade unionism is an indispensable feature of any democratic society. There is not one single dictatorship in the world, Communist or Fascist, which co-exists with free trade unions – and they have a duty to support that democratic society. To do so convincingly, their own democracy should be above reproach and that is far removed from the existing situation. Yet the unions cannot talk authoritatively to the Government without knowing that they really speak with the voice of their members.

The TUC General Council is part of the establishment and its role, at that level, is clear. On the shopfloor, the ordinary union members take very little notice of their unions, let alone the TUC, except when a pay deal or a strike occurs. The fact is, there is often a vast gap between the members and their representatives. The trade union movement that the public hears about is that of the activists, but however important they may be, they are not the union. Too often, they are zealots who must be kept in their place within the structure of the union, not frozen out, but not allowed to control and perhaps ruin it.

People at factory level have a fair idea of what they want without knowing much about their unions, their policies, history and so on, and they cannot relate today's grievances to past union actions on the workers' behalf. Unions tend to be bureaucratic and slow to respond; unless a large number of members are involved, they may not respond at all. So there must be more and better two-way consultation and communication between the unions and their members, not merely the provision of platforms for hot gospellers. We cannot cuddle everyone up into the decision-making process but we can try. Shop stewards with a place in the structure, for instance, usually behave realistically and will not just come together to carp and criticise.

But above all, the organisation must be membership based, not activist based. That change is vital if the movement is not steadily to fade. If we seek renewed membership growth, we must recognise that most workers are mainly concerned with their family, their car, their holidays and the television. They will not attend branch meetings, especially when they are dominated by boring Marxists or their like. We must not discourage our members, take their dues and forget them. We must remove every possible obstacle to maximum participation; that means, above all, secret postal ballots. The present Government's latest legislation, punitive and anti-union in parts, is pusillanimous and equivocal on this. My own private representations to Tom King, successor to Tebbit as Employment Secretary, seem to have been brushed aside and it is hard to avoid the conclusion that the Government wants to further weaken the unions. I want them strengthened.

Secret postal ballots will ensure that union leaderships rest on a firm representative base and can properly guarantee that small politically-motivated minorities cannot imperil the structure. Postal ballots also mean that individual unions can cede more of their autonomy to the TUC whose representatives, unlike much of the present General Council, will reflect the views of the bulk of the nation's trade unionists. Left union leaders who hang on will be reluctant to flout the wishes of working people if they face periodic re-election by ballot of all their members, as I have done in the EETPU. The TUC could then speak without the constant fear of repudiation by its affiliates: its policies would carry the movement's seal of approval.

Free trade unionism is a guarantee of democracy, but its abuse can be a threat. We are handicapped in our criticisms of other institutions so long as we need to put our own house in order. The damaging contradictions in trade union behaviour are obvious and the NGA dispute is only one more in a dismal chain of conflicts which provides ample ammunition for our opponents and threatens our very existence.

I do not believe that the pursuance of higher wages, at any cost, has anything in common with those who sacrificed to build our organisation. I do not believe that those pioneers who fought against the horrors of mass unemployment and who strove to create a fairer society, would be proud of those who endanger the jobs of others and who seem prepared to use any means to achieve often transitory goals. A strike is one thing, but a strike that threatens to kill is quite another – that is precisely what I told our EETPU shop stewards, some of whom wanted to intensify our go-slow action in the power stations under the Heath Government. The action that I attacked during the 'Winter of Discontent' had no part of our trade union tradition. Hanging in my office is a banner, printed in 1865 for the plumbing section of our union, which bears the slogan 'United to support, not combined to injure'.

The trade union movement must reassert its principles and rediscover its purpose and responsibilities and we need far more than a generalised strategy, however worthy that may be as a first step. We need to form a bargain with society that protects our freedoms and the freedoms of all. We need a bold new initiative that is specific. If trade unionists had to swear their own Hippocratic oath, it might include:

a total repudiation of violence in industrial disputes;
a pledge not to strike before agreements expire;
a commitment to use strike action only as a last resort;
a pledge not to initiate strikes which can ruin the lives of other

citizens, usually innocent bystanders, without first, totally exhausting all other channels and second, holding a secret ballot;

a pledge to take no industrial action whatsoever that might cause death or physical injury;

a disavowal of strikes for political purposes and a commitment to seek to change the law through the ballot box;

the right of a worker not to join a union if he or she has a conscientious objection with a simultaneous acceptance, to deal with free-riders, that the equivalent of union dues should go to an agreed charity.

Could any government refuse a fair return to a trade union movement that offered that kind of deal, that desirable co-operation? The political risks of a mulish response are obvious enough.

Far from betraying trade union interests, TUC acceptance of such a way forward would give a new impetus to us and provide a new standing for the unions in society. Once more, though, I am likely to be the odd man out in suggesting a position which would find overwhelming support from the rank and file, but which would enrage the recalcitrant left and will thus be largely ignored in Congress House. There is a further move required to bring the unions up-to-date: that is to jettison the impossibly irrelevant belief, rooted in the movement's history and enshrined in my union rule books, that the means of production, distribution and control should be owned and controlled by the workers. The grim conditions of early capitalism merited such a position, but today its significance is confined to historians and to those political extremists who use it to justify the need for permanent conflict in society. It is time they were stripped of an outdated weapon which they wield only to stir unrest and confrontation.

There is one more crucially important prerequisite for trade union recovery and growth. My 1983 claim that we must decide on 'Socialism or Survival' is every bit as valid today. We cannot subordinate to a distant dream our current efforts to protect trade unionism, to achieve jobs, to halt the rundown of essential services. Can we really settle for fifteen years of Conservative Government that could do irreparable harm to our organisation and rights? Can we realistically pin our hopes on Labour to pull back from the catastrophic defeat it suffered at the polls, to repair its deep divisions, to withstand the threat the Tories present to its funding? Labour's electoral base has steadily declined for twenty years and its lack of appeal to the young stares us in the face. It looks more than ever like a party of permanent opposition.

I have argued consistently for proportional representation. If trade unions want to claim that Mrs Thatcher lacks majority support, they must do so by endorsing PR, for otherwise they are supporting a system which they themselves know produces disreputable results. It is not only trade union democracy which is in urgent need of reform. We will not, though, achieve electoral change under this Government, which has a clear-cut vested interest in the status quo. Instead, we must redefine our relationship with Labour and face the probabilities. It is highly unlikely that extremist policies will be jettisoned, that straight answers will replace fudge, that infiltrators will be ousted – unity, however shallow, will remain the priority. It is important then, that not only should we cease to be an electoral liability to Labour, undoubtedly the case in the past, but that Labour should not prevent us from dealing with any non-Labour Government, or from maintaining a dialogue with all the major parties. Both wings of the Labour movement must move towards greater independence.

There are signs that this is happening: within the TUC, the strains of our political links are increasingly obvious, especially for unions not affiliated to Labour. The Government plan to force unions to ballot their members over maintaining political funds could hammer Labour's finances and put the Tories in an almost unassailable position: that is its blatantly one-sided purpose. Many union members, however, do resent paying the political levy because they dislike Labour's policies. Millions of trade unionists have consistently shown in public opinion polls that they oppose the union–Labour tie-up. Contracting out of the levy is an available option in theory, but it can be a very difficult matter to arrange in practice.

I admire the American system where unions back candidates, not on the basis of party, but on their voting record on labour issues – not on what politicians say but on what they do. That system would bring some interesting shifts in support here. But there is one sensible way to beat the Tories next time round, almost certainly the only way in the short-term. It is through an agreement between Labour and the Alliance parties not to fight each other at the polls.

With its present policies, Labour is likely to be minced again in 1988. The last election showed that there are far more people in the country who feel threatened by Labour's policies than by those of the Tories and it will require an incredible shift of opinion to swing things Labour's way. Conservative politicians are openly contemptuous of Labour, sure that they have less to beat than ever. Only their own internal divisions pose any danger to them – divisions that only exist through the luxury of a huge Parliamentary majority. Those same Tories continue to see the Social Democrats as a more potent threat: electoral volatility cannot be discounted and it is the middle ground that is the most unpredictable.

Unity candidates, straddling the three minority parties, need not share identical platforms, but would simply show a determination to steer the country on a different economic course and a readiness for coalition government if they succeed. Admittedly, there seems to be no prospect of such an agreement. Personal rivalries and enmity between the parties and their leading personalities run deep. Labour's left, especially, prefer to retain their near-domination in a political vacuum and it may take another defeat by the Tories to knock all the relevant heads together.

I remain a reluctant Labour Party member, in disagreement on almost every major policy issue with the leadership. I certainly shall not vote for or support any candidate who backs unilateral nuclear disarmament, EEC withdrawal without a referendum and an economic policy that offers only the notion that we can spend our way out of recession. Am I supposed to stand behind and hawk around a phoney panacea when there isn't a single socialist system in the world that can be sold on the doorstep with honesty. Labour left-wingers who defy the Party's collective wisdom seem to be accepted, while the right are vilified. I may yet hit trouble again. Labour has seemed to be on its deathbed before and revived; it could astound me and do so again, but I am less optimistic than ever before. The moderates lack the raw courage, the sense of direction and the political will to evict the unprincipled left alliance that is deeply embedded in the Party at every level.

In any event, we must live with a Conservative Government for some years. The trade union movement cannot relinquish its responsibilities to argue and negotiate with, to dissent from and where necessary to oppose, that Government. Its members' interests cannot be represented by sulking and by token demonstrations of weakness, not strength. The Government, too, must think again and accept the importance of trade unionism, with all its shortcomings, in a modern society. There are no simple solutions to our industrial relations and other problems, and they will not be removed by the application of ancient political and economic doctrines. Only by removing deep suspicions and mistrust can we provide a lasting basis on which to build the unity of our nation and achieve the economic success and future stability that must be our goal. No political dogma or prejudice should blind us to that fact.

I hope that I have made my contribution over the years towards easing the nation's troubles. I have seldom left room for doubt about my views or intentions, right or wrong. I have made the sparks fly. As I told my union's conference in my farewell speech, it hasn't been 'a bundle of fun for me'. I've always done it the hard way, often alone.

But there have been many compensations and I have few regrets. I leave my job as General Secretary of the EETPU knowing that my union is industrially and politically robust and healthy, financially sound and that it is undoubtedly the most democratic of all Britain's trade unions. I need no other testimonial.

# POSTSCRIPT

My always qualified optimism in the wake of the 1983 TUC Congress has soon vanished. The unions are more confused, more bewildered and more fragmented than ever. So much for the TUC's so-called 'new realism'.

Congress 1984 is set to be a bloody battlefield with brother fighting brother in a bitter conflict which can only do still further self-inflicted damage to our ailing movement. The pre-conference manoeuvring shows plainly enough that the left will be in full cry against those they contend betrayed first the National Graphical Association and then the miners. In their venomously simplistic book, if you weren't for the strikers, you were against them. They have no interest in the merits or demerits of the issues involved.

It could have been so very different. For 1984 gave the unions their best opportunity in very many years to secure much-needed public sympathy and support. The Tory government's arrogant dismissal of the case against the ban on trade unionists at the Cheltenham intelligence headquarters was an extraordinary gift. The gain though, was remarkably short-lived: the TUC's muddled and ill-judged Day of Action and ridiculous boycott of Neddy, the National Economic Development Council, tossed away a valuable advantage. Union leaders matched ministerial intransigence with their own typical bloody-mindedness.

David Basnett, for instance, somersaulted and renounced his own previous insistence on the need to keep a tripartite dialogue going between government, employers and unions. Len Murray wobbled precariously and eventually managed to head off extravagant moves to withdraw trade union representatives from a host of public bodies that the movement has fought for a hundred years to join and often to establish. My own union gave forthright advance notice that we would ignore any absurdly indiscriminate action of that kind and would go it

222

alone in continuing to attend such bodies, if necessary. In the event, we were not put to the test.

But the TUC enabled the Government to conjure, if not a full-scale propaganda victory, then at least a draw, out of what would otherwise have counted as a resounding public relations defeat. Once again, the unions appeared to be sulking to no sensible purpose. The withdrawal from Neddy, in particular, has given its long-time reactionary right and revolutionary left detractors a weapon with which to kill it off. Unless the 1984 Congress demands a TUC return to the Neddy table, it could be curtains for this uninspiring but nevertheless useful and workmanlike forum which until now has survived under governments of varying political colours.

Walking back to Neddy was never going to be an easy option for the unions and it will be astonishing if the TUC delegates, stoked up to emotive protest, are prepared to let the General Council backtrack. I tell them now that permanent withdrawal will only comfort the Government and will be totally counter-productive for trade unionists, whose views and needs should be pressed home whenever and wherever possible.

If the Cheltenham GCHQ affair was a fiasco, the miners' dispute was a dangerous tragedy. Only a headstrong few of those directly or indirectly involved had either the heart or the stomach for it. The miners were the victims of Arthur Scargill's determination to use them in his blatant political class war bid to topple the Government. They were his expendable cannon fodder. He produced what no miners' leader before him could claim: he split his own anguished union right down the middle. It was a stoppage that should not and need not have happened. Mr Scargill dragged in other trade unionists whose culpable or gullible leaders allowed them to be grossly misled by the miners' President's heady rhetoric and phoney presentation of his union's case. Yet the TUC stayed silently on the sidelines while the miners' split precipitated a similarly deep and wounding division in the wider trade union movement and while picket-line violence earned widespread public condemnation. The TUC's only early statement on the miners was a fudge. It might properly have issued a stern reminder about its own code of conduct on orderly and peaceful picketing. That code was drawn up in Jim Callaghan's last days of office and in the aftermath of the Winter of Discontent. It was intended to help Labour at the then oncoming General Election, but it is no less relevant today if Labour's electoral fortunes are to stand any chance of restoration.

Labour's National Executive Committee is as irresponsible as ever. It ran true to form by blaming the police for the fracas on the miners' picket lines. The Labour leaders chose to ignore the fact that without the massed pickets, the police presence would have been unnecessary. They conveniently forgot that the police were there to make sure that miners who voted to work on were not bullied into staying away by unwanted militants from other coalfields.

Neil Kinnock, the Labour leader, once more kept his head down when boldness and bravery were required. His performance was a good imitation of a political eunuch. He was aware that outright backing for Mr Scargill would send his own opinion poll ratings plummeting. He knew, too, that outright condemnation would earn him the wrath of the left and could well cause a major rumpus within his Shadow Cabinet and the left-wards-lurching Parliamentary Labour Party. He ended up with the worst of both worlds. He belatedly backed a miners' ballot – when that cause was already lost. He ultimately associated himself with the strike and with the National Executive Committee's call for donations from Labour supporters to the strike fund.

He always appeared to be running scared – firstly of public opinion and then of Arthur Scargill. Riding two horses is a painful affair, as Mr Kinnock discovered. Moreover, Labour's increased entanglement served to emphasise the political nature of the whole sorry affair. It brought Labour into line with the Communist Party which had repeatedly endorsed each and every extravagant Scargill demand or distortion. The TUC's deliberately low profile reflected similar mixed and unworthy motives to those of Mr Kinnock. Their responsibility was more direct than that of the politicians. Mr Scargill was unwilling to seek TUC help and risk a rebuff and he scorned genuine consultation with other unions affected by the miners' actions. Too much was at stake to allow this rogue elephant to trample on the movement, virtually unchallenged from within.

The TUC leaders are not romantics. They knew that high cost coal from uneconomic pits has no ready market, that only the non-coal energy producers are boosted if clapped-out pits stay open and that the Government would become more determined than ever to see that alternative sources of energy supply are available to the nation. They knew that the ongoing taxpayers' investment in the coal industry is vast but is not inexhaustible. They knew that voluntary severance pay for a long-serving miner was tantamount to winning the football pools and was the envy of most other industries. They knew, above all, that Mr

Scargill was desperate to avoid a national ballot vote. His domino theory, in which pro-strike coalfields forced the rest to join them, was a crude rather than a clever ploy. It was a constitutional wangle. Mr Scargill relied on his flying pickets to keep him on course, that was the ugly truth.

He pontificated about the emergence of a police state in Britain to add to his distorted picture. In those East European countries with which he seems so ready to identify, there are no democratically elected governments or free trade unions. Strikers are starved out, marched to work, jailed or even shot. Whatever the distaste for Tory legislation, it is exaggerated nonsense to compare it with tyrannies of that kind.

The TUC should have asserted itself and promptly. It should have declared unequivocally that a strike involving large sections of British industry is the prerogative of the whole Trade Union movement, not of an unrepresentative part of a divided National Union of Mineworkers. It should not have appeared to acquiesce in such action and in the constitutional sleight-of-hand which accompanied it. I spelled out my union's position. I pointed out that our power station workers have the capability to cause devastating hardship and social havoc. They had not used that strength on their own behalf and would not be compelled or manipulated to do so for some other group with the muscle to throw up a blockade. That would have set an awesome precedent. I went further: I urged the TUC to suggest an independent examination of pit closure proposals as a reasonable way to avoid an industrial virility test each time the axe was poised.

Mr Scargill and his more avid supporters appeared to be prepared to see an ungovernable Britain. His aversion to the ballot box in the miners' dispute is matched by a similar refusal to accept the verdict of the electors at the last General Election. He has made plain his belief in extra-parliamentary action to overturn policy decisions of an elected government and has used the Communist *Morning Star* to call for 'total mobilisation of the trade union and labour movement'. One thing is certain. The remarkable events of 1983 and 1984 ensure that the movement will never be the same again.

Those who think it necessary to destroy the past to build some revolutionary new order on the ruins will doubtless believe they are steadily marching to victory along with Mr Scargill and Mr Mick McGahey. Presumably a sheepishly militant Mr Kinnock and an utterly out-manoeuvred Mr Roy Hattersley will continue to wretchedly bring up the rear. My assessment is very different. It has been a calamitous period in which working people and their families have been shamefully betrayed. Len Murray, struggling and inadequately supported in his bid for realism, retires prematurely from a sorry shambles that he was unable to prevent. His successor faces a daunting task.

Trade unions today, more than at any time since our movement was founded, must justify their existence to an increasingly sceptical national audience, including their own mostly shrinking membership. If the broad left advance continues, if their bankrupt and destructive policies are unchecked, that once great movement will lose still more of its members, money, influence and already severely waning power. A government that has piled on anti-union laws can convincingly add to them. Unions will be turned into increasingly meaningless protest organisations. Governments and employers alike will take note of their views – and forget them even more promptly than is the case today. Those unions that have fought against and emphatically rejected those deadly and desolate left tendencies will hopefully survive and thrive. They will deserve to do so. I am certain that the EETPU will be among them. How many other unions will successfully stand with us in the years ahead can only be a matter of conjecture. There are not so many who are entitled to escape a fate they will have brought upon themselves by a mixture of timidity, ineptitude and sheer funk.

The situation is not beyond retrieval but there are few signs of a rescue. It will be a prodigious test of trade union resolve. The record suggests disaster rather than delivery.

# INDEX

227